REVOLUTIONS

HOW WOMEN CHANGED THE WORLD ON TWO WHEELS

Hannah Ross

NO LONGER PROPERTY OF
ANYTHINK LIBRARIES/
RANGEVIEW LIBRARY DISTRICT

PLUME

PLUME

An imprint of Penguin Random House LLC
penguinrandomhouse.com

Copyright © 2020 by Hannah Ross
Penguin supports copyright. Copyright fuels creativity, encourages diverse
voices, promotes free speech, and creates a vibrant culture. Thank you for
buying an authorized edition of this book and for complying with copyright
laws by not reproducing, scanning, or distributing any part of it in any form
without permission. You are supporting writers and allowing Penguin to
continue to publish books for every reader.

Plume is a registered trademark and its colophon is a trademark of
Penguin Random House LLC.

Photo credits:
Page vii: (top) © Picture Art Collection/Alamy;
(bottom) © Alice Austen House.
Page viii: (top) *The Referee & Cycle Trade Journal*, 15:12
(July 18, 1895) Smithsonian; (bottom) © Peter Zheutlin.
Page ix: (top) © Eland Books/Dervla Murphy;
(bottom) © Signal Photos/Alamy.
Page x: (top) © William Wilson; (bottom) © Michael Tant.

LIBRARY OF CONGRESS CATALOGING-IN-PUBLICATION DATA
Names: Ross, Hannah (Cyclist), author.
Title: Revolutions : how women changed the world
on two wheels / Hannah Ross.
Description: New York : Plume, 2020. |
Includes bibliographical references and index.
Identifiers: LCCN 2020003218 (print) | LCCN 2020003219 (ebook) |
ISBN 9780593083604 (trade paperback) | ISBN 9780593083611 (ebook)
Subjects: LCSH: Women cyclists—History. | Cycling for women—History. |
Cycling—Social aspects. | Cycling—History. | Bicycle racing—History.
Classification: LCC GV1057 .R67 2020 (print) |
LCC GV1057 (ebook) | DDC 796.6082—dc23
LC record available at https://lccn.loc.gov/2020003218
LC ebook record available at https://lccn.loc.gov/2020003219

Printed in the United States of America
1   3   5   7   9   10   8   6   4   2

BOOK DESIGN BY TIFFANY ESTREICHER

While the author has made every effort to provide accurate telephone
numbers, internet addresses, and other contact information at the time of
publication, neither the publisher nor the author assumes any responsibility
for errors or for changes that occur after publication. Further, the publisher
does not have any control over and does not assume any responsibility for
author or third-party websites or their content.

*For Mike. And to the "bump," who
I hope grows to love cycling too.*

CONTENTS

The Italian cyclist Alfonsina Morini Strada, who in 1924 became the first and only woman to ride in the Giro d'Italia.

Maria "Violet" Ward supports Daisy Elliott on a bicycle during the photo shoot for her book, *Bicycling for Ladies*, 1895.

Katherine "Kittie" Knox, circa 1895.

Annie Kopchovsky, before setting off to cycle around the world. Boston, 1894.

Dervla Murphy
on a tour of
Spain, 1956.

Elsa von Blumen,
US high-wheel
competitive cyclist,
circa 1882.

Marguerite Wilson when she stopped for tea at Ford Pass, near Exeter, on her record-breaking Land's End to John O'Groats ride, 1939.

InternationElles at the start of stage 15, Limoux to Prat d'Albis, July 20, 2019.

LA PETITE REINE

La petite reine, the little Queen, is how the French have long affectionately referred to the bicycle. Which is ironic since the impression you might get from most accounts of over a century of cycling is that it hasn't involved many women. Turn on the TV or look at the sports pages every July and it's hard to avoid coverage of the travails of almost two hundred cyclists battling it out over several thousand miles across France in one of the biggest sports events of the year. Every one of those taking part is a man. Look around you in most cities and towns in the world and you are likely to see more men on bikes than women. On this evidence, cycling certainly would appear to be more of a boys' club than anything to do with little queens.

This is of course not the whole story. As far back as the late nineteenth century, when suffragist Susan B. Anthony told a newspaper that the bicycle "has done more to emancipate women than anything else in the world," cycling has been a feminist issue.

When the bicycle emerged in the 1880s, it triggered a revolution for its unique dual qualities as both a practical and efficient machine to cover distances with comparatively little effort, taking people to places they might never otherwise have ventured, and for how fun it felt to pedal one. Even now, when there are so many ways to travel, people still love to bike. That feeling of pedaling along, the wind in one's hair, feeling close to flying on a descent—it never gets boring.

If you ask people what they like most about cycling, the words that you will hear come up again and again are "freedom" and "flying." Yet as I started researching the history of the bike it was striking how often women had their wings clipped. Whereas men have never had to think twice about jumping into the saddle and pedaling off, for women cycling has always been politically charged, with opinions raging, even today, about what they can and can't do on one.

In the 1890s, as the bicycle craze swept across large parts of the world, around a third of owners in the U.K. and North America were women. An impressive statistic when you consider that a woman on a bike at that time raised more than just a few eyebrows. In an age when women's bodies and behavior were heavily policed and controlled, with little freedom to use their bodies so physically and publicly, a woman cycling was nothing short of revolutionary. Despite having insults—and in some cases stones—hurled at them, they also had to contend with the hazards of impractical long skirts, petticoats and other cumbersome garments deemed essential to public decency. Undaunted, these women embraced this new machine with elan. And they didn't stop when they were told it would ruin their looks, leave them infertile or lead to promiscuity.

The bicycle was expanding their world and they were determined to seize the opportunity. Some would go as far as circumnavigating the globe on two wheels. But even those that never made it farther than the local park were riding over the established view that women were frail creatures, who—if their financial situation meant they didn't need to work—were best suited to a stifling and genteel life indoors, indulging in suitable pastimes such as needlework or flower pressing. This first wave of female cyclists set a match to such restrictive notions of femininity. Though most cycled for pleasure, it was a political act to be seen using their bodies in this way. It's no coincidence that the women fighting for universal suffrage, to be treated as equal citizens, were also enthusiastic cyclists—bicycles were nothing short of feminist freedom-machines.

• • •

A century after women got the vote, it seems astonishing that we still account for less than a third of cyclists in the U.K. and North America. How is there still so much gender disparity when women today have so many more freedoms than their Victorian sisters? Whether for sport or leisure, the benefits of cycling are wide and far-reaching and it should be open to all. As those early pioneers demonstrated, gender is no barrier—although unwieldy skirts and corsets might be.

By getting people where they need to go cheaply and easily, the bike has proved a powerful tool for change. It can mean the difference between getting an education or earning a living—or not. It can also have profound health benefits, both physical and psychological. Ask anyone who cycles to say what it means to them and one thing they are likely to say is that it makes them happy, with some reporting they *need* to bike to stay sane. We live in a world where there are bikes to suit every need and preference—featherlight road bikes for the more competitive, electric bikes to provide extra power where it's needed, adapted bikes for those with mobility issues. It's widely recognized that getting more people cycling could transform our cities from poisonous gridlock to quieter, cleaner and happier places with significantly lower carbon footprints—a no-brainer when we are currently tipping over into climate catastrophe.

That there are people who feel cycling isn't for them suggests there is still a long way to go in making it fully inclusive. A big part of that is having better cycling infrastructure to make it safer and more inviting, something proved by countries like the Netherlands and Denmark, who lead the way as cycling nations and boast an even split between genders. Representation matters. When we see people who look like us doing something, we're more inclined to give it a try. For too long cycling has presented too narrow and exclusive an image, making it appear a closed shop.

My aim is to present a different picture. I want to put women and girls at the center—the queens of cycling—by telling some of their extraordinary stories. Stories of freedom, empowerment and revolution which for too long have been pushed to the margins, forgotten or unrepresented. Whether they were going after medals, exploring the world or spreading the word about votes for women, these female cyclists are an inspiration. *Revolutions* tells the story of over a hundred and thirty years of women on bikes, from Europe and North America to Afghanistan, India and beyond.

When I told people I was writing this book, many assumed I would focus only on those competing at the highest level of the sport. These formidable athletes are an important part of the narrative, but there is more to cycling than medals and power meters; to suggest it is all about sports is restrictive and limiting in its own way. You don't need to have the most expensive bike and most Instagrammable kit. There is not one type of cyclist, but a huge variety of women from diverse backgrounds who have fallen in love with two wheels and used them in so many different ways. That's what I hope I will show here.

Part I starts with a revolution—the emergence of the bicycle, an event which rocked the western world and beyond in the late nineteenth century, and the early cycling pioneers who bravely endured the torrent of abuse and misinformation thrown at them. In Part II, we meet women who have used their bikes in the name of liberty, equality and sisterhood. Then we go onto the open road in Part III, with those who pedaled roads less traveled, certainly by women, and encouraged their contemporaries to follow. Finally, Part IV turns the spotlight on some who have raced at speeds and distances many assumed impossible for their sex, starting in the days when the bicycle was still a novelty—and women racing them even more so. We will end with some of the incredible women who not only compete at the highest level, but engage in activism to transform the sport, calling for equal pay, better conditions, more visibility and inclusivity.

The time for a more female-centered version of cycling history is long overdue. This is a story for everyone: those of us riding our bikes today and wondering why it's not as diverse an activity as it should be; those who haven't yet realized that; and those who will come after and will hopefully never have to question their place on the road, mountain trail and track.

PART I

THE
REVOLUTION

CHAPTER ONE

MAD ABOUT THE BIKE

Cambridge Mob Rule

It is May 21, 1897, and a large, raucous crowd of male students—some armed with eggs and fireworks—have gathered in Cambridge's medieval Market Square. A few women students, looking a bit apprehensive, stand at the edge of the crowd. Above everyone's heads, suspended from the second-floor window of a bookshop facing the university senate, hangs an effigy of a woman on a bicycle dressed in a blouse and bloomers. Why is she here and why is there a mob of undergraduates swarming below her?

They had all gathered to await a decision from the university's senate, which had been debating a proposal to grant full degrees to women studying at the university. Although they had been attending and sitting exams at the women-only colleges of Girton, Newnham and Hughes Hall since the late 1860s, women were not entitled to be awarded degrees at the end of their studies; they also had to ask permission from a professor before attending their lectures and were not considered full members of the university. While they could just about study, they could not graduate—though they were in a slightly better position than their predecessors in the 1860s, those first five female students who had to study thirty miles away, lest their presence upset the male students.

The protestors outside the senate were not challenging the gross unfairness and inequality of the situation, they were outraged at the possibility that the proposal might be passed, even though other universities in the U.K. were already awarding degrees to men and women on an equal basis. The proposal was so divisive that extra trains had been put on from London to enable graduates to return to cast their vote. Many held aloft placards that made their feelings clear, such as "No Gowns for Girtonites" and "Varsity for Men."

When the news broke that the Senate had rejected the proposal, with 661 voting in favor and 1,707 against, the male students' delight was palpable. They tore down the effigy in a frenzy, ripping off her head and tearing her body into pieces before posting her remains through the gates of Newnham College. The women students locked inside—disgusted and possibly terrified—looked on as a mob tried to break down the gates. As far as these men were concerned, they were the moral victors; women needed to know their place and stop making outrageous demands that were encroaching on male privileges.

It was another fifty years before women would be granted degrees at Cambridge on equal terms to men—the last university to hold out against the tide of change. It wasn't until 1988 that the last of its all-male colleges accepted women, and once again the male students protested—though less violently this time—by donning black armbands and flying their flag at half-mast.

To understand why the 1897 protest targeted that female cycling effigy, we need to trace two movements that intersected in the run-up to that raucous event. One was the emergence of the "New Woman"—the term for feminists who, in short, wanted to throw off the restrictive shackles imposed by late-Victorian patriarchy and were demanding the same social and political rights as men, as well as educations and careers: women who many thought were trying to inhabit spaces or partake in activities that should be the sole preserve and prerogative of men. This was to be an important decade in the history of feminism that had been building since at least the late eighteenth century, with the publication of Mary Wollstonecraft's *A Vindication of the Rights of Woman* (1792), and that would ultimately evolve into the large-scale movements for suffrage in the early part of the twentieth century. The other was the "bike boom," triggered by the invention of a new type of bicycle. This was a time when interest in cycling was at its absolute peak, becoming a mass activity in Western Europe and North America, not least with women, who took it up in droves. First, though, we must understand the revolutionary potential of this new machine, and why some men were intent on keeping it for themselves.

Two-Wheeled Genesis

In 1885, Coventry's Starley & Sutton company launched a new bicycle called the Rover Safety. It wasn't the first bicycle, but it was the one that would stand the test of time and have the most seismic impact, its basic design forming the blueprint for the machines we ride today. Although the reverberations of this unveiling weren't felt immediately, with some tweaks and refinements it would become the must-have accessory of the following decade.

Looking at pictures of bicycles before the launch of the Safety, it's easy to see why they were superseded. The first was designed by German inventor Baron Karl von Drais, who had set out to create a horseless carriage and launched his "Laufmaschine," or "Running-Machine," in 1817. "Running" was the pivotal word, as that was exactly what the rider was required to do on a contraption that was essentially two carriage wheels joined together by a wooden plank, with a cushioned seat for the rider and a rudimentary steering mechanism. The rider propelled the machine by running along the ground while seated. Apart from looking quite silly, this wasn't an easy thing to do when going uphill, and the absence of brakes didn't make the downhill any more comfortable. But the appetite for a self-propelled wheeled device, pre–motor age, was clearly there; in spite of its drawbacks, and high price tag, it was soon seen in fashionable cities such as London, Paris and New York. But as a craze it was short-lived; the novelty of running along while seated—wearing quickly through the soles of the rider's shoes—was destined to have limited appeal.*

In the years between Drais's invention and the Rover Safety in 1885, countless aspiring bike builders had a go at improving on the concept. But it wasn't until 1867 that the first pedal-powered bicycle rolled onto the scene in Paris.† This much-improved machine designed by Pierre Michaux, a Parisian blacksmith, featured pedals attached to the hub of the front

---

* Drais's design hasn't become entirely obsolete—the wooden balance bikes that children now use to learn to ride bear some similarity.

† Some believe the first ever pedal-driven bicycle emerged as early as 1839, created by Scottish blacksmith Kirkpatrick Macmillan. Since he never patented his design, it was never commercially available, making it impossible to prove conclusively that he was indeed decades ahead of his time with his invention.

wheel—no more running! Despite the prohibitive cost (250 francs, nearly $1,600 today), velocipedes became a relatively common sight in France and beyond. Michaux's machine has since been dubbed "the boneshaker" because of the deleterious effect the all-iron frame and wooden wheels had on the rider, with air-filled rubber tires still a few decades away. It became a popular pastime for a few years with those who could afford one. Theater and circus performers incorporated the machine into their acts, and the more competitive enthusiasts took part in the world's first organized bike races.

As inventors worldwide competed to refine this new style of two-wheeler, patent offices were deluged with variations on Michaux's theme. In the 1870s, the craze for the boneshaker was eclipsed by the arrival of the "high-wheeler" or "Ordinary." Perhaps the most emblematic of all Victorian-era inventions, with the cyclist perched above an enormous front wheel and a diminutive rear wheel providing counterbalance. Its British name of "penny-farthing" comes from the wheels, which resemble a large penny coin and more diminutive farthing. The design now looks so outlandish and impractical it seems it must have been invented by someone with a loose grasp of reality. Yet there was something about this strange new beast that stuck, at least for the few decades after 1871 when Starley & Sutton put their model on the market with its 48-inch big wheel.

This new bike was also much lighter and, perhaps most important to many, it was remarkably nippy. Even without the luxury of air-filled tires, the oversized front wheel meant the rider was much farther from the lumps, bumps and ruts that were endemic of roads at that time.

As the decade progressed the wheels continued to expand and speeds increased, with riders competing in races that attracted large crowds and where they were soon busting the three-minute mile, as well as covering progressively longer distances. Demand grew so great that by 1880 there were over a hundred Ordinary manufacturers in the U.K., with consumers in the United States—after overcoming some initial skepticism—no less enthusiastic. One convert was Thomas Stevens, an emigrant from the U.K., who in 1884 became the first to cross the United States on two wheels when he rode a U.S.-made Columbia Ordinary from San Francisco to Boston. That was just the start of Thomas's cycle adventuring, and the following year he set off from London, cycling through Europe, the Middle East, China and Japan, to become the first to pedal around the world.

You may be wondering why the evolution of the bicycle didn't stop with the Ordinary if it had so much going for it. First, they were dangerous: it was a long way to climb up onto the saddle, and a long way to fall, and falling was an occupational hazard for the high-wheel enthusiast. Even for experienced riders, strong winds, ruts in the road and other obstacles (such as fellow cyclists who'd hit the deck) could prove deadly. Serious head injuries—dubbed a "cropper," "header" or "imperial crowner"— were common, and were enough to stop most from giving it a go. The tag many of its detractors gave it as "a young man's game" is telling, and even then, it was only a certain type of young man who was willing to put up with the bicycle's potentially fatal design quirks. It also wasn't inexpensive (though far cheaper than Michaux's boneshaker), so largely only middle- and upper-class men of means could splurge on one. All this meant it was somewhat exclusionary; cycling's pleasures as well as its dangers, were denied not just to sensible, aged or less affluent men, but to women.

While some women did take to the machines—a few intrepid female riders even raced on them, drawing large audiences—it's fair to say female fans of the high-wheel were in the minority.

The dangers of falling aside, if social norms required you to wear long skirts and petticoats made up of yards of material that drag on the floor when you walk—as women were largely required to do at this time—then just getting up into the saddle is going to be near impossible. Even if they had managed such a feat, all that fabric would inevitably jam in the spokes and send them plummeting back down to the ground.*

Instead some women—and men—took up the tricycle, a three-wheeled machine propelled by foot levers that gained popularity in the late 1870s. No straddling was required, which accommodated standard Victorian dress, and knees could be kept firmly together, which made them appropriately ladylike and uncontroversial. So much so that Queen Victoria bought one for herself and her daughters in 1881. But like the high-wheel, they had a few fundamental flaws. First, they were extremely heavy and cumbersome: getting uphill required a helping hand, as pedaling was insufficient against such a weight. And while the rider didn't need much in the way of lessons, they weren't without their dangers—while not overly common, rolling over was one possible hazard. Their size meant you couldn't exactly store them in your hallway. If you didn't have a coach house, then you might be a bit stuck. More to the point, if you weren't wealthy enough to own a coach house, then you probably couldn't afford a tricycle.†

* Implausible as it may sound, Starley did create a sidesaddle design featuring a rear wheel offset to one side as a counterbalance. However, it's hard to find evidence anyone actually rode one.

† Tricycles have in fact since made a comeback, albeit with far lighter and more user-friendly versions, to enable older people or those with disabilities to cycle who aren't able to use standard two-wheeled models. Many users find getting

Meanwhile, the high-wheeler remained an exclusive boys' club—though that probably suited a lot of its fans—and clubs started springing up specifically for them. Some were positively lavish: the Massachusetts Bicycle Club was housed in an imposing four-story town house in Boston, financially supported by the Pope Manufacturing Company. Its members could cycle straight into the building via a handy ramp to make use of its washroom and library before settling down in the parlor to enjoy post-ride drinks and cigars in front of roaring log fires. While not all clubs were quite as grand, with many taking whatever space they could find, such as a room above a pub, they all placed high importance on uniform, with members turning out in caps and jackets in their chosen colors and emblazoned with their club's badge. There was a sense of pride in being part of this elite group of young men who adventured, raced and diced with death, so it's no surprise the students of Oxbridge formed their own clubs, with Ivy League universities in the United States following suit.

However, high-wheeler fans could cling to their caps, badges and deadly giant wheels all they wanted—they would soon start to look somewhat anachronistic when a new type of bike that would democratize cycling arrived. It was long overdue.

Safety First

John Kemp Starley got straight to the point when he named his successor to the high-wheeler the "Rover Safety" back in 1885.

---

around on them easier than walking. Whereas once the three-wheeler was for the privileged few, they are now about making cycling accessible for more people than ever.

With its two standard-sized wheels, it was exactly that: a safe choice compared to its seemingly absurdist predecessor, for here was a machine low enough for the rider to place their feet on the ground when they stopped. While the early designs featured a slightly larger front wheel, there was only a small disparity, so anyone who was reasonably mobile could mount one without difficulty. It's iconic diamond frame, still the basis for bikes today, proved the design breakthrough all those aspirational inventors had been hoping to get to first. But, as with most objects that become design classics, it was a few years before it really took off, and even Starley is unlikely to have predicted how revolutionary it would become. Devoted high-wheelers initially spurned the Safety, believing proximity to the ground to be most undignified, but change was a-wheel in the bicycling world, and the Rover was soon being shipped all around the globe.

Three years later, another design breakthrough finally set the wheels turning for a true bike boom. Its creator was John Dunlop, a Scottish veterinarian based in Belfast who, in his spare time, had been experimenting with fitting air-filled rubber tires to his son's tricycle to make it more comfortable. Realizing he was onto something, he quickly registered a patent. There were the usual naysayers who thought it would never catch on, and early sightings sometimes attracted a crowd, but a quick spin on a Dunlop was all that was needed to prove that riding on air-filled, shock-absorbent tires was preferable to a solid wheel. When the tires were fitted to bikes at a race and the average speed was increased by a third, there was no doubt that they would become a permanent fixture. With this winning combination, the western world was about to go bike crazy.

Boom Time

My great-grandfather Samuel Moss, a printer on London's Fleet Street, was one of those who was bitten by the cycling bug. By the middle of the 1890s, he was competing regularly at the newly opened Herne Hill Velodrome in London. The trophies he won for his efforts were proudly displayed on a side table in my grandmother's house.

While racing was a big thing by then, most people were content with the novelty of going for a sedate spin around the local park. The enjoyable sensation of coasting along with relatively little effort would have been unlike anything most had experienced before, and if they wanted to go further, what was to stop them? We live in a time when people think nothing of covering hundreds of miles a day in a car, but at a time when steam trains or horse power were the only options for covering long distances, it would have been revolutionary for our ancestors, who could now explore so much more of the world around them, independently and under their own power. It would have been even more life-changing if you lived in a village or small town with no train line, where many inhabitants would not have been farther than they could walk in a day.

Horses were expensive, and far from an option for everyone, and they weren't necessarily much of a match either: in an average day of cycling, it's possible to cover twice the distance compared to traveling on horseback. While trains were more efficient, they couldn't take you everywhere.

With a bicycle, the world would have expanded dramatically for fin-de-siècle Victorians, particularly as bikes became increasingly affordable, bringing new experiences and opportunities, and perhaps even new romantic liaisons. Sociologists now credit the bicycle with a decrease in genetic faults associated with in-breeding in the U.K., and as early as 1900, the U.S. Census Office identified the invention as a game-changer: "Few articles ever used by man have created so great a revolution in social conditions as the bicycle."

The late Victorians embraced the Safety with feverish enthusiasm, making the end of their century the most significant period in the history of the bicycle, taking it from minority activity to mass pursuit in just a few years. In 1890 in the United States, there were just 27 factories making around 40,000 bicycles a year; by 1896, upward of 250 factories were producing over 1,200,000, and many factories were working through the night to meet demand. Pope, then the largest U.S. cycle maker, was producing one bike a minute by the middle of the decade. Meanwhile, the U.K. had established itself as the world capital of cycling with its 700 factories.

Early models were expensive, but as the decade progressed new mass production techniques brought prices down from around $150 in the early 1890s—six months' pay for a worker at a Pope factory—to an average of $80 by 1897, with some models priced much lower. In addition, options to pay by installment, and a growing secondhand market fueled by wealthy consumers upgrading to the latest model, soon put machines within reach. By the end of the decade, bicycles on the streets of Western Europe, North America and beyond, used for both recreation and transport, were a commonplace sight and not just a plaything for the elite.

Copenhagen and Amsterdam, today's great cycling cities, were early adopters and by the beginning of the 1890s were buzzing with bikes. Toronto also became a cycling city at this time, as the town's governors liked the bike's association with modernity, which they saw as helping identify the city as urban and modern. In the U.K., pedal-powered machines were the most fashionable thing to be seen on in the Royal parks of London in 1895, and by 1896, Hyde Park had as many as three thousand cyclists parading their machines along its paths each day. That same year, a silent film by one of the pioneers of British cinema, recorded in grainy black and white, shows a continuous flow of smartly dressed men and women cycling down one of the park's grand avenues, watched by an audience who line the thoroughfare. *Hyde Park Cyclists*, which runs to just twenty seconds, gives an extraordinary glimpse into the world of those fashionable park cyclists.

France too was identifying itself as a cycling nation, and it wasn't long before it was dictating the cycling fashions of the day, with the Bois de Boulogne in Paris as the epicenter of *le cyclisme à la mode*. Enthusiasts would meet daily at the park's Grande Brasserie de l'Espérance or Chalet du Cycle, handing their mount to the cloakroom staff in exchange for a numbered ticket, so they could sit and enjoy a coffee or glass of wine before cycling the park's tree-lined avenues. It was a mixed crowd, which could include President Jean Casimir-Perier, who rode a tandem with his wife and children; stage actors like Sarah Bernhardt; artists and writers, such as Fernand Léger; and even waiters on their lunch breaks. The Italians were also busy putting themselves on the cycling map, but riding for leisure wasn't quite so compelling to them—it was all about the racing.

In Australia, the bike wasn't just a fashionable accessory but a practical tool in their challenging climate and geography. During the gold rush it was taken up by prospectors who needed to travel long distances across inhospitable terrain, and it rapidly became an economical alternative to horses for many working in the country's remote mining towns, as well as by itinerant shearers traveling between farms.

In the face of cycle-mania, Germany took a rather different view and was instead trying to repress the seemingly unstoppable rise of the new velocipede. In certain regions the authorities insisted cyclists pass an examination, and it was banned from the centers of cities like Berlin, Dresden and Munich. Each region of this only recently unified country seemed to have its own regulations—particularly confusing for foreign travelers—and plainclothes policemen lurked ready to catch offenders. Some areas required cyclists to attach a sign to their bikes with an identification number, but even this didn't stem the rise of this practical and pleasurable machine, and by 1896 half a million Germans identified as cyclists. Russia also went through a phase of setting exams for cyclists, even though Tsar Nicholas was a fan, and women who wanted to cycle weren't entitled to sit the exam until 1897.

The German and Russian authorities weren't the only ones who were far from enamored, as other manufacturing industries began to complain that people were spending all their money on bicycles. Some companies tried to get in on the act, including the jeweler Tiffany & Co., which produced a gold-plated machine with pearl handlebars and studded with amethysts valued at $10,000 (around $300,000 today). It was commissioned by businessman "Diamond" Jim Brady, who gave it to his girlfriend, the performer Lillian Russell.

This high-water mark of cycling-related conspicuous consumption, in what would come to be referred to as America's Gilded Age, would certainly have added to the church's deep suspicion of the mania, with prominent members of the clergy in cycle-mad cities decrying the activity as distinctly profane. They did have a vested interest though, since increasing numbers of their flock were choosing to go out cycling on a Sunday instead of sitting on a hard pew to be chastised for their sins.

Even outside the church there were many, including enthusiasts themselves, who thought cycling could be morally ruinous, at least for a certain sector of society, namely women.

What was with all the outrage? This was a time when women were too often denied agency and had few rights, when they led lives that were decidedly unfree, both socially and physically. They were not supposed to be independent, to pursue an education at elite universities or take off on two wheels.

CHAPTER TWO

WILD WOMEN ON WHEELS

Ladies Who Pedal

It was Starley again, designer of that original Safety bicycle, who was visionary enough to design a bike that would specifically appeal to women. Released in 1887, the Psycho Ladies' Safety featured a frame with a sloping top bar—a step-through—so that the rider didn't have to straddle a crossbar in cumbersome long skirts, and a chain guard to prevent the layers of fabric getting mangled and causing an accident.*

It was the Psycho that members of Harriette H. Mills's women's cycling club ordered in 1888 all the way from the U.K. to their hometown of Washington, D.C. Harriette owned a U.S.-produced Ladies' Dart bicycle, but the company couldn't produce them fast enough to supply the sudden demand. Another

---

* Admittedly "Psycho" seems an odd choice of name if you want to attract a new sector to your market, but it didn't have quite the same connotations as it does now, largely thanks to Alfred Hitchcock's film of the same name.

company called their ladies' model "The Witch," which perhaps seems a counterintuitive marketing strategy at a time when the term had yet to be reclaimed by feminism. What was clear, though, was that manufacturers realized they could sell more bikes if they were specifically marketed and adapted to women.

Family history does not say if while Samuel Moss was winning racing medals in the 1890s, his wife, my great-grandmother, had also caught the cycling bug. But we do know that by the middle of that decade women were making up a third of the bicycle market in the U.K. and North America—something that would have seemed an impossibility during the peak of the high-wheel craze.

Some of the most publicized of these women were members of the upper echelons of society, who very much embraced and accelerated the boom. The Duchess of Somerset, for instance, often hosted fifty or so of her friends for breakfast in Battersea Park's lake house before pedaling circuits of the park together. They also enjoyed night rides through the city, with Chinese lanterns lighting their way, before dismounting for a grand supper. Bicycles could be spotted gracing the marble halls of the aristocracy across London, and each morning they would be carefully placed in carriages to be driven to the local park along with their lady owners. Boys in uniform were poised ready to polish the cherished bike on its return.

For society cyclists, it wasn't just about being seen on a bicycle, it was also about whether you had the latest model and what you were wearing. Daisy Greville, the Countess of Warwick (mistress of the Prince of Wales, future King Edward VII), was described as having caught the "rabid disease commonly known as cyclomania," a pursuit that reputedly led to her becoming the inspiration for the music hall staple "Daisy Bell," who the narrator thinks will "look sweet on the seat of a bicycle built for two." The press fixated on what the countess wore, eagerly reporting the changing colors of her mount and coordinating outfits to match the seasons—moss-green for autumn, all-white for summer and brown and gold for spring—with tailors poised to copy whatever she was sporting.

The cycling press at the time was filled with interviews with these society ladies—as well as some famous actresses—who were so taken with their new hobby that they had incorporated it into many of their favorite pastimes. For instance, when inviting guests to weekend parties at their country houses, they urged them to bring their bicycle so they could go on picnic rides and partake in games or fancy-dress bicycle parades. Some even switched their usual equine mount for two wheels in order to follow along with the local foxhunt.

The ladies of New York society were equally enthusiastic. In 1894, *Cycling* magazine reported how "as early as five o'clock in the morning, a large number of ladies are seen riding with their maids or footmen upon Upper Fifth Avenue and the Boulevard." Some of them might have joined the rarefied Michaux Club based on upper Broadway, which catered to the likes of the city's elite "Four Hundred" group, a list drawn up by the doyenne of the social scene, Caroline Astor, and included the Rockefellers and Roosevelts. In 1896, *Harper's* magazine reported that the club comprised "many of the fashionable folk of the city, and quite as many women as men are enrolled"; with an upper limit of just 250 members, it quickly established a long waiting list. Their premises boasted a library, a lounge for taking high tea and an indoor school for the winter months, where members cycled to music and performed synchronized routines—like a nineteenth-century equivalent of today's Peloton or SoulCycle spin classes.

A reporter from *Munsey's Magazine* was spellbound by the

sight, declaring that "the intricate figures performed by the cyclists, as they follow their leader around the spacious hall, to the music of the band, make one of the prettiest sights in all Gotham." In spring and summer, group rides were organized to scenic destinations like Riverside Drive, where they would stop for lunch. The city planners responded to the craze by creating a bicycle path in Brooklyn that went all the way from Prospect Park to the resort town of Coney Island on the Atlantic. It was so popular that within a month it had to be repaired from overuse and widened to accommodate the high number of users.

In Italy, Queen Margherita of Savoy was a convert, with gossip columns reporting that she rode a bicycle with solid gold wheels. And Queen Amélie of Portugal was encouraged to take up cycling by her husband, who worried she was spending too much time reading books about physics. She embraced the pastime enthusiastically, though I hope she still found time to pursue her interest in science. The impact of the aristocracy's fervor for cycling could even be felt as far away as China, where Shanghai's Sing-song girls (the Chinese equivalent of the geisha), who were always quick to adopt the latest fashions, could be seen cycling around the city's parks.

By the close of 1896, society cyclists in London, New York and elsewhere had started to let their bikes gather dust and were no longer frequenting the parks in quite such numbers. The fad was over for them almost as quickly as it started—it was now less rarefied since bicycles had become more affordable for the masses. It was far from the end of the road in wider society, though.

By this point even some sectors of the clergy had begun to accept that the invention wasn't going away, with forward-thinkers installing bike racks so their congregation could combine the two activities. There were even bicycle weddings, such as that of an Italian couple who married in a church in London's Leicester Square in 1897, with the wedding party pedaling up the street followed by the bride and groom in wedding dress with their mounts covered in flowers. The scene attracted so much interest that the police were dispatched to deal with the crowd. It wasn't just holy matrimony being celebrated a-wheel either. In 1896, *Lady Cyclist* magazine reported a christening where the baby and nurse arrived on a tandem, with the rest of the party on as many as eighty bicycles bringing up the rear.

Cycling honeymoons also became a thing, often with the newly married couple on a bicycle made for two. Tom and Helen Follett were one such couple, spending their two-month honeymoon riding from New Orleans to Washington, D.C., in 1896, after being gifted a tandem by an uncle. Despite bemoaning the deplorable state of the roads in the South, Helen was smitten with life on two wheels, describing it as the "grandest" of experiences and that the sense of elation it gave her made her feel like "a bird, sailing over flower-covered prairies; you fancy yourself a greyhound bounding after a breathless and frightened jackrabbit; you even compare yourself with a flash of lightning or a whizzing cannon-ball. You realize how Monte Cristo felt when he climbed upon that rock and declared that the world was his."

In France during the previous year, the physicist Marie Curie and her husband, Pierre, celebrated their nuptials with a cycle trip. The wedding was a simple affair, stipulated by Marie, with no white dress, gold rings or wedding breakfast, and certainly no religious element. Their daughter Eve wrote in her biography of her mother that the only indulgence on the day was the two "glittering" bicycles the couple had bought the day before with money sent as a wedding gift. Immediately after, "at the cost of some thousands of pedal strokes and a few francs for village lodgings, the young couple attained the luxury of solitude shared between them for long enchanted days and nights" and that "during these happy days was formed one of the finest bonds that ever united man and woman."

Cycling would remain a fixture in Marie's life, a way to unwind from her demanding work, research that would lead to her becoming the first woman to be awarded a Nobel Prize. Each summer, Pierre and Marie would explore part of rural France on their bicycles. Eight months pregnant, she was still cycling—the couple traveled to Brest, covering distances no different from her pre-pregnancy days. The trip was only cut short when Marie returned to Paris to give birth.

You Can't Ride Sidesaddle on a Bicycle

Before high society made it fashionable in the mid-1890s, albeit in a distinctly genteel way, the early women of cycling often met resistance and disapproval similar to the female students on lockdown at Cambridge. This ranged from harassment and possibly even violence to questions about their femininity or supposed lack of it, and even suspicions about their sexual morality.

Helena Swanwick, a suffragist and writer, described the reaction she experienced when biking in London in the early 1890s: "Bus drivers were not above flicking at me with the whip, and cabmen thought it fun to converge upon me from behind. I was once pulled off by my skirt in a Notting Hill slum." Despite this she remained undeterred, judging the benefits of cycling to outweigh the prejudice and that her life had been "greatly enlarged" by the activity. She and her husband enjoyed exploring the countryside together on their bikes from their home in Manchester, as well as touring other parts of the U.K. and France.

Helena was educated at Girton College, Cambridge, so it's possible she may have helped inspire that infamous effigy.

The writer Evelyn Everett-Green, like Helena, also seemed to offend cab drivers, who regularly called her a "hussy," with even some women calling her "disgusting" for doing no more than riding her bike in London. Friends and family tried to discourage her as they felt that it was "not quite nice." They may have changed their tune a few years later for, as Evelyn wrote, "in April of 1895 one was considered eccentric for riding a bicycle, while by the end of June eccentricity rested with those who did not ride."

Other women cyclist pioneers faced similar opposition, which could sometimes veer into physical violence. A Lady Dorothea Gibb had stones thrown at her when she started riding her Safety in York, but she wasn't thrown off her pedal strokes and even encouraged her daughter to have a go. Emma Eades, reputedly one of the first women to cycle in London, was pelted with bricks by both men and women and told to go home. Like many others, she carried on regardless. When she took up performing cycling tricks before an audience at the Alhambra, a music hall in Leicester Square, her family was so scandalized they refused to speak of it.

Those female students on lockdown in their Cambridge college and the braying mob of men outside with their cycling effigy are a good analogy for how gender norms in the nineteenth century were constructed. Men and women were supposed to exist in separate spheres, with women confined to the family and home, not gadding about for all to see, while men existed in the social and public world of work, politics and learning. This was a time when a woman could cause a disturbance simply by walking alone down the street, with some instances of women who did so being wrongly arrested for prostitution. With their new bicycles, women were escaping their domestic prison and visibly taking up space in the streets—men's territory—and like the women in Cambridge, they weren't always welcome.

Women indoors—the "Angel in the House," preoccupied with domestic issues and with no political power or complete freedom of movement—were of course much easier to control. Defined as the weaker sex, they were told they risked complete disintegration should they exert themselves mentally or physically, a construct of femininity that helped keep many prisoners in their own homes. They weren't even legally free, with married women for most of that century required to give their property and bodies over to their husbands, as well as their wages if they worked.

It was also about the appropriate way for women to display and use their bodies, with cycling, an overtly physical activity which takes place in a public space, making women conspicuous. Prostitutes made spectacles of their bodies on the street, women and girls who were brought up "properly" didn't; "nice" girls hid them away under long skirts and petticoats and stayed indoors as much as possible. While it may have been fine for working-class women to toil away, the daughters of polite society were considered too fragile and precious to break a sweat. In Jane Austen's novel *Pride and Prejudice* (1813), archconservative Caroline Bingley was scandalized by Elizabeth Bennet walking just three miles alone to nearby Netherfield to nurse her sick sister, deeming her a social pariah in her muddy skirts.

Before the Safety, if women did sports at all, they were largely genteel and "ladylike"—for the moneyed leisure classes, taking place away from prying eyes, behind walls or in private gardens, such as croquet, archery, golf and lawn tennis. Even swimming remained segregated on the whole until the 1920s, so risqué was the idea of a woman in a bathing costume, even though women's swimming apparel at this time more closely resembled a burkini than a bikini, with knee-length woolen bathing dresses worn over bloomers and black stockings, not an outfit that could facilitate too many lengths of the pool. When women's soccer matches began in the mid-1890s, they were quickly shut down by protests before being revived again, to great popularity, in World War I. Not that there weren't also examples of women having successfully defied such limited and restrictive ideas of their capabilities to do physically arduous feats—such as scaling alpine peaks and glaciers—but they tended to be the exception.

Helena Swanwick and others taking up space on the streets on their new machines, no longer hiding the fact that they were in possession of a pair of legs in good working order, were putting a rocket under rules that sought to contain and control them. In the limited worldview of many Victorians, these were dangerous, wild women who were disrupting the established order. Many believed they should be kept under surveillance, so it's perhaps unsurprising that local newspapers ran stories about the first women to cycle in their town. Ethel Smyth, a suffragette and composer of numerous orchestral works and operas, described how the London papers in the early 1890s were full of pictures of "wild women of the usual unprepossessing pioneer type" riding their bicycles. As someone who would go on to compose the women's suffrage anthem "The March of the Women" and spend two months in Holloway prison for breaking an MP's window, it makes sense that she was attracted to these nonconformist and independent women. Encouraged by her mother, she immediately decided to buy a bicycle. Other family members told her it was an "indelicate" activity for her to do, not suitable for "nice" women. Their pleas fell on deaf ears. Why should men be the ones having all the fun?

While an interest in women's suffrage wasn't a prerequisite for these early women cyclists, there is evidence that the type of women who were attracted to the independence and excitement offered by a bicycle also had more than a passing interest in gender equality. Many of them would have identified as what the writer Sarah Grand defined as "New Women" in an essay in 1894. Not least was Kate Sheppard, a prominent New Zealand women's suffrage campaigner whose work was key to the country becoming the first to establish universal suffrage in 1893, and who also found time to set up their first women's cycling club.

"New Women" wanted an education, the right to pursue a career, and might also have thought they too deserved the right to vote—they wanted autonomy over their lives. They weren't the first, but during this period marked by transition, there was a groundswell that it would no longer be possible to contain, a movement that was disrupting restrictive ideas of Victorian womanhood. The New Woman became synonymous with cycling, not least in the press, since both were about empowerment, freedom and change. It also helps explain why those Cambridge men thought a bicycling woman was equal to a Cambridge-educated one—and why both were a dangerous thing to the established order.

In 1896, *Munsey's Magazine* declared that for men the bicycle is "merely a new toy," but for women it is "a steed upon which they rode into a new world." Marguerite Merington, who had once taught Latin and Greek at a women-only college in the United States before going on to become a playwright, would have agreed. She prescribed cycling as the best means for women to break the chains of domesticity in an article in 1895: "Now and again a complaint arises of the narrowness of woman's sphere. For such disorder of the soul the sufferer can do no better than to flatten her sphere to a circle, mount it, and take to the road."

The following year, Susan B. Anthony, the U.S. women's rights campaigner, described the bicycle as a "freedom-machine" which she believed "has done more to emancipate women than any one thing in the world. I rejoice every time I see a woman ride by on a wheel. It gives her a feeling of self-reliance and independence the moment she takes her seat; and away she goes, the picture of untrammeled womanhood."

Just as studying at university offered new opportunities outside of the home, the Rover Safety, with its promise of movement and new worlds to explore, was so much more than just a fashionable thing to own, and instead symbolized and actualized the exact opposite of what for many women had been a life of confinement and enforced inactivity. Is it any wonder that women were so eager to embrace this "freedom-machine" and to be so visibly seen to do so? Suffragist and writer Elizabeth Haldane even went as far as to say that the inventor of the new bicycle should have a national memorial built in his honor on behalf of the women whose lives it had so revolutionized. Though like the men in Cambridge, not everyone was quite so convinced about such new female freedoms.

Call the Doctor

At a time when women's bodies were heavily policed by the patriarchy, just sitting on a bike saddle became the focus of intense debate, bad science and misinformation. Many objected to how the bicycle would take women away from the watchful gaze of their families and guardians, which could lead to them getting up to all sorts of morally reprehensible things.

The U.S. Women's Rescue League came down firmly on the side of cycling having a negative moral impact on its female enthusiasts. Its leader, Charlotte Smith, was so convinced that it would lead to women's undoing that she petitioned Congress to get the activity banned, condemning it as "the devil's advance agent," bringing about their moral and religious demise and "swelling the ranks of reckless girls who finally drift into the standing army of outcast women of the United States." In short, Charlotte believed it would turn them into prostitutes. She also strongly felt the activity wasn't decorous or ladylike, and many in the church and elsewhere agreed.*

Women had of course been riding horses for centuries by this point, so why was exchanging four legs for two wheels so controversial? What made one acceptable and the other not partly came down to how you sat on your chosen mount. If you were horse riding, you would have been expected to ride sidesaddle, with both legs demurely draped down one side, which accommodated long Victorian skirts hiding those scandalizing legs. In fact, it would take a world war to kill off this tradition, but sidesaddle wasn't an option on a bicycle. The very act of sitting on a bike seat was assumed by some to lead directly to a woman's downfall, an idea that stems from the prudish and misguided idea that to sit astride a bicycle, or horse, is an overtly sexual act and could also be perilous to women's reproductive organs.

Some men—and a few women—who considered themselves

---

* Including one reader of Washington, D.C.'s *Sunday Herald* who, in 1891, described a woman on a bicycle as "the most vicious thing I ever saw in all my life . . . I had thought that smoking was the worst thing a woman could do, but I have changed my mind."

medical professionals (I use the term loosely here, bearing in mind some doctors at this time thought traveling in fast steam trains might lead to brain damage) felt science was on their side. American gynecologist Dr. Robert Dickinson believed that women cyclists went to great lengths to set up their saddles so as to "bring about constant friction over the clitoris and labia" and that the "pressure would be much increased by stooping forward, and the warmth generated from vigorous exercise might further increase the feeling." I think this says more about the state of Dr. Dickinson's mind than anything else. He was certainly wrong about many things—not least his endorsement of eugenics and his opinion that homosexual women were a threat to society, devoting much of his career to trying to "cure" them.

Others went as far as to say cycling led to promiscuity, a misconception that persists to some extent now in more conservative cultures, and perhaps also explains why women in supposedly more liberal countries often report being subjected to more sexual harassment when they ride a bike than when they are walking.

Victorian manufacturers were quick to cash in on the controversy by producing new types of saddles that they claimed prevented sexual stimulation. Labeled "anatomical" or "hygienic," most models featured a seat with a deep groove down the middle and a shortened nose. Whatever the design, they all claimed the result was elimination of "perineal pressure" or of "relieving the sensitive parts of the body from pressure of any kind." In short, their lady riders wouldn't be getting off by using one of their new saddles, with one company proudly declaring "You do not Straddle the Duplex Saddle."*

---

* This argument seems ironic now, given that many female cyclists, even with today's technological advances, consistently report that their saddles cause huge discomfort, despite there being a plethora of designs on the market which are

In 1896, Dr. Frances Oakley, a doctor who was both a woman *and* a cyclist, had no truck with the saddle stimulation myth and told readers of *Harper's Bazar* that the "freak" saddles marketed in response to this misinformation were constructed on entirely "wrong anatomical premises" and their proliferation was a confusing and distressing distraction. Sadly, this didn't shut down the argument, with some doctors going beyond genitalia and on to the reproductive organs. One thought cycling increased painful periods, and others went as far as to declare it caused infertility. The dominant, though entirely incorrect, medical discourse at this time was that women's gynecology made them the "weaker sex" and any exertion would put their reproductive ability at risk. That bicycling was physical, and that the saddle was in direct contact with women's genitals, made it a huge concern.

According to some, there was no part of a woman's anatomy that might not be ruined by riding a bike, from the head down to the toes. Cynthia, an anxious would-be cyclist, wrote to *The Lady Cyclist* magazine in 1896 to ask for help. She wanted to know if it was true that cycling would make her feet grow. The respondent assured her there was no possibility of that happening, but that what was doubtless true was that there would be a stack of periodical articles arguing the opposite. Indeed, there was a doctor in New York who thought he could detect something he called "bicycle walk" in his cycle-mad patients. He de-

---

supposed to combat this. At the extreme end, Paralympian cyclist Hannah Dines recently revealed she had to undergo surgery on her vulva due to trauma from hours spent training, leaning forward in the race position, which puts pressure on that sensitive area. She described the lack of resources being put into developing designs to make women more comfortable as "laughable," another example of women's needs not always being taken seriously in the industry.

scribed this as the feet moving in a circular instead of a forward motion. Others were worried that the act of leaning forward to reach the handlebars might give them an unsightly "bicycle hump" and, accordingly, women's bicycles at this time were designed with high handlebars to ensure an upright position, an acceptably ladylike riding posture. Any angling down toward the frame, despite being far more aerodynamic, was discouraged.

It was the head, though, that excited as much debate about the potential perils of cycling for women as the reproductive organs, with much concern focusing on so-called "bicycle face." In 1899, Dr. Arabella Kenealy, another eugenics fan, claimed her patient Clara was afflicted. She describes how Clara's face had once had a subtle feminine charm which, since she had taken up cycling and other sports, was now replaced by "muscular tension": "the haze, the elusiveness, the subtle suggestion of the face are gone; it is the landscape without atmosphere." Another doctor suggested that women over forty are the most afflicted by the "ravages" of cycling: "I have seen them rapidly decline in the 'good looks,' become thin and wrinkled, and quickly lose any freshness of appearance they might have had previously." *Harper's* magazine recommended chewing gum to keep the effects at bay.

Men could also develop the condition, with a *New York Herald* journalist describing how he saw "bicycle face" among most members attending a meeting of the League of American Wheelmen in New Jersey. Doctors were more concerned about how it affected women, however, because they felt the loss of femininity was at stake, and that these cycle-mad women would soon be indistinguishable from men. Dr. Kenealy also claimed cycling had made Clara a domestic slattern, given her a manly gait and, worst of all, would result in her "squandering" the "birth right" of her future children. If cycling was robbing women of their femininity, grace and even fertility, then the future of the nation was surely at stake. If they weren't freewheeling into a life of prostitution, then it was making them barren, or even worse, turning them into men.

Perhaps it's unsurprising so many were convinced cycling would make women sick in mind and body, when many doctors at this time were prescribing the "rest cure" to treat mental health issues such as depression and a range of symptoms then generally labeled as "hysteria" or "neurasthenia." The treatment is famously critiqued in Charlotte Perkins Gilman's feminist short story of 1892, "The Yellow Wallpaper," where the narrator, described as exhibiting signs of "temporary nervous depression," is confined to her bed by her doctor husband. She is not even permitted to write, her one true pleasure. Trapped and inactive, she says he "hardly lets me stir without special direction," behavior we would probably label today as coercive control rather than a necessary medical intervention.

The narrator progressively loses touch with reality, obsessing over the design of the bedroom wallpaper and encountering visions of a woman crawling on all fours behind the pattern, and "all the time trying to climb through. But nobody could climb through that pattern—it strangles so." In her mania she tries to free the imagined woman by tearing the wallpaper from the walls, with the trapped woman of course a projection of the narrator's own psyche, and also the author's. For Charlotte Gilman had herself been prescribed her own period of complete inactivity—or domestic imprisonment—by Dr. Silas Mitchell, the architect of the rest cure, to treat her postnatal depression. This "treatment" she describes as having nearly driven her to mental breakdown, and she decided to stop it against doctor's orders. She also left her husband, rejecting suffocating Victorian domesticity to become a full-time writer, describing the decision to leave as the only way to keep her sanity.*

Dr. Mitchell would have strongly disapproved since he was opposed to women working or indeed doing anything that would make them equal to men: "The woman's desire to be on a level of competition with man and to assume his duties is, I am sure, making mischief . . . She is physiologically other than the man."† The treatment echoed a wider culture that wanted to clamp down on women's physical and intellectual independence, with Dr. Mitchell (willfully) blind to the reality that it was in fact women's lack of political, social and physical enfranchisement that was ailing them.

If only the doctor had listened to the many women who claimed that since they had started cycling, they had never felt better. How could they not if the alternative is staying at home to stare at the same four walls? One woman writing to *The Cyclists' Touring Club Gazette* held that her new pastime was the

---

* The writer Virginia Woolf was also subjected to the rest cure to treat her depression, and initially she too was forbidden to write during her treatment, a diktat which seems unimaginably barbaric, not to mention absurd, though eventually she was permitted to work on her novel for just a few hours a day. She too would use fiction to lampoon his methods.

† If it's not obvious by now, Dr. Mitchell had a ludicrously binary approach to gender. While he was prescribing bed rest to his female patients, he was promoting the benefits of the outdoors and exercise to some of his other patients, specifically men who were deemed, according to the rigid gender expectations of the time, to be overly intellectual and too effeminate. His "West" cure had them sent off to Midwestern cattle ranches to do stereotypically "masculine" activities like cattle herding and hunting. Patients included Theodore Roosevelt, who had previously been described as resembling Oscar Wilde, but years later, as U.S. president was seen as epitomizing a more rugged masculinity; and also the poet Walt Whitman, who is now widely considered to have been gay, and who I hope had more of a *Brokeback Mountain* experience with the cowboys on the ranch.

cure for all her ailments: "I have never enjoyed robust health, and for years had been a martyr to neuralgic headaches, accompanied by vomiting—symptoms which baffled the skill of the ablest physicians. Some years ago, I commenced cycling with my husband and daughter, with the result of a great diminution of my old painful malady, and general increase of strength. I am convinced that all women would be better if they too had enough out-of-door exercise." Another enthusiast described how she had previously suffered poor health and fatigue, but since taking up cycling had been energized and could manage up to seventy miles a day.

There were also doctors who were convinced of its benefits for all manner of afflictions. A Dr. Albutt started prescribing moderate cycling to his patients and claimed there was a distinct improvement in all who followed his advice. A woman doctor writing in a cycling magazine in 1896 was unequivocal about the impact the activity had on women's mental and physical health: "When women began to understand the needs of their own organisms and to bring those disused and unvalued members, their muscles, into action, the whole being responded with a joy born of its new freedom. Derision and croaking availed not; the wind tossed their hair, the sun kissed their cheeks, the blood warmed and reddened on their leaping pulses, and they grew strong in body and refreshed in spirit."

French physician Dr. Oscar Jennings countered the idea that cycling led to infertility by suggesting it might have the reverse effect, prescribing it to patients who suffered with any problems associated with their reproductive organs. Similarly a Dr. W. H. Fenton lambasted his peers for spuriously telling women that cycling is harmful, declaring that "there is nothing in the anatomy or the physiology of a woman" that should stop her getting on a bike, that women can "cycle with as much impunity as a man."

He stuck the boot in the misguided medicalization of Victorian women and the rest cure by claiming that 90 percent of cases are a result of ennui and the lack of opportunity to work off energy, with "already thousands of women qualifying for general invalidism" having been "rescued by cycling." Women weren't so frail and helpless after all; exercise wasn't going to kill them or make them infertile, but only make them stronger, which was also useful if you were going to rise up and demand better conditions and opportunities for your gender.

Cycling on Prescription

Dr. Fenton was on to something. The benefits of exercise are now backed up by extensive scientific research, not least the 2017 study published in the medical journal *The Lancet*, which reported that people are as likely to die early from inactive lifestyles as they are from tobacco. An outcome that, albeit unknowingly, patriarchal Victorian culture was willing to force on the female population to keep them under control.

Scientists have also discovered that regular biking, particularly daily commuting, can nearly halve the chance of early death. Research published in *The British Medical Journal* outlined that cycling to the office, as opposed to commuting by car or public transport, is linked with a 45 percent lower risk of developing cancer, and a 46 percent lower risk of cardiovascular disease, as well as reducing the risk of a stroke, type 2 diabetes and other life-threatening conditions. While you might skip the gym if you don't feel like it, if cycling is your way of getting to work then you are more likely to keep doing it. For many people it's also more pleasurable than hitting the treadmill or lifting weights in a gym, which goes a long way in motivating us.

In another study, cycling was shown to slow down the aging process, keeping the immune system young and preserving muscle mass. Certainly, the man and woman in their eighties I recently saw happily cycling up a long, steep climb in the south of France looked like they were reaping the health benefits of their years in the saddle. For schoolchildren too, the impact is just as beneficial, with boys aged ten to sixteen who cycle regularly to school 30 percent more likely to meet recommended fitness levels, while girls are seven times more likely to do so. Inspiring statistics compared to the figure of one in five children in their first year at school in England who are classed as obese or overweight.

The impact on mental well-being is just as significant, with the psychological health of people who commute by car being far worse than those who opt to pedal instead. While it might not be practical for everyone to bike to work, particularly for those commuting longer distances, regular bike riding has an unarguably positive impact on mental health. The cardiovascular workout results in lower levels of adrenaline and cortisol, the stress hormone responsible for spiking levels of tension, and the endorphins released help alleviate anxiety and the symptoms of mild to moderate depression. Numerous studies have also shown that cycling boosts feelings of self-worth, all evidence that it would have been far more sensible for those doctors to have prescribed cycling instead of confinement in bed.

I know from my own experience that cycling is a mood-booster, and I've come to rely on it. On days when I feel a bit low or stressed, I know that if I can motivate myself to get out on my bike it will disrupt any negative thought processes I've sunk into and give me time to think in a more expansive way. It is overwhelmingly restorative. Even commuting a few miles to work each day, despite dealing with London traffic, has an undeniably positive impact on my mental well-being. I'm in control of my journey, I won't be held up by crowds or delays, and getting my blood pumping around my system helps start my day with a burst of energizing endorphins.

Cycling isn't just making us happier; it also apparently expands our brains. A study in the *Journal of Clinical and Diagnostic Research* showed people scoring higher on memory, reasoning and planning tests after thirty minutes of cycling. Exercise creates more blood vessels in the brain and stimulates the growth of proteins that are responsible for forming new brain cells, suggesting that cycling can improve brain health and might even help reduce the risk of cognitive diseases such as Alzheimer's.

On account of compelling evidence that many incidences of type 2 diabetes, stroke, breast cancer and depression could be prevented if more people cycled, some doctors in the U.K. have started prescribing cycling to their patients, and health professionals are lobbying governments to invest in cycling infrastructure to enable more people to reap the proven health benefits. If only more of those nineteenth-century doctors had had the same idea, it would have improved the lives of so many more at a time when women were discouraged from any sort of exercise, at a great cost to their mental and physical health.

CHAPTER THREE

YOU'RE NOT GOING OUT LIKE THAT

Who Is Wearing the Trousers Now?

If fierce disapproval from late nineteenth-century reactionaries and misguided doctors wasn't enough to stop women cycling, then the next problem was how to do so when the clothes they were expected to wear were far from comfortable—or safe. Dr. Fenton recognized this and went as far as to describe women's fashions of the time as nothing short of a "handicap," preventing them from doing much in the way of any physical activity.

Lady Harberton, aka Florence Wallace Pomeroy, would have strongly agreed. On April 5, 1899, she brought her years of campaigning to do away with her generation's fashion staple of long skirts and corsets into the courtroom. The previous October, Florence had been enjoying a bicycle ride through Surrey when she stopped for a caffeine fix at the Hautboy Hotel in Ockham. Making her way to the coffee lounge, she was barred by the hotel's manager, Mrs. Sprague, who said she couldn't enter—"not in that dress." She was redirected instead to the public bar, a traditional boozer with a spit-and-sawdust floor. A space that was, in Florence's opinion, "abominable. It smelled of spirits and all the horrors of a drinking bar."

The hotel would learn that nobody puts a lady in the bar when they found themselves summoned to court for contravening licensing laws. Though perhaps it would be more accurate to describe the charge as discrimination on the grounds of dress. The reason Mrs. Sprague had not wanted Florence in her coffee lounge was on account of her not wearing a skirt. To Mrs. Sprague, Florence may as well have been naked from the waist down as she was wearing "rationals," which was considered by some to be about as scandalous and unacceptable as arriving in your birthday suit.

"Rational" dress came in various forms, but what distinguished it from any other women's apparel was the bottom half—bloomers or knickerbockers instead of a skirt. These were essentially short, baggy trousers tapering to just below the knee—the same worn by that Cambridge effigy.

For many Victorians, women who opted for what was then seen as an overtly masculine outfit were at risk of turning into men. In the nineteenth century, only men were entitled to wear the trousers, both figuratively and literally, and many wanted it to stay that way. Satirical features in the press that aimed to poke fun at the "New Woman," whom they generally saw as a threat to the status quo, almost always pictured her in bloomers and often cycling. In one picture from 1900 captioned "Mind the children, finish the washing, and have dinner at 12," a woman in voluminous check bloomers stands by her bicycle while her apron-wearing husband kneels to tie her laces. In an illustration from *Puck* magazine, an oversized, stern-looking woman in rational dress rides a bike with a man half her size perched on her handlebars under the heading "The New Woman Takes Her

Husband Out for a Ride," and in others men are shown mistaking women in rationals seen from behind, and even face-on, for men. Their meaning was clear: these women were a grave threat to what they saw as the natural order of things, and they needed to be put back in their place.

The bike industry took a different view. Aware of the importance to their revenue of their more liberated women customers, they ran numerous campaigns that celebrated strong, independent women in rationals. Ads for Elliman's Universal Embrocation ointment, a muscle rub, featured athletic women in knickerbockers unashamedly speeding ahead of male cyclists, including one showing the man taking a tumble as the woman passes by. Though even *The Lady Cyclist* magazine, while praising rational dress as contributing to "the greatest blessing of modern womanhood— perfect physical freedom," was alarmed by what it saw as the "swagger" of some of the wearers and their tendency to "use boyish gestures and talk," which they thought "shockingly ungraceful." It's hard to understand now just how shocking it was then for women to wear such an outfit and why so many thought it represented the end of civilization, with one wearer describing the efforts to gain acceptance for rationals as a beleagured "great war."*

Lady Harberton wasn't just experimenting with this risqué fashion, she was the president of the Rational Dress Society, which had been campaigning against the dangerous excesses of

---

* A war they might think that in 2019 they still hadn't won, with the Cannes Film Festival reportedly banning women from appearing on the red carpet unless they are wearing high heels, while the health and labor minister of Japan rejected a petition started by women in the country to ban workplaces making heels a requirement, by telling them that "it is socially accepted as something that falls within the realm of being occupationally necessary and appropriate."

Victorian women's clothes since 1881. Cycling had put the issue of women's dress in the spotlight again, and her spat with the hotel was an opportunity to make rational dress the cause célèbre of the day, with the Cyclists' Touring Club (CTC) the organization progressive enough to bring the case to court on her behalf. While the press was captivated by Florence in her knickerbockers, they generally came down on the side of Mrs. Sprague, as did the British justice system, which concluded that as the Hautboy Hotel hadn't refused to serve her entirely, the charge didn't hold. The jury had also been swayed by photographs of the bar that had been spruced up with white tablecloths and jugs of flowers for its day in court. The CTC retaliated by removing the Hautboy from its list of recommended hotels and advised women members to take a skirt to throw on over their rationals when out touring in order to avoid being thrown out of conservative-minded establishments. Again, it would take a world war before women could wear a bifurcated garment without the risk of having to go to court to get served.

Dying for Fashion

Many women, like Florence, continued to wear rational dress regardless of the opposition and ridicule they encountered, for it offered a freedom of movement sorely lacking in standard nineteenth-century women's fashions, when woman's skirts and petticoats alone could weigh as much as fourteen pounds. Such long skirts dragged on the floor, picking up dirt and germs, and presenting a constant tripping hazard. Their voluminous nature was also problematic: it wasn't unheard-of for women to die of immolation after catching the fabric on an oil lamp or open fire, or even getting pulled under the wheels of a passing cart. If walking was dangerous enough, then it was hardly surprising that women like Florence didn't want to wear them cycling. The only purpose they really served was preventing the wearer from getting very far—perhaps by design—and the richer you were, the bigger and more impractical your dress.

Writing in *The Rational Dress Society's Gazette*, Florence connected the limitations inflicted by women's clothing with their status as the "weaker" sex: "By force of habit, the world forgets that these disabilities are artificial and in consequence the status of women generally, becomes lowered." She was also forthright about who was responsible for contorting women's bodies: "the widest part is on the ground, measuring about seven or eight feet in circumference, tapering up to a round waist not so very much larger than a good-sized throat should be . . . In this form, which may literally be called the work of men's hands, not only are the true lines of Nature ignored, but they are positively reversed."

While it would be some time before common sense prevailed over the desire to cinch the waist to the size of a throat, many women had already decided to banish the corset. Not a small thing when corsetry had been de rigueur, even at times for men, from the sixteenth century onward. Some doctors were ready to back them up, deeming it injurious as well as uncomfortable. Dr. Victor Neesen charged the corset with pushing the organs and stomach upward against the heart and that "the pressure on the large vessels causes a stagnation of blood in the valveless veins of the sexual organs—a potent cause of many of the ailments peculiar to women." I can't attest to whether this is scientifically correct, but it's certainly true that overtight corsets restricted blood and oxygen flow, causing fainting.

One woman writing to *The Lady Cyclist* magazine in 1895

likened the lives of women who partook in the fashions of the day to "one long suicide" and a "living death," with their corsets responsible for "fainting, hysteria, indigestion, anemia, lassitude, diminished vitality and a host of other sufferings." She held up cycling as pivotal in helping the cause of dress reform, which she felt long overdue: "Such is the woman of old, now happily dying out. Dress reform is one of the great factors in this result, and the cycle is an aid to this reform. Therefore, the cycle is to be gratefully welcomed, and its use promoted by all thinking women." Alarmed at the number of women abandoning their corsets, the American Lady Corset Company started offering free hundred-dollar bicycle insurance with every new corset purchased.

Bloomer Brigade

Florence wasn't the first to start a movement to consign the corset and the crinoline to the dustbin. The original agitator for the rationalization of women's dress gave her name to the article of clothing that offended so many: Amelia Jenks Bloomer.

In the 1850s, Amelia, alongside fellow feminists Elizabeth Cady Stanton and Elizabeth Smith Miller, started wearing billowy Turkish-style trousers which came to the ankle and a knee-length skirt or dress over the top. It was named the "freedom dress," much as Susan B. Anthony later referred to the bicycle as a "freedom-machine"—both represented independence and autonomy through freedom of movement.

The group had a keen interest in women's liberation and had previously been part of the Seneca Falls Convention in 1848, the first recorded women's rights gathering. Amelia toured the United States and the U.K. and wrote articles in her women's newspaper, *The Lily*, to encourage others to adopt the costume. Some did, with the actress Fanny Kemble one of the most visible enthusiasts. Further afield, women were wearing versions of the outfit for practical rather than political reasons, such as frontierswomen who needed something better suited to the harsh pioneer life. One woman on a Midwestern prairie farm eulogized about how much she could get done in her new style of dress: "I can do the work for 16 cows, and 18 persons in the family; can walk 7 miles and be none the worse for it." These women were mostly out of sight and not the focus of the media who were going wild over what they were dubbing the "bloomer costume." This—to our eyes now—demure and feminine outfit was causing quite the culture shock and was ruthlessly satirized in the press, which ran caricatures of masculinized women dressed in the outfit.

Elizabeth Cady Stanton's husband was also the victim of media prejudice against his wife's choice of outfit when he ran for a second term in the Senate, with lines such as "Twenty tailors take the stitches, Mrs. Stanton wears the breeches," which undoubtedly helped diminish his majority. Wearing bloomers in public was also attracting the wrong type of attention, and Susan B. Anthony had firsthand experience of it on a visit to a post office in New York City. She had to be rescued by a policeman after she was surrounded by a mob of jeering men, forcing her to rethink whether the world was yet ready for women wearing something akin to trousers.

It wasn't long before the original advocates, even Amelia Bloomer, gave up wearing the costume, as they believed it was detracting attention from the pressing issue of women's rights. It was another forty years before the next generation of women who wanted to comfortably ride their "freedom-machines" would push the idea of "freedom dress" into the spotlight again.

Amelia died in 1894, sadly without seeing the swaths of new converts and the controversy they were attracting.

"A Lamentable Incident"

Despite the obvious benefits of rational-style outfits for the cyclist, debate over whether it was acceptable raged on throughout the decade. In 1893, almost exactly five years before Florence's bloomers got her turned away from the Hautboy, Angeline Allen of Newark, New Jersey, and her cycling outfit were making the news. One of the most popular U.S. men's magazines of the day, *The National Police Gazette*, ran a story under the headline "She Wore Trousers," where they described how Angeline had shocked her neighborhood when out for a bicycle ride clad in bloomers and black stockings, "a costume that caused hundreds to turn and gaze in astonishment," with the wearer seemingly "utterly oblivious of the sensation she was causing." That might not have been quite accurate, as when interviewed by another journalist, Angeline said she wore bloomers *in order* to be looked at. The crowd probably wasn't so unsuspecting either—only a few months previously she had caused a scandal among her fellow swimmers at Asbury Park for wearing a bathing dress that stopped several inches above her knees. The shocked, and not unexcited, crowd made such a scene that she was escorted back to the bathing hut to change under police protection. Soon residents of Newark were running to their windows whenever they heard she might be cycling past.

The same year that Angeline was causing curtains to twitch in New Jersey, sixteen-year-old Tessie Reynolds from Brighton, England, became the focus of fierce debate when she attempted to break a new women's cycling record, the 120-mile Brighton to

London and back. She achieved a time of 8 hours, 38 minutes, an astonishing feat when a woman on a bike was still not universally accepted, let alone a woman getting competitive with it. Afterward, a medical professional examined her and confirmed that it had done no damage, though many might have refused to believe it. Tessie was one of those "wild women" and had already been cycling for at least three years by this point, probably seriously if this performance was anything to go by. Her father, who acted as timekeeper for the event, was also cycle-mad, running his own bicycle shop and racing at the nearby Preston Park Velodrome, and with their family home doubling as a boarding house for cyclists.

Newspapers across the country and as far away as the United States reported on Tessie's achievement, though many were far from enthusiastic about women racing. *Cycling* magazine declared it "a lamentable incident" that would pain anyone believing in the "innate modesty and sense of becomingness in the opposite sex." They were equally fixated on her outfit. Like Angeline and Florence, she chose not to cycle in a skirt, preferring knee-length wool knickerbockers, with a long jacket in the same fabric. One British newspaper called it "a caricature of the sweetest and best half of humanity," though much of the cycling press was more forward thinking, recognizing the advantages for female cyclists. The women's page of *Bicycling News* said they wished to "congratulate Miss Reynolds on her courage in being an apostate of the movement," and in the same publication, a male writer called her "the stormy petrel heralding the storm of revolt against the petticoat."

Whether people approved or not, Tessie had become a celebrity. Soon Brighton shops were selling postcards of her dressed in her rationals. Her unapologetic embrace of bloomers may have given other women the confidence to follow suit. Certainly sightings of women in similar outfits were becoming more common, causing one outraged woman to write to *The Daily Telegraph*: "I protest, in the name of every self-respecting woman, against the shocking and painful spectacle which has, for the last fortnight, disgraced our public thoroughfares in some of the suburban districts—that of women who, in addition to the degradation of riding a bicycle, have further unsexed themselves by doing so in man's attire. I contend that this proceeding is demoralizing and calculated still further to lower the standard of man's respect for woman." She went on to ask whether this movement can "be stopped on the score of illegality? If it be illegal for a man to wear woman's attire, is it not equally so for a woman to assume that of a man?" Though judging by the fan mail Tessie received, including one marriage proposal, not all men found her outfit repellent.

Tessie would continue to be a vocal advocate of rationals and may have been the reason why Brighton came to be regarded by some as the home of the bloomer. A reader writing to *Cycling* magazine in 1894 was unimpressed, singling out the rationals-wearing women of the seaside town as being of a particularly unladylike sort, reporting that he saw one on Brighton Pier drinking with men in a bar and that most of them were "shop girls" wanting to "create a small sensation." In other words, real ladies didn't wear bloomers.

Meanwhile, across the pond, some U.S. states had criminalized what they defined as "cross-dressing." France took a different view, with the fashionable women of Paris's Bois de Boulogne enthusiastically adopting the bloomer costume without causing mass moral outrage. Somewhat surprising given it had been illegal since 1799 for women to wear trousers in the city, with the only exceptions allowed on health grounds and requiring a permit—a decree that had come into effect following the Revolution, when Parisian feminist revolutionaries had worn trousers.

In 1892, the law was modified to allow an exception if the trousered woman was "holding a bicycle handlebar or the reins of a horse"; otherwise she had to seek permission from the police to "dress like a man." Though there were of course women who wore trousers regardless, risking arrest. The writer George Sand favored a more traditionally masculine outfit that allowed her to move freely around Paris and access places where women were unwelcome or even barred.

The law wasn't formally repealed until 2013, though it had been long since disregarded. It may have been the novelty of the new decree which was behind the sudden popularity of bloomers, but at least the government at the time had been clear-sighted enough to see that wearing long skirts on a bicycle wasn't practical or safe, even if they weren't going to go the full hog and let women wear such a garment doing whatever they pleased. The editor of the ladies' page of *Cycling* commented enviously: "Parisian women are riding and enjoying themselves, blissfully ignorant of the meaning of posing as a pioneer in a rational dress."

Paris, a city always at the forefront of fashion, was soon inspiring women's cycling fashions elsewhere, with most of the cycling magazines—and even *Vogue*—regularly reporting on the latest styles sported in the Bois. Much of the press was enthusiastic about the Parisian women's bloomers, often cut in fine and delicate pale fabrics, describing them as "graceful" and "feminine," suggesting that even when the general concept was accepted, too many still focused on whether the style was ladylike or not. By contrast, the more practical and less fashion-orientated U.K. rational wearers, in their hard-wearing wool serges and tweeds, were still too often regarded as on the more male end of the Victorian gender spectrum.

Even the Parisian women in their fashionable bloomers didn't manage to convert everyone to the idea of women abandoning their debilitating skirts. Helen Follett on her tandem honeymoon in 1896 was warned by a local in New Orleans that he thought a woman would be "lynched" for wearing bloomers in the Southern states. Even Helena Swanwick, who described how her skirts regularly caught in her pedals, hurling her to the ground, felt unable to wear bloomers except under cover of darkness. Then she experienced such a feeling of liberation from the constraints of her gender that she would find herself singing a German ditty which included the line "What glorious rapture to be a he-man!"

Creative Needlework

While some women believed the benefits of bloomers far outweighed the negativity they aroused, others opted to get creative, adapting their existing outfits so they could pass as what was defined as a respectable Victorian woman, while avoiding a spill. To do this, some were simply raising their hems a little and rationalizing the amount of fabric to create a narrower skirt, often inserting weights into the hem to avoid the fabric flying up and exposing an eyeful of leg, while others were using clever devices to create a skirt that could be transformed into a cycleproof, but noncontroversial, garment.

Clothing for women on a bicycle in the 1890s was a complex puzzle, with the tension between what was practical and acceptable, and countless women were trying to solve it, with many registering their designs with the patent office in the hope of turning their interest into a commercial enterprise.

One such was Alice Bygrave of Brixton in London, who had

success with her patented Bygrave Convertible Skirt in 1896. Fashion brand Jaeger, then Dr. Jaeger's Sanitary Woolen System Company, bought the design and produced the skirt in a range of fabrics, and Alice traveled as far as the United States to promote it. Her design featured a sophisticated system of weights, pulleys and buttons so the skirt could be raised both at the front and the back when mounted, with the material ruched around the hips. The crucial thing for the rider, which the ads boasted, was that it could be "instantaneously raised or dropped," so on dismounting, the wearer could seamlessly transition back into the acceptable standard for Victorian feminine dress.

Alice had her sister-in-law Rosina Lane, a cyclist who raced at London's Royal Aquarium, wear the skirt when she competed to promote the benefits of the design. Soon it was possible to send off for patterns for many of these new-style garments, so they could be run up at home if you couldn't afford a tailor.

An equally successful and popular way of avoiding unwarranted attention was with a divided skirt, or *jupe-culotte* as it was called by the fashionable Parisians of the Bois. These pleated wide-legged trousers were indistinguishable from a full skirt when the wearer was standing, but gave them freedom of movement without risk of exposing flesh. They also came with the approval of Oscar Wilde, an arbiter of fashion if ever there was one. In an essay entitled "The Philosophy of Dress," which was published in the *New-York Tribune* in 1885, Oscar made the case that women's clothing needed to be simplified—rationalized— and came down in favor of the divided skirt, which he saw as giving "ease and liberty" to the wearer. Though he was less keen on the idea of using so much fabric so as to "pass" as a skirt, since he didn't feel that would help the long-term goal of women's dress reform: "Let it visibly announce itself as what it actually is, and it will go far towards solving a real difficulty."

The fact he had come to dwell on the problem of women's fashions was doubtless down to his wife. Constance Wilde was often pictured in her own elegant divided skirt, campaigned alongside Florence Harberton as part of the Rational Dress Society and was editor of its gazette. Dress reform would have been far from Oscar's thoughts by the time he was tragically imprisoned on charges of sodomy and gross indecency a decade later, though women in trousers, like homosexuality, were still perceived as a threat to Victorian masculinity. *Jupe-culottes* enjoyed a comeback as a result of the bicycle, with Parisians, those early embracers of the bloomer, considering it the height of fashion for a season at least and with women who weren't quite ready to make such a statement with bloomers finding it was a neat solution for riding a bike without breaking their neck.

Out with the Corsetry, In with the Lycra

Thankfully women today, in the West at least, are relatively free to choose what they wear whatever they are doing. Florence Harberton would have been thrilled by the streamlined and nonrestrictive cycle-specific clothing available for women now. Just observing the cyclists in London, you see women in a huge spectrum of outfits, from those on the way to the office in heels and suits to others in head-to-toe Lycra. Sadly, despite this, we know there are still fewer women cycling than men, at least in the U.K. and U.S. The lack of safe cycling infrastructure is one of the main reasons, but another significant barrier is the extent to which women feel they are judged by how they look. We may have more options than our Victorian sisters, but our appearance continues to dictate what we feel we can and can't do.

When I was cycling through France in 2018, a male hotel owner made a comment about my bike shoes which exemplified the pressure women are subjected to. The hotelier pointed to my cleated shoes and told me, sarcastically, that they were "very sexy." He was making a joke, one that derives from the assumption that it is a woman's responsibility to look attractive and feminine at all times. The shoes help me pedal more efficiently, which had come in handy since I'd cycled ninety miles that day, and their sex-appeal wasn't a consideration. Is it any wonder that some women don't get as far as putting their workout clothes on when such attitudes are so pervasive?

Pressure from the press and social media are large factors in why insecurity about body image is so endemic, particularly in western societies. People are literally dying from botched surgery in their quest to look more like a Kardashian. Sport England, whose remit is to encourage greater participation in sports, has found that concerns about body image are often cited by women and girls as a reason for avoiding physical activity. Many feel that they don't have the right body shape, that they will look unattractive working out and are too self-conscious to get active.

The assumption that you have to dress like a Tour de France contender, in skintight shorts and jerseys, might be enough to stop some women from taking up cycling. Some are also worried that they might be perceived as looking "unfeminine" if they appeared too sporty, sadly suggesting that our ideas around gender haven't progressed much since rational wearers were called "unwomanly" or "ungraceful." This helps explain why there is a huge drop in girls cycling to school when they hit their teens and why fewer women exercise in general than men.

Happily, body positivity is finally filtering into the mainstream, with ad campaigns beginning to include people who are more representative. Sport England's This Girl Can campaign shunned celebrities and professional athletes, opting instead for women of all ages, abilities, ethnic backgrounds and body shapes to share their positive experiences of working up a sweat. A film they made unashamedly celebrates ordinary women—complete with cellulite, sweat and wobbling flesh—on massive endorphin highs from getting their blood pumping. The inclusive nature of the campaign's imaging challenges entrenched ideas about what women and girls should look like when they are being active, as well as redefining what being athletic looks like. Sport England claims that within a year 2.8 million girls and women aged fourteen to forty reported they had done more physical activity as a result of the campaign; 1.6 million of them didn't previously exercise.

There's still a long way to go before the culture completely changes, with many professional female athletes reporting that they feel that the public and media value what they look like more than what they achieve in their sport—a pernicious consequence of our image-saturated culture in the social media age. Even professional women athletes are expected to look sexy as well as being at the top of their game. Not least is the first ever winner of soccer's prestigious Ballon d'Or Féminin award in 2018, Ada Hegerberg, who was asked by the prize's host to twerk onstage when she collected her award. She refused.

Countless professional sportswomen have also complained that they have been subjected to derogatory comments from other professionals. It seems "skinny = good" prevails even within the industry, regardless of achievement. Olympic cyclist Jess Varnish brought a lawsuit against the technical director of British Cycling for, among other serious allegations, insulting her size and shape. In athletics, Olympic gold medal–winning heptathlete Jessica Ennis-Hill claimed a senior figure in British Athletics called her fat. Numerous female, and even male, professional cyclists have reported developing, or coming close to developing, eating disorders due to the immense pressure to be lean and light, and report that their trainers regularly make digs about their weight.

If women at the top of the game are feeling pressured to look a certain way, then it's understandable that many nonathletes feel it's not for them. They are missing out on the huge proven health benefits of exercise. Without more realistic and representative images of women being active, that's unlikely to change. It has also been proven that just a few weeks of moderate exercise can help improve someone's body image, even with little or no change to their physical appearance, and the good thing about endorphins is that once they start kicking in, they become addictive, with one revolution of the bicycle wheel leading to another revolution.

CHAPTER FOUR

TRANSMISSION

Pedal Power

It's a blowy day on Hackney Downs in East London. A foreboding gray sky is offset by the autumn leaves which give a much-needed pop of color. I'm here with a group of female refugees and asylum seekers who have signed up for women-only cycling lessons run by a charity called The Bike Project. They are all at different stages in their learning, with some attempting to master balance as they walk-wheel across the asphalt ball courts, while others are circling the perimeter, practicing hand signals, changing gears and emergency braking. I bring up the rear of a group of riders who have all been attending long enough that they confidently ride away from the practice court to take their learning to the next level, following their instructor on a cycle skills lesson along the park's tree-lined avenue and navigating around dogs, joggers and a group of schoolchildren. A park-keeper, seeing this crocodile of women cyclists wearing helmets and high-visibility clothing, calls out proudly that his daughter is also learning to ride and has just moved beyond stabilizers, a major stepping-stone on the way to becoming a cyclist.

Most of the women and girls attending these "Pedal Power" sessions never had the opportunity to learn to ride as children, so this is a new—and not a little daunting—skill they are hoping to master. When they talk about why they come and what they get from the experience, it's often about de-stressing, relaxation, learning new skills, with one participant describing how "cycling gives you wings, you're flying. It brings such happiness and joy." These are all appealing and freeing experiences for anyone, not least if your refugee or asylum status means that you don't have the right to work and are living in a constant state of uncertainty about whether you will get to stay or be sent back to the country you fled. Not to mention the pressure of having to survive on the equivalent of forty-eight dollars a week.

An Iranian woman tells me she had been a nurse before she came to the U.K., but now living with her daughter and not being allowed to work, she feels she has lost much of her freedom, both financial and personal. She has been in London eight years but is still waiting for a decision from the Home Office on whether she will be granted permanent right to remain. With little autonomy in this process, it's understandable why she's drawn to these sessions where learning to ride offers both a sense of empowerment and the physical pleasure of self-propelled movement and speed, not to mention access to an economical form of transport.

In the beginners' lesson, an Eritrean woman who is still wobbly on her wheels takes a tumble. Undeterred, and ignoring the instructor's suggestion to take a break, she gets straight back in the saddle. Despite the falls, she is one of the group's most enthusiastic learners, telling me that "every time Friday comes, I am so excited. It's like being in love with a guy and going to see them. I've never had such joy since I came to the U.K." Soon, many of the learners will be expert enough to graduate from the group and will be given a bicycle they can take home, a second-hand bicycle that has been donated to the charity and expertly restored by its mechanics: wheels of their own so they can continue to enjoy their newfound pastime and explore their new home city for free.

For many, learning to ride a bike is a childhood rite of passage. It was my dad and siblings who helped me make the jump from trike to bike. Everyone in my family rode one, my mum had previously used hers to get to work and my dad used his to de-stress out of the office. My eldest brother had taken up racing while the other preferred mountain biking. My sister, meanwhile, had a brown vintage sit-up-and-beg–style bike and she would often seat me on the comfy sprung saddle and pedal me to school. There was no question that at some point I too would be riding around on my own set of wheels.

I can still picture that first bike, acid yellow with fat white tires, that one of my brothers had found abandoned in a Bristol woodland and had expertly made roadworthy again. He was forever taking apart and reassembling his own growing collection of bikes, so he knew what he was doing. The width of the tires was an asset when it came to balancing, but I was soon progressing to bigger bikes with skinnier wheels. Later, I would explore the neighborhood on my pink Raleigh Bianca shopper with friends who had also been bought bikes or inherited them from older siblings. I was jealous of the Raleigh Chopper ridden by the brother of a friend; those bikes modeled on motorcycles—

with the large seat with a backrest, very high handlebars and gearstick—and for a time I hankered after a BMX, which all the cool kids rode.

Learning to ride was an intrinsic part of growing up, like tying my own shoelaces, and I've been surprised when friends have told me that it wasn't part of their journey to adulthood. Though of course it relies on having someone to teach you and access to a bike, not to mention the motivation.

For many of the learners at Pedal Power it just wasn't something girls did in their countries; they had no opportunity to try it even if they had wanted to. Others didn't have a bike they could practice on. As an adult learner it's no easier, and possibly more difficult. It's not like swimming, where you can go to your nearest pool and sign up for lessons. There are cycle sessions for adults, but they are relatively few and far between since keeping and storing a bank of bicycles for would-be cyclists, as well as supplying instructors, is expensive and needs lots of space—though there are some excellent organizations who do just this. It's also physically more challenging as an adult since it's harder to balance, farther to fall—tougher on our bodies when we do—and we are inherently more aware of our vulnerability. When you've been riding a bike for years, it requires little more thought than walking, but watching the women at Pedal Power go through the stages of mastering balance while propelling themselves with enough speed to keep going, it appears it's more complicated than it may feel to someone who has been doing it long enough that it's second nature.

When I returned to the sessions after a month, the Eritrean woman who had been unsteady before—falling enough to make someone less determined reconsider whether this was something they really did want to do—was now pedaling around Hackney

Downs with confidence. Through grit and determination something had finally clicked. Her refurbished Raleigh—her "Lamborghini" as she called it—was going to be coming home with her so she didn't have to wait for Fridays to cycle. She is now part of a rich history of women who have been helped by other women to find empowerment, freedom and enjoyment in cycling which stretches back to when women first started taking to two wheels.

Back to School

Learning to ride in the late nineteenth century was also not without its challenges. Many who were keen were long past childhood, and anyway, given it was considered an adults-only activity, children were generally discouraged from learning. A degree of dedication and bravery would have been required—not least for women who were also fighting against moral panic—but luckily great numbers exhibited these qualities and thought the effort and disapproval a small price to pay for mastering a machine that would bring both pleasure and freedom.

The sheer number of people wanting to learn to ride in the bike-mad 1890s gave rise to cycling schools, which overtook the ice rink as the popular venue to while away a few hours.

One particularly exclusive school was Kingstone & Co. on London's Sloane Street, which *The Lady Cyclist* described as a "school for the upper-classes." Here novices would start on the "auto-instructor," a machine suspended on rollers to practice pedaling and balancing without the risk of falling. The magazine was careful to point out that pupils were fitted with a leather belt with a handle, so the male instructors wouldn't touch them.

Over in Belgravia, H. G. Thomas's school was in a former

sculptor's studio with its marble statuary filling the waiting room and a grand piano to provide musical accompaniment. Not all cycling schools were quite so rarefied, as many of the bicycle shops springing up quickly realized that including cycle instruction for new riders would boost sales. Just as people came to see the cream of London society cycling in the parks, some cycle schools became a place to watch friends and family come to grips with this new sport, such as Le Petit Ménage on the Champs-Elysées in Paris, which also had a bar to keep spectators well lubricated.

Instruction wasn't restricted to cycling schools—many women penned manuals to share their know-how and encouragement with their sisters. One such writer was American suffragist and president of the Woman's Christian Temperance Union, Frances Willard, who in 1893 became a keen cyclist at the age of fifty-three and thought her story might inspire other women.

Frances had been suffering with poor health and had come to recover at Reigate Priory, the English stately home of her good friend Lady Isabella Somerset. Frances describes how she had been close to what sounds like a breakdown, brought on by the death of her mother in addition to years of working without a break. Instead of a rest cure, she was prescribed an exercise regimen to build her strength. Isabella, a keen cyclist herself, encouraged Frances to learn, gifting her a bicycle which she named "Gladys." The two women had a deep emotional bond, with Frances describing Isabella as "my beautiful picture gallery and library, landscape and orchestra"—and with Isabella calling Frances "the earthly anchor of my happiness." It's unsurprising she followed her advice without hesitation.

Frances was truly taken with her new "freedom-machine," which helped recapture the feeling she had experienced as a child when she "ran wild" on her Wisconsin farm. A sensation that had ended abruptly at age sixteen when she was forced into the strictures of Victorian female adulthood of long skirts, corsets and a life indoors. In her imprisoning new garments walking was such a trial that she was deprived of the pleasures of the outdoors—despite being "born with an inveterate opposition to staying in the house." She had instead pursued her freedom through education, becoming dean of the women's college of Northwestern University before moving on to the Temperance Union. In addition to sobriety, she campaigned for women's education, suffrage, an end to domestic violence, and better prison and working conditions.

Frances had also planned to write a novel imagining the life of the first female president of the United States, but her campaigning work was all-consuming, and she never got on to it. She would be shocked that over a century after she had this idea, a female president still hadn't existed outside of fiction.*

Frances did however find time to write *A Wheel within a Wheel*. It is appropriately dedicated to Isabella, the woman who initiated her into the cycling world, just as she hoped to do in turn for her readers. On the cover and within the pages of my edition are photographs of a serious and determined-looking Frances on her bicycle, almost always surrounded by one or two other women, underlining the message that this activity also belongs to women. These are doubtless the series of teachers, her "devoted and pleasant comrades," who supported the bicycle while she learned to balance, offering advice and encouragement. She doesn't gloss over that becoming an accomplished wheelwoman takes time, patience and strength of will, but she sees

---

* In 1913, readers of London's *Evening Standard* in 1913 voted her dear friend Lady Isabella the woman they would most like as a female prime minister.

these as attributes essential to mastery of life in general. Indeed, she goes as far as to say that she found a "whole philosophy of life in the wooing and the winning of my bicycle." She identifies fear of judgment as one of the biggest obstacles in learning this new skill, for "we are all unconsciously the slaves of public opinion," which is certainly true now and was even more so then, not least for an unmarried woman in her fifties. Yet such prejudices had no bearing for Frances, and she was adamant that the bicycle could advance women's cause, citing the positive impact it could have on rationalizing dress, as well as eroding entrenched opinions about what women can or can't do. In fact, she saw it almost as her duty as a woman in the public eye, one whom so many looked up to, to prove that gender is no obstacle.

Frances quotes doctors who were convinced of the benefits of the exercise for women, a sensible tactic when the voices of reason were often drowned out by a chorus of unreason. She also imparts her advice on how to successfully master your own Gladys, including how balance requires more precision than mathematics, that if the mind wobbles then so does the wheel, and how looking down is guaranteed to end in a fall. Within three months of practicing for ten to twenty minutes most days, Frances was happily cycling off on Gladys without being propped up by her mentors.

Cycling wasn't a fleeting interest for Frances. With her girlhood love of adventure reawakened, in 1896 she set off on a cycling tour to the south of France with Lady Isabella. (The tour was cut short when they decided to go to Marseille instead, to help the Armenian refugees who had just arrived in the city having fled the massacre in their country. They set up a center in a disused hospital, housing and feeding them, as well as successfully organizing resettlement for many in the United States and the U.K.)

The same year that Isabella and Frances had temporarily put cycling aside for humanitarian work, Maria Ward, a member of the Staten Island Bicycle Club in New York, was publishing her *Bicycling for Ladies*. A photograph taken the previous year of Maria (nicknamed Violet) and her sister Caroline shows them standing with their safety bicycles alongside other members of the club, and unusually for a club photo of this time, the group is made up of at least as many women as men. Maria is in the center wearing what looks like rationals, with the other women mostly in long skirts, puff-sleeved blouses and fancy hats, while the men wear knee-length breeches, long socks and straw boaters. The text on the back invites the recipient to join the club on a ride departing from St. George at 4:30 p.m. on June 25 before returning to the clubhouse for tea. The photo was taken by Alice Austen, another member and one of the first women documentary photographers. Alice took the many photographs in the book, which all feature gymnast Daisy Elliott illustrating different positions in her knickerbockers.

Maria's book is an instructional primer on everything women would need to know to become accomplished cyclists. While Frances Willard took a more philosophical approach, this guide is thorough and extensive, covering which type of bicycle to choose, what to wear (bloomers ideally, or a skirt that comes to no lower than halfway between knees and ankles), and how to get on and stay on, as well as the rules of the road and how to teach others.

While Maria emphasizes the practical benefits of cycling—transport and exercise—she is most rapturous when writing about the opportunities for exploration and discovery. She meditates on how "the road stretches out before you" with its "succession of wonderful possibilities" and "instead of a few squares, you know several towns; instead of an acquaintance with the country for a few miles about, you can claim familiarity with two or three counties; an all-day expedition is reduced to a matter of a couple of hours." The possibility for adventure, a novelty to so many Victorian women, is the rich reward if you follow Maria's guidance, a sentiment echoed on the cover of the lavish leather-bound original edition with its gold embossed lettering on deep blue, featuring an image of a euphoric woman in rationals coasting down a hill, her feet resting on the foot pegs on her front wheel, hat flying off behind, while on the back cover a little dog dashes down the road after her.

Maria's repeated use of words like "conquer," "mastery" and "achieve" drive home the goal to become an active agent. While she suggests female friends can assist each other in learning to ride, she is also adamant that it's possible to do so simply with the support of a fence post. *Bicycling for Ladies* stresses the freedom that lies in store in being independent and self-sufficient— quite radical when women of her era were so often defined by their very dependence. Though clearly keen on the social aspects of cycling, with her teas and group rides, she also wants her readers to be "ready to meet any emergency" and not be reliant on anyone else to fix or maintain their machines. Those who can accomplish this are, in Maria's view, the most "keenly alive," and least likely to be stranded helpless on the roadside with a puncture or broken chain.

For where is the freedom of the open road if you must wait for someone else to come along to fix your problem? Maria describes in detail the geometry of the bicycle and how the different parts fit together, instructing her readers to examine each nut and screw to determine its purpose. In a chapter titled "Women and Tools," she sets out to demystify the idea of working with hardware, severing its connection to masculinity by suggesting that "any woman who is able to use a needle or scissors can use other tools equally well." Hammers and wrenches are no more alien to Maria than the staples of domesticity, though possibly the reference may date the book for contemporary women readers—I'm sure I'm not alone in being able to mend a puncture but unable to darn a sock. She takes the reader on a tour through the various uses of the tools required in a bicycle workshop before setting them the task of taking a bicycle apart entirely, cleaning its constituent parts before reassembling—all to be done in a room where the door can be locked to avoid interruptions. It seems that the room of one's own that Maria prized was one with a workbench and strewn with bicycle parts, a room she describes in detail, with everything in its proper place—a place where she has already spent a fair bit of time, judging by the confident way she imparts her knowledge.

That same year in the U.K., Lillias Campbell Davidson published the *Handbook for Lady Cyclists*, her contribution to the growing library of cycling self-help for and by women. Lillias was born in Brooklyn in 1853 but had been living in the south of England for some years by this point. She had previously written a handbook for women travelers, so it's safe to say that Lillias wanted women to get out and see the world. Like Maria, she also wanted them to acquaint themselves with the mechanics of their machines, especially for those who wanted to cycle alone in rural areas. Where she may have differed from Maria is in her advice that there is no need for a woman to be "constantly airing her knowledge in conversation." Knowledge may be power, but for Lillias it wasn't always advisable to draw attention to the fact you were in possession of it. She was already practiced in hiding things that weren't seen as appropriate to her gender: when she started cycling in the late 1880s, one of those pioneer women, she had restricted herself to the early mornings to avoid being spotted.

One thing Lillias refused to compromise on was what women should wear, stating that it is "out of the question" for women to use their normal clothing on a bicycle. She prefers a shorter, narrow skirt with knickerbockers instead, a costume she thought should be adopted for all daily activities. She bemoans how men can jump on a bike just as they are, unaware of the "terrible hampering a woman suffers from with a flapping, sail-like mass of draperies" which is the source of a woman's "most profound anxiety, her deepest sorrow." For Lillias, having to change outfits just to get in the saddle turns the activity into "a grave affair of premeditation," making the bicycle far from the complete "freedom-machine" it could be.

Rationals, or the bloomer costume, seemed to Lillias the most sensible outfit for cycling, but only if carefully cut and tailored for the wearer—while she was a vocal advocate for women cyclists, in her book as well as her column in the *Cyclists' Touring Club Gazette*, she still hadn't quite left behind her days of swerving into a side street to avoid shocking the vicar. Throughout her handbook she fixates on how women cyclists need to retain their "feminine grace and dignity" and that those who didn't were "fearsome apparitions." For Lillias, it was the natural way of things for women to want to look as nice as possible whatever they are doing, and although she is writing a guide for other women, she holds inexperienced women teaching their friends responsible for the fact that, in her opinion, 99 percent of women cyclists are "defective in style." According to Lillias, appearances are everything and "if she looks loud, fast and simply a fright, she is doing [cycling] infinite harm."

This compulsion to encourage women to take up cycling

while simultaneously insisting they do so in an appropriately feminine manner was a common trait in manuals and the cycling press at the time. Even women's cycling magazines, like *The Lady Cyclist* (edited by a man), fixated on women's correct deportment and dress on a bicycle, and while they were often happy to recommend rationals, they would insist they be properly tailored so as not to repulse any passing men. They featured short stories that almost always centered on cycling-based romantic liaisons of well-behaved middle-class heterosexual women, reinforcing their message that women who cycle can—and should—still be feminine and desirable. Women's bodies were continually policed across their pages, with certain shapes deemed unsuitable for particular items of clothing, one writer even commenting that some women who have "peculiarities of figure and form" will never look good on a bicycle. With so many newspapers and women's magazines today still body shaming, despite women now being largely so much more enfranchised than our Victorian sisters, it's sometimes hard to see how far we've moved on.

Another contributor declared that there is no sight "more distressing to the refined mind than that of a gaudily dressed woman returning travel-stained and untidy after a long day's cycle on dusty roads," and recommended a small vanity mirror be fixed to the handlebars for "there is no disputing that one's hair does become disarranged in the course of a long tour, and that smuts do sometimes settle on the nose, and one's hat just a trifle tip-tilted."

It isn't clear among all this advice whether it's less about abiding by patriarchal norms and more about ensuring women can cycle without attracting the wrong sort of attention. For while that may sound like a limiting view, working within the existing codes rather than breaking them down would at least have helped deflect the idea that it wasn't an appropriate pursuit for a woman and, more important, encourage less socially rebellious women to give it a go. Perhaps this was an understandable tactic when even the U.K.'s first female salaried journalist, Eliza Lynn Linton, was regularly using her columns to single out cycling for what she saw as its deleterious effect on Victorian womanhood. Eliza, an ardent antifeminist, held the bicycle as helping usher in what she saw as those "dangerous" new feminine freedoms symbolized by the "New Woman."

While Lillias couldn't be defined as a rebel—although it's notable she never married, preferring to live alone or with other women—she did want as many women as possible to experience the same benefits that she did from cycling, particularly getting out and seeing the world. There was safety in numbers; the more it became an everyday occurrence, the less it could be deemed inappropriate. To her, every woman on a bicycle was an "advocate," "the best advertisement for the sport," while "slovenly" and ungraceful cyclists were letting the side down by frightening rather than encouraging all-important new recruits.

A Club of One's Own

Hackney Downs is an appropriate place for the Pedal Power pupils to be learning to ride bicycles—it was the original home of one of the first ever cycling clubs, the Pickwick Bicycle Club, formed in 1870, the year of Charles Dickens's death and named in his honor. Uniquely, the club combined cycling with an interest in the author's work. Still in existence today, its members carry on some of the original traditions, including taking on the soubriquet of a character from *The Pickwick Papers*, such as Count Smorltork, Augustus Snodgrass and Dismal Jemmy. Members are referred to en masse as The Pickwick Fathers, an appropriately gendered term as this is a men-only institution, even in 2019.

Photographs on the club's website of their annual garden party show a sea of white men filling the Grand Connaught Rooms with its crystal chandeliers and vaulted ceiling—it seems fitting that this venue was also once the home of another fraternal and exclusive society, the Freemasons. Many of the members wear the club's uniform of straw boater and gold and black tie, and are heralded by buglers and other pageantry. The club's stated commitment to spreading "fellowship and conviviality" only seems to apply if you are the appropriate gender. You'd think a club like this would have died out with the penny-farthing, but it seems not, and fittingly a club member is photographed alongside one. It may appear an anachronistic organization in the twenty-first century, but apparently there is a seven-year wait list to join its ranks.*

Despite women making up a third of cyclists in the U.S. and U.K. by the mid-1890s, the Pickwick wasn't the only club to cling to its outdated boys-only rule, though most clubs had the sense to start opening their doors to women members. In Boston

---

* When former Olympic cyclist Chris Boardman challenged the club about their men-only policy, a member responded on Twitter that "most real ladies wouldn't want to be on our table #boystalk." He's probably right—they'd die of boredom. I wrote to the club to ask about the rationale for their men-only policy, but I didn't get a response. The more I discover about the Pickwick Fathers, though, the more it excites me that a new generation of predominantly nonwhite women cyclists are falling in love with cycling in the original home of their exclusionary club, helping rewrite the rules of who is allowed to ride a bike.

in the United States, one club went the other way and voted in 1894 to exclude their existing female members, causing the women in question to form a new club along with male members who disagreed with the ban.

The Cyclists' Touring Club in the U.K., the same organization that had gone to court on behalf of Florence Harberton's bloomers, was more forward thinking and had been open to women since 1880. Even so, many women wanted to form their own club, and soon women-only cycling clubs were springing up around the U.K. and North America, such as the Knickerbockers in Chicago, and Viscountess Harberton's similarly clothing-inspired Chelsea Rationalists. Women's cycling clubs were popping up so fast in Chicago that the Illinois Ladies' Cycling Association was founded to support the clubs and run women's races, attracting thousands of spectators. Some were also modeled along the same lines as exclusive gentleman's clubs. Like New York's Michaux, members of these high-end institutions would socialize over tea in their clubhouse's lavish dining rooms, perhaps even meeting with their tailor to decide on the designs for their new cycling outfit. The Woodbridge Cycle Club in Boston even had their own bugler for their rides. However, most clubs were a bit more egalitarian, such as the Ladies' South-West Bicycle Club, which would simply meet by a pond on Clapham Common in London every Wednesday at three p.m.

Lillias Campbell Davidson also recognized that there were many women who wanted to cycle exclusively with members of their own sex, which led her to found the Lady Cyclists' Association (LCA) in 1892. Operating as a networking association, the LCA helped connect women cyclists across the U.K. so they could form their own local clubs to go on social rides. It also published a list of hotels and inns across the country that were hospitable to women cycling on their own, rationals or not. The monthly magazine connected members, reassuring them they were far from alone in their interest, and featured exclusive discounts for tailors and bicycles.

It's understandable that many women felt there was much to be gained from female comradeship a-wheel and wanted to carve out a safe space on their own terms, particularly when they would have been far outnumbered by men in most clubs, with many put off by the more competitive aspects of club life. According to a 2017 Department for Transport study in the U.K., men make three times as many cycle trips as women and cycle on average four times as far. I belong to a London club that works hard to support its women members, but we still make up just a fraction over 20 percent of the membership, which is not unusual today. To arrive at the meeting point on a Sunday morning to a flock of—mostly white—men in Lycra can be daunting and possibly not an experience that is going to shift the scales the other way without a lot of work to be even more inclusive and welcoming to minority groups.

Lillias wasn't keen on club uniforms, arguing that it would be hard to settle on an outfit that suited all members, which could be a deterrent for would-be members. Some clubs, though, were founded on what they wore—members of Lady Harberton's club were only permitted to wear rational dress in order to help promote and further the work of her society. In contrast, the Countess of Malmesbury led a ride from Richmond Park in Surrey each Wednesday where only women wearing skirts were accepted. This was to encourage more conservative women who might otherwise be put off from joining a group in which some wore bloomers. Most clubs didn't have such rigid dress codes, however, and instead their members sported a range of styles from the period, depending on their personal preference. Even so, most did have a badge at the very least, and sometimes specific club colors to identify their cycling crew, just as members of most clubs today, including my own, wear jerseys featuring their insignia and colors.

As an active member of her local (mixed) club on Staten Island, Maria Ward was keen to recommend to her readers the benefits of social rides. She also had some advice about how to start a club, suggesting that the purchase of two bicycles to share among its members was a good way to begin, a sort of time-share approach to bicycle ownership. The more members that joined, the more bicycles should be purchased, presumably with membership fees covering the cost—a club based on cooperative principles that would have benefited anyone who couldn't stretch financially to wheels of their own. This egalitarian and inclusive approach was similar to that of London's Mowbray House Cycling Association, founded in 1892 by Florence Harberton again and the aristocratic cycling humanitarian Lady Isabella Somerset. It even received support from the Countess of Warwick, aka Daisy Bell. What distinguished this club was that it was aimed specifically at working women who would not have earned enough to purchase bicycles of their own.

To start out, Florence and Isabella, with the support of liberal newspaper editor William Thomas Stead, used their own money to purchase a fleet of cycles. Anyone wanting to join paid a modest fee for use of a bicycle for one or two weeks every month. By 1897, they had twenty-four bicycles shared among 150 members. Not only was this a way to give their members some independence by providing them with their own affordable transport, they were also offering much-needed relaxation and pleasure outside their working hours. No wonder suffragist Millicent Garrett Fawcett was a supporter, and she wrote to readers of the upmarket *Wheelwoman* magazine asking them to donate their old bicycles to the club.

Mowbray House offered training for their inexperienced members. Once they were confident, they could join one of the regular social rides out to rural spots on the edge of London. Members also had the option to take full ownership of a bicycle by paying it off in installments. Additionally, the organization owned a gypsy caravan, a large canvas tent and a cottage, all located in countryside south of London, giving members the chance to enjoy an economical cycling-based weekend break, the only holiday many could afford. The members also met regularly at the club's home in the offices of W. T. Stead's newspaper, *The Pall Mall Gazette*, in central London, where they would discuss club matters and finances and listen to talks on rational dress and other social and women's issues of the day. With Florence as a founder, many of the members adopted rational dress, and all wore a Mowbray House badge which featured a butterfly symbol, as well as dressing in the club's colors of blue and white.

This wasn't the only club specifically for working women: London's Guy's Hospital started a club for their nurses in 1896. Miss Florence Nott-Bower, the hospital's matron, described how cycling gave their "weary and worn out staff nurses" an opportunity for "change of thought and exercise after day and night confinement in the depressing wards." It's not clear how long the club was in existence, but its legacy continues today with the newly founded Royal London Hospital Nurses' Cycling Club in East London, a charitable initiative which was also started to help female nurses benefit from physical activity. Half of those participating reported that they previously did less than thirty minutes of exercise a week, and over 75 percent were new to riding a bike, with one participant commenting that she had been "trying to find suitable and affordable sessions to learn to ride for the last 5 years and this is the first group that is regular enough, and where I feel safe and not embarrassed." A club that is affordable and provides a nonjudgmental safe space was also core to the foundational principles of Florence and Isabella's project over 120 years before, and both are part of a long history of women who encourage, nurture and support each other in joining a community of cycling sisters.

Kitchens for Bikes

Today, the London Bike Kitchen in Hackney, East London, with its tools and bicycle parts lining the walls and suspended from the ceiling, and a blackboard showing a bicycle with all its constituent parts labeled, is somewhere Maria Ward would feel right at home. But far from locking its doors to avoid interruptions, this nonprofit bicycle maintenance workshop is open to anyone who wants to fix their bike and benefit from extensive know-how and the necessary tools. It provides a way to pass on knowledge and encourage self-reliance, like Maria set out to do, but also a place in which to do it. This is particularly important in a city where space is at a premium, with so many living in small flats and house shares, where the idea of a dedicated space for a bicycle workshop is the stuff of fantasies.

Californian Jenni Gwiazdowski, London Bike Kitchen's founder, describes what they do as "pulling back the curtain" on what goes on in a bike workshop, making the information accessible for the many people who feel mystified by the alchemy that happens behind the workshop doors when they hand over their bicycle for repair. They also run a series of practical seminars covering a range of maintenance subjects, from adjusting gears to building a bike from scratch. Inspired by a similar concept in Los Angeles, the idea is not only to empower their users through know-how, it's also about challenging perceptions about who gets to participate.

The Bike Kitchen has more women mechanics than most, but Jenni is keenly aware of the gender bias. When she did her training to qualify as a bicycle mechanic, she was the only woman in the course. Despite Maria's *Bicycling for Ladies* having been published nearly 125 years ago, the bicycle workshop remains a predominantly male domain. Gender politics in the toolshed still need overhauling—largely, women aren't encouraged to be interested in fixing things, just as men are expected to be innately handy with a hammer and wrench. A 2015 study by the Association for Psychological Science indicates this might go back to childhood development, with boys encouraged more—through marketing and other social forces—to play with construction or complex puzzle games which foster "spatial reasoning," cognitive skills that are important in STEM (science, technology, engineering and math) subjects. It also normalizes the idea of technology and mechanics being a boy's domain. This imbalance is seen as one of the reasons there is an underrepresentation of women in science and tech, as well as in a bike workshop.

Jenni, undaunted by the prospect of entering such a stereotypically masculine profession, was "hell-bent" on getting her open-access workshop off the ground. Her first tutor was a woman, a Native American named Therese who had been working in London bike shops for several decades and who had achieved legendary status within the industry. She helped guide Jenni in setting up the workshop, and was keen to help her former student succeed.

When the Bike Kitchen opened its doors seven years ago, there were almost no women using their facilities. That has changed now, in part due to its bimonthly women and gender-variant—WAG—night. Jenni started these classes in recognition that these are the people least likely to feel confident, able or willing to come to any of their other sessions. Just as women might find joining a cycling club that is 75 percent men off-putting, many would feel similarly—maybe more so—about entering the stereotypically male environs of a workshop. When I went to one of these sessions, there were around ten of us crammed into the intimate workshop for a session on chain care run by Jenni. We were taken through the process, step by step, of getting our chains and corresponding parts in good order and encouraged to ask whatever we wanted, no question being too basic.

Jenni hopes that her WAG sessions will be a "back door" into—and a way to get comfortable in—an area that may have appeared a closed shop or alien environment. They are about "getting rid of the idea that it is something that you're not allowed to do," even if mending a puncture might take you out of your comfort zone. It's all about providing a safe, nonjudgmental space where no one will be ridiculed for thinking a cassette was a retro medium for listening to music.

The sessions cover the staples of keeping your bicycle in good working order—as Lillias and Maria argued, the advantages of self-reliance and independence can only be achieved by knowing how to do at least the basic repairs to keep your wheels turning. It's also a lot more economical than taking it to a shop to get it fixed each time you have a problem. Testament to the "stepping-stone" nature of these WAG classes, the gender split in the Bike Kitchen's other sessions is now much more even. This is something to be celebrated when too many still don't feel they are the right "fit" for the cycling world.

PART II

RESISTANCE AND REBELLION

CHAPTER FIVE

FIGHT FOR YOUR RIGHT TO BIKE

Kittie Fought the LAW

It's a fine summer's day in July 1895 and the press have descended on Asbury Park, New Jersey, for the League of American Wheelmen (LAW)'s annual meet. Thousands of members are arriving from all over the country to take part, but the press is focused on one particular cyclist, Katherine "Kittie" Knox, a twenty-one-year-old seamstress from Boston. It isn't her sex that is causing a media sensation though, it is the color of her skin. Kittie is mixed race, and the previous year the organization had passed a controversial "color bar," excluding anyone who wasn't white from joining. As a result, all eyes are on Kittie and the LAW to see what, if anything, will happen.

At a time when racial prejudice was ingrained in every facet of life in the United States, a Southern faction of the LAW led by a Colonel W. W. Watts of Louisville, Kentucky, had successfully campaigned to transform it into a whites-only organization, overturning its 1892 declaration that "all races are eligible for membership." The colonel had been petitioning for the exclusion of black people—and for the Californian branches to refuse prospective Chinese members—for three years. One Southern member who supported the ban said it had once been an "honor" to belong to the organization, but that it would "cease to be such if any number of objectionable people should get in. And that the Negros as a class are very objectionable to a majority of the people is undeniable." He wasn't alone in his racist views, and in a secret ballot the colonel got his way by 127 votes to 54, with Southern members voting unanimously for the Jim Crow–style amendment. The constitution was consequently changed to "none but white persons can become members of the League."

Not all members agreed with the new policy, with more enlightened branches refusing to implement the ruling. The Massachusetts division, true to Boston's abolitionist roots, was one of these groups, and they were not averse to ruffling the feathers of the Southern racists by showing up with their black members at the annual meet. In any case, grossly discriminatory though the new ban was, theoretically it didn't apply to Kittie since she was not a new applicant but a card-holding member of the League when the ban came into force. Despite this, the press, and I'm sure Kittie and her fellow Bostonians, were preparing for a clash of some sort on the day.

As a woman of color on a bicycle, Kittie was subject to more scrutiny and moralizing than white women on bicycles. In addition to her race and sex, her outfits caused a stir; like Tessie Reynolds in Brighton, she'd put her sewing skills to use to make herself a rational dress outfit consisting of baggy gray knee-length bloomers with a matching jacket, completing the ensemble with long boots buttoned down the sides. An outfit well suited for the men's crossbar bike that she rode, and which led Chicago cycling magazine *Referee* to declare her "a beautiful and buxom black bloomerite." It had also won her a prize in a cycle costume competition at what must have been a progressive Massachusetts bicycle event. (This being the less enlightened 1890s, there were still murmurings from some quarters about the prize being awarded to a nonwhite participant.)

Kittie also belonged to the Riverside Cycling Club. Founded in 1893, this was one of the first ever black cycling clubs in the country. She was such a keen cyclist that, again like Tessie, she had ridden in several competitions, including participating in century (100-mile) races. While she may not have been surprised that the press was so interested in her attendance at Asbury, particularly given that she had already been featured numerous times in newspapers and cycling magazines, she may have wondered why the reports that emerged were so conflicting.

It is still not entirely clear what happened that day. The least likely account is that she was denied from even entering the meet, though it seems most probable that she did pedal into the park along with fellow members. Indeed, *The New York Times* reported that Kittie demonstrated some "fancy cuts" in front of the clubhouse. But what happened next is much less clear and centers on whether the LAW accepted her membership card when she presented it to them. *The San Francisco Call* reported that her card was refused and she "withdrew very quietly," though it believed that 99 percent of members expressed regret for what had occurred. Other papers reported that a member of the executive committee, a fellow Bostonian, demanded they acknowledge her as a member and accord her the privileges she was entitled to, while the *Boston Herald* said that Kittie had no complaints whatsoever about her reception at Asbury and was perplexed by the media furor. Other accounts which filtered through to the press from members left some journalists frothing at the mouth, such as those who said she had not only been welcomed at the event but had been the belle of the ball in the evening, dancing with white men, though some witnesses claimed that as a consequence the women members had staged a mass walkout in disgust at what they deemed her flagrant behavior.

With the Southern press in particular spewing racist bile in response to Kittie's attendance, this issue wasn't going to go away anytime soon. *The New York Times*'s conclusion that "this episode will result in temporarily opening the color line question" for the LAW and that some of its members "will protest against permitting Miss Knox to remain a member" was sadly accurate, if not much else had been.

Although Kittie's fellow Bostonians had defended her on the grounds that she was an existing member, they were ultimately unsuccessful in overturning the discriminatory new rule for prospective nonwhite members. Nor did they manage to stem the flow of rising racial discrimination in the cycling world, with more clubs—including ones in Boston—implementing their own ban on nonwhite members. It was a policy that would directly curtail Kittie and others from joining certain clubs and participating in what had previously been open events such as the Boston Wheelman's century ride, an event she had previously excelled in.

The LAW—today known as the League of American Bicyclists—didn't publicly renounce their controversial "color bar" until 1999, though the policy had long since been ignored. When they made the retraction, they announced they would be doing more to support diversity in cycling. This was long overdue and continues to need addressing, since according to 2018 figures, women still make up only 25 percent of cyclists in the U.S.—27 percent in the U.K., according to a 2007 Department for Transport report—and women of color make up only a small fraction of that number.

Whatever happened on that day in July 1895, Kittie had been justifiably determined to be part of this event, exhibiting remarkable chutzpah in the face of a rising tide of agitation for segregation in the country, which is why many Bostonians today call her the Rosa Parks of cycling. She resisted in the face of grossly unfair and prejudiced attitudes and actions that were intended to block her participation for no other reason than the color of her skin. Kittie remained defiant and holds a place in a long line of women who have continued to ride their bikes despite being told it isn't for them, with some resisting to this day, even in the face of threats of extreme violence. Their fight reveals the extent to which the bicycle remains at the center of intersecting discourse around the politics of race, gender, public space, climate change, urban planning and more.

Psyco Sisters

A 2019 survey carried out in San Francisco showed that only 13 percent of cyclists in the city are women of color, with Asian and Hispanic women the least represented—a low figure when you consider that 34 percent of the population of the city are women of color. Many of those interviewed said that "women like me" don't bike, that they saw it as a predominantly young, white, male activity. As ever, representation matters. The problem isn't isolated to San Francisco, but an issue across the country and elsewhere.*

---

* This is far from a problem just in the United States. In London, for instance, black, Asian and minority ethnic groups—across both genders—account for only around 15 percent of the city's cycle trips despite making up 41 percent of the city's population.

When African-American Monica Garrison started cycling in Pittsburgh in 2014, she soon became aware that there were few women who looked like her riding bikes in her city. In an interview she admitted she struggled with the distinct lack of representation in the cycling community: "I have to admit that I used to have preconceived ideas about who cyclists were and what they looked like. I was unsure of where I fit in."

As a result, she founded Black Girls Do Bike (BGDB), which she describes as a "pep rally for black girls on bikes." Like Lillias Campbell Davidson's Lady Cyclists' Association, BGDB connects women, specifically women of color, with other cyclists in their area. Now there are chapters across the country, with more opening all the time, set up by women who have been supported and inspired by the organization. They arrange group rides, support new learners and share skills such as basic mechanics, creating a supportive and nurturing community to make cycling a more diverse and inclusive activity. The aim is for their members to feel empowered and at home, helping change the narrative of who gets to ride bikes that has been ongoing since women first started pedaling.

In Los Angeles, a lack of diversity in the bike community is also a significant problem. In this distinctly cycle-unfriendly city—one built for the motor age, with highways bifurcating every neighborhood—just getting on a bike is an act of resistance. Unsurprisingly, when road safety is frequently cited as one of the major barriers for women's participation, only one in five cyclists in the city is a woman. The number of women on bikes in a particular area is seen as an indicator of how safe it is to do so, with countries that have good cycling infrastructure, such as the Netherlands, having a more favorable gender split. In the East L.A. neighborhood of Boyle Heights, though, a group of predominantly Latina women, like BGDB, are challenging the city's overwhelmingly white male cycling culture, combining cycling with activism to reclaim the streets.

The Ovarian Psycos Bicycle Brigade, also known as the OVAS (Overthrowing Vendidxs, Authority and the State— Vendidxs meaning Mexican-Americans who have sold out their culture in favor of the dominant American one), are a cycling sisterhood for "womxn"* of color from their neighborhood. Unlike Kittie Knox, they haven't been officially barred from joining other clubs, but they felt they needed to carve out their own cycling space in a way that is representative of their values and daily reality as women of color in a marginalized community. Though images of the Psycos riding as a group, wearing black bandannas over their faces printed with the group's ovary and uterus imagery, may make them look like a biker gang, they couldn't be further from that.

An overtly feminist and politically engaged crew, the Psycos was founded in 2010 by Xela de la X, a musician and community activist. When Xela's car broke down and she couldn't afford to get it fixed, she started commuting to her job in downtown L.A. by bike. She was subjected to catcalls and other overtly sexist harassment during her daily rides to a degree she had not experienced as a pedestrian, an experience that illustrates that sadly women are still often subject to greater prejudice and observation as cyclists. Regardless, being able to weave freely through the city's notorious traffic jams made her think "this is what freedom feels like, this is what it feels like not to have

---

* The Psycos often use the gender-neutral and nonbinary term "Latinx," as well as "womxn," which denotes the inclusion of transgender women and women of color.

obstacles blocking your movement." She wanted other women to have a chance to experience this liberating and empowering feeling, not alone and harassed, but together and supported in a bicycle brigade. Thus the idea for the first Luna ride was born, a full-moon night ride for female-identifying and nonbinary cyclists in her community who may not have previously had the confidence to ride out on the streets alone, but who might do so if they were surrounded by people like themselves.

Xela's Eastside neighborhood of Boyle Heights is a stone's throw across the Los Angeles River from the sprawling city's downtown, but a world away from its gleaming skyscrapers and other emblems of capitalism, though creeping gentrification is beginning to change that. The Chicano civil rights movement was centered here in the 1960s, a movement to empower Mexican-Americans, and its population is still of a predominantly Mexican heritage. The Psycos proudly connect their community's history of fighting for social justice with what they are doing with the Bicycle Brigade, referring to themselves as "warriors," though their focus is specifically on the issues affecting them as women of color from this area.

Freedom, mobility, autonomy and fearlessness are core to the group's ethos, something Xela felt she was acutely lacking when she was growing up. While her brothers were free to roam, she was largely confined indoors—taking up space in the streets with her cycling sisters is an act of defiance. Some of the other members say they also weren't encouraged to ride as children, because their parents' generation didn't think it was something girls should do; others said that they rode as children but gave up when they got older due to harassment or disapproval. Now they are rewriting the rules together of what they can do with their bodies and where they can go, sending a strong message that through group solidarity they will no longer be scared away from moving freely around the streets, especially at night.

On a Luna ride, they cruise the neighborhood, riders two or four abreast, chanting "Whose streets? Our streets!," the power of the group allowing them to fearlessly inhabit the streets they may have previously avoided alone at night. As Xela says, "When you are riding with a group of women it feels like I'm supported, I got backup. You feel like you could win the war. You feel like nothing, absolutely nothing can stop you. It was women not being scared of riding our bicycles or just claiming space in very dangerous zones." Another group member says that the feeling she experiences of cycling as part of the brigade, the sense of safety and empowerment it provides, is "one of the most liberating feelings in the world."

As part of their activism, the Psycos have been known to organize rides to areas where young women from the community have been murdered or kidnapped, to raise awareness of systemic violence against women and reinforce the message that they won't be driven off the streets by fear. Their physical presence inspires other women to join their movement, women who might not have seen others who look like them riding bikes before. Much like the gangs of women cyclists in Lizzie Borden's 1983 feminist dystopian film *Born in Flames*, who rescue women who are being threatened or assaulted on the streets, many of the rides are themed. They also host talks on issues relevant to members, such as women's health and self-defense, or they have a humanitarian focus, such as distributing care packages to the homeless. Their longer annual rides—around thirty miles—are known as "Clitoral Mass," a play on the popular Critical Mass* rides, which the Psycos see as too white and male, in L.A. at least, to be fully inclusive. No rider is left behind—if someone has a puncture then the whole group waits with them. As member Maryann Aguirre says, "We're not about who can ride fastest, we're about sisterhood." It's an experience wholly different from when the group rides into mostly white and upmarket neighboring areas like Echo Park and Pasadena, where they say they are regularly stared at in a way that makes them feel that they don't belong there and which they don't think they would experience if they were all on expensive bikes and kitted out in cycling gear.

When I look through the comment section underneath an online LAist article on one of their recent Clitoral Mass bike rides, it's clear that this group of feminist cyclists are seen as a threat by some, including one reader who described them as "Femtards" and "deluded hysterical female" and suggests people "throw sticks in their spokes" to "see how tough they are." But the group is still going strong and has become increasingly active on issues impacting their community, particularly the gentrification of their neighborhood, which they see as ushering in rent hikes and evictions, and the government's policy on the U.S.–Mexico border, which includes the inhumane detainment of migrant children and enforced separation from their parents.

---

* Critical Mass originated in 1992 in San Francisco, where cyclists gathered monthly to ride through the streets, using the safety of numbers to take back the space from motor vehicles, raising awareness about climate change and the safety of cyclists on the road. The event now takes place in cities across the world as both a celebration of cycling and a form of activism to reclaim the streets for greener modes of transport.

Bicyclists of Bamiyan

Across the world there are still women who are not just discouraged from riding bikes but actively forbidden to do so by their families and community. Some continue regardless, including in Afghanistan, where women who cycle have been labeled "infidels" and threatened with violence and even death. Though Afghan women gained the right to vote in 1919, only a year after the U.K. and a year before the U.S., their country was ranked in a 2018 Thomson Reuters poll as the second-worst place in the world to be female, with women and girls facing severe gender-based violence, abuse, illiteracy, poverty, and other human rights offenses. This is a result of fifty years of instability in the country, which has seen Soviet occupation and then years of civil conflict in the 1980s and '90s between mujahideen groups and government forces, followed by a repressive and violent Taliban rule.

Women's rights under the Taliban were pushed over a cliff. Legislation was introduced banning girls and women from going to school, working, being involved in politics and leaving the house without a male chaperone, as well as requiring them to wear a burqa at all times when out in public. The punishments for noncompliance were violent and sometimes deadly. Not surprisingly, bicycling, with its connotations of freedom, independence, mobility and pleasure, was not permitted. When the United States invaded the country in 2001 to remove the regime, citing their appalling women's rights record as one of their motivations (though the reality is of course more complex than that), the situation began to improve for women in some parts of the country. Education was reinstated and women were even running for parliament, becoming judges, taking a greater role in commerce and generally gaining visibility in public life again.

The adventurer and campaigner Shannon Galpin has spent over a decade visiting and running women's rights projects in Afghanistan. She spoke to me over the phone from her home in Colorado, where she lives with her daughter when she's not traveling. She remembers 2007–8 as a particular high point when it seemed that women's and other important rights in the country would continue to progress unabated. One thing she never saw then, though, despite all the new freedoms, was a girl on a bike—that was still "too controversial." Shannon, a keen mountain biker, decided this wouldn't stop her from biking across parts of the country to experience the breathtaking landscapes in ways no other form of transport would have allowed, enabling her to see a country known to foreigners mostly for war, terror and poverty in a completely different way, a country that, far from being monolithic, is in fact one of myriad cultures.

In 2010, Shannon became the first woman to bike the Panjshir Valley in the high mountains north of Kabul and was the first woman most people she encountered had seen cycling. As a foreign woman she discovered she was exempt from the strict social codes that prevented Afghan women from doing the same, and felt she was viewed as more akin to "a curiosity, like a circus bear juggling." It was also an icebreaker, with men who would never have deemed it appropriate to approach this American woman had she been traveling in a vehicle as part of a convoy like most foreigners, coming up to talk to her: "Whatever that restraint was, it had gone. The curiosity overrode the restraint of cultural boundaries." The open desire to interact often extended to invitations into homes for tea.

In one instance, traveling with a female translator, Shannon was also able to have an uninhibited conversation just with the women members of a family—who felt able to speak freely with no men in the room. The Afghan women started by asking about contraception and women's health, before Shannon took the opportunity to ask them about women's lives in the country. After the fall of the Taliban, women's participation in certain sports started to flourish, including soccer, volleyball, cricket, tae kwon do and even boxing, since it had become increasingly accepted that it was important to women's health for them to be active. According to the women she talked to, these sports were acceptable because they could be done behind closed doors and walls; cycling, however, remained taboo since it was largely something you did in a public space. Since Afghan culture has traditionally encouraged women to dress modestly, and in some areas to stay indoors and out of sight, women on bikes are considered by some to be too visible and open to the male gaze.

Shannon believes that the other reason cycling remains so controversial in Afghanistan, and in other religiously conservative countries, is still down to the idea of a woman physically straddling the bicycle seat, which may be viewed as offensive, suggestive of promiscuity and overt sexuality, and thus taboo.*

The same is true in Iran, where Ayatollah Khamenei, the Islamic Republic's supreme leader, issued a fatwa in 2016 against women cycling in public on the false grounds that they pose a threat to morality: "Riding a bicycle often attracts the attention of men and exposes the society to corruption, and thus contravenes women's chastity, and it must be abandoned." Many women continue to cycle in Iran, although some have been arrested for doing so. Their bikes were confiscated and they were

---

* Like the person I saw commenting on a 2018 *Arab News* article about women in Saudi Arabia riding bikes, who wrote that as a result of this they are "expecting AIDS to enter Saudi soon."

forced to sign statements to say they will desist. In 2019, authorities in Isfahan, an Iranian city renowned for its high concentration of cyclists due to its extensive network of bike paths, said that women who ignore the ban will be subjected to "Islamic punishment." Apparently they are working on a covered bicycle for them instead.

Shannon also believes that in Afghanistan, where virginity tests are often still carried out on prospective brides, many would see cycling as a direct threat to the highly prized intact hymen, even though many other activities pose a similar risk. One man she met had a different view, telling her that riding a bike takes a lot of intelligence and that's why women couldn't do it. While Shannon felt that her biking in Afghanistan showed that this was something women could and did do elsewhere, she recognized that as a foreigner she would never be able to change perceptions about Afghan women and girls doing the same. Unbeknownst to Shannon, while she was biking around the Panjshir Valley, there was an Afghan woman a few hundred miles to the west who was risking disapproval and violence by riding her bike, and in so doing helping to normalize the idea of others like her doing the same.

Zahra, now in her twenties, had started cycling at thirteen when she was living in Iran, despite much disapproval. Her parents had died when she was a small child, and she was raised by an elder sister whom she has described as treating her more like a boy in the hope it would give her more freedoms and courage than most Afghan girls. It seemed to work, as Zahra has not shied away from pushing against boundaries that have tried to prevent her from doing things because of her gender, including demanding to attend school.

When she was eighteen, Zahra moved to the province of

Bamiyan, just northwest of Kabul, to study archeology at the university that had been reopened after the Taliban were removed from the area. She was soon attracting attention for cycling to her classes. Local boys would bike to the university, but there were no other women or girls doing the same even though there were no buses, and it could take as long as two hours a day to walk there and back. Regardless of the risks, Zahra believes quite rightly that "girls deserve to have the same opportunities as boys, whether that's education or the right to ride a bike."

When I spoke to Zahra down the line from Kabul, where she is continuing her studies, she told me that when she first started getting around this way, the religious scholars in the area were so angry that they said she should be stoned. No one would have blamed her for deciding to go back to walking, that it was too dangerous a fight, but Zahra continued. Eventually she convinced them that it was necessary in order to continue her education. She became well known in the area as the woman who cycled, and it wasn't long before others wanted to join her, the first being Zakia, who had learned to ride in Iran and had missed it since she hadn't felt able to continue after returning to her home country.

Zakia's father ran a bike shop in their city and was supportive of women taking part, but understandably she didn't feel confident going it alone, so she stopped Zahra on the street to talk to her and soon they were going on rides together. Before long, other girls also wanted to join them and it was at that point that they decided they would start a team, with training sessions and races. Of course, purchasing a bike can be yet another barrier to participation since they cost around an average month's salary in the area. The father of one team member was so supportive of his daughter's desire to join the group, though, that he even borrowed money to buy her one.

The women began meeting regularly, gathering first to chat, eat, warm up, clean and fix their bikes before heading out onto the road. On the busy highways which they share with large trucks and farmers with donkeys piled high with produce, they ride single file, spreading out to ride two abreast on less busy roads, forcing any traffic to slow in order to pass. They often ride past the historic cave complex where the giant sixth-century buddhas of Bamiyan carved into the sandstone cliffs had stood until they were blown up by the Taliban in 2001.

In 2015, the group took part in the Tour of Bamiyan bike race, the first race in Afghanistan to allow women. Yet they still struggle to be accepted, and years after forming they still sometimes attract the wrong sort of attention for being a group of girls on bikes. Some of the local mullahs have labeled them "infidels" and "sinners," declaring that what they are doing is shameful and that they risk losing their "honor." The mullahs said they didn't have a problem with them riding bikes if they did it somewhere private, but that they are risking violence by "parading around in groups." They were also falsely accused of riding without headscarves or dressing inappropriately, even though the members all abide by the country's dress code for covered arms, legs and head hair.

Many of the members were understandably scared, yet Zakia and Zahra remained convinced that they were doing nothing shameful. They organized meetings with the more progressive governor of Bamiyan to obtain his support and it was gladly offered, though of course he can't protect them from any sudden acts of violence that they might encounter. Shannon, who has since biked with Zahra and her team, described her as "one of the strongest women" she knows, and it's not hard to see why.

Five years later the group is still going strong. Members are now generally accepted by the community, with some locals even proud that this team is part of the identity of the region, including boys who see them out riding and tell them that they are going to teach their sisters. Though there are still men who won't let their daughters or sisters take part, Zahra is optimistic it will become more and more accepted in her country that anyone can ride a bike, though she has since had to pass on the role of director and trainer of the team to Zakia, now that she is studying full-time in Kabul.

The team members, a little like those of the Victorian Mowbray House bicycle cooperative, share the club's six mountain bikes, their training sessions split between mornings and evenings. On Fridays, when there is no school, they often transport the bikes farther into the high mountains of the Hindu Kush to the country's first national park, Band-e-Amir, to do a longer ride of around sixty miles, something that would have been inconceivable before Zahra started defiantly pedaling through the streets of her town. The group continues to inspire other girls and women to have a go too, for sport or transport, and there are also women's teams in Kabul and Mazar-i-Sharif that they compete against, though there are still many areas in the country where it would be unsafe to do so. Even though it's often been a battle for the members to bike, and not always felt entirely safe, Bamiyan is comparatively progressive and liberal compared to many other regions, and has fewer land mines left over from the wars. It is also peaceful, whereas some other parts of the country are once again under Taliban control, making it impossible for women there to demand basic rights such as education—let alone to cycle to classes.

While Zahra uses her bike to get to her classes and to visit archeological sites as part of her studies, as well as for sport, too many others are denied that kind of essential mobility in Afghanistan, especially in rural areas where very few have cars and public transport is limited.

There are other countries where historically it has not been a cultural norm for women and girls to cycle, including many southern African or Southeast Asian countries, but where girls in rural areas are now using bikes to get to school and to access health care or job opportunities. Their lives have been transformed by their two wheels—once they may have dropped out of education because the journey took too long on foot, but they are now getting to school quickly, easily and safely which, among many other benefits, improves their job prospects and gives them greater control over their own lives.

Shannon believes that bikes are a powerful tool for social justice, and if more women in Afghanistan were permitted to cycle, then they too would experience similar advantages. It can mean the difference between "a life fulfilled and a life of oppression." The charity World Bicycle Relief backs this up by reporting that school performance and attendance increases among the girls to whom they have donated bikes.

While the future for women's rights in Afghanistan is uncertain with the resurgence of the Taliban, it is undeniable that there are currently many more girls and women on bikes in the areas where it is safe, many of whom have been inspired by pioneers like Zahra. There is also a women's national cycling team in Kabul, which is rebuilding itself after it was brought down by alleged corruption on the part of their male coach. If the team can go on to represent Afghanistan one day in international races, or possibly even the Olympics, then it will be harder to rationalize denying other women the same opportunities.

A Green Bicycle

To the west of Afghanistan, Saudi Arabia, one of the world's most conservative and closed countries, recently granted women the right to drive cars after decades of campaigning. They were the last place in the world to do so, a historic moment for women's rights in a country which has repeatedly sought—and still does—to limit their freedoms in what many regard as a totalitarian dictatorship. In 2015 they were finally granted the right to vote and stand in local elections. Less well known is the fact that in 2013 a ban on women riding bicycles, which had been enforced by Saudi Arabia's Committee for the Promotion of Virtue and the Prevention of Vice—the religious police—was also overturned.

The film *Wadjda*, released in 2012, explored the taboo of girls cycling in Saudi Arabia by telling the story of the eponymous heroine's desperate desire to own a bike at a time when only boys were permitted to. The director, Haifaa al-Mansour, was the first Saudi Arabian woman to make a feature film in her homeland, and she has an intimate understanding of the struggle to pursue a goal that is in opposition to her society's rigid gender expectations. In the film, Wadjda's best friend, Abdullah, teaches her to ride a bike in secret and she pleads with the local bike shop not to sell the green bike she has fallen in love with until she has saved enough to buy it. Her mother tells her that "here girls don't ride bikes. You won't be able to have children if you ride a bike," that if she persists she won't be able to marry. Nevertheless Wadjda remains focused on her goal. The news that a Quran recital competition at her school is offering prize money that would pay for the bike turns her into a model student. Wadjda goes on to win the competition. However, when she tells her teachers, whose duties include policing the behavior of their girl pupils, how she will spend the money, they are horrified and donate the money to Palestine on her behalf. Not long after, when her father takes a second wife, Wadjda's mother rebels by buying her daughter the bicycle. As the film closes, we see Wadjda beating Abdullah in a bike race, her face beaming with delight.

While the 2013 decree would have made it legally permissible for Wadjda to bike, few did, since it was still a long way from being a cultural norm in this ultraconservative country. The stipulations that women ride while wearing their abayas (modesty robes), that they can only ride in parks and other designated areas, and should be accompanied by a male guardian, made it far from the exercise in independence and freedom that it ought to be. The other telling stipulation for a country that is well known for curbing women's freedom of movement was that it can't be used for transport—only recreation.

Today, in the east coast city of Al-Khobar on the Persian Gulf, groups of women can be seen riding together along the beachfront, but it's taken years to get to this point. One of these women is Fatimah Al-Bloushi, who started cycling in the city in 2017, after deciding to take part in a weeklong charity bike race in Europe. She had learned to ride as a child but largely stopped when she reached adulthood, as did most girls she knew, if they had learned at all. Only when she traveled abroad to cycle-friendly cities like London and Amsterdam would she take the opportunity to go for a ride.

To prepare for her upcoming race, which would require her to cycle up to sixty-two miles a day for seven days, Fatimah decided she would need to train back home. At that time, she never saw any other women in Al-Khobar riding. Not wanting to draw attention to herself, she opted for quiet areas early in the morning or at night. She told me that despite there being no law against what she was doing, she was often pulled over by the police, who would reprimand her, asking her to sign something to say she wouldn't do it again, that she could face legal action if she did, telling her that they were just worried for her safety as a woman out on her own. However, the only hassle she experienced was from the police themselves. Fatimah thinks they were acting out of personal prejudice—men she sees as having opinions and the power to enforce them, who don't like that she is challenging the norms for women in her country. One even declared, "Where do you think you are? You are not in America. We didn't reach that level where you get to go out like that."

Fatimah was rejected by the all-male Saudi team that was taking part in the same charity race, fearful they would get in trouble with the authorities for letting a woman ride with them, so instead she had to join an international team of riders. When the press reported that a woman from Saudi Arabia had taken part— the first to do so—she was inundated with messages from women and girls back home who said they wanted to learn to ride a bike. Some even hoped they could ride with her in the race next time; the majority were women who didn't feel confident riding around the city on their own.

To respond to the demand, Fatimah formed the group Her-Ride, leading its members twice weekly along the city's only bike path, on the corniche along the sea where it is traffic-free. The following year, four of them, including Fatimah's sister Yasa, traveled to Europe along with hundreds of other cyclists from around the world to take part in that same charity race, which this time started in Sweden and ended in Germany. When they returned, Fatimah felt that the tide was finally turning and women on bikes, at least in comparatively more liberal cities like

Jeddah and Al-Khobar, were becoming an accepted part of life in the Kingdom.

It had certainly come a long way since before 2017, when physical education wasn't even on the school curriculum for girls. Women were not permitted to take part in the Olympics until 2012, when two women were included among the competitors sent from Saudi Arabia—much to the consternation of many hardliners—then four in 2016. This and the fact that exercising in public has traditionally been strongly discouraged, with many women resorting to walking circuits around shopping malls just to burn off some energy, meant that there are higher rates of obesity, cancer and other diseases in the female population. Sports and exercise were largely the preserve of Saudi men, with women banned from watching competitions and matches in stadiums until 2018.

Despite the slight loosening of regulations, there are still many who are extremely unhappy about women doing sports, citing a variety of repressive reasons, including the fear it will make them less feminine and cause a relaxation in strict clothing rules, much like the kind of moral judgments that women cyclists came up against in western countries in the late nineteenth century. One female cyclist in Jeddah reported that when she first started going out on her bike with friends in 2015, unhappy members of the public sometimes called the police to come and stop them.

Women who want to bike in Saudi Arabia now have a government supporter, Princess Reema bint Bandar Al-Saud—the Kingdom's ambassador to the United States. She's the first ever female envoy and was previously the president of the Saudi Federation for Community Sports, where her remit was to make sports more inclusive of women, from its administration to participation. She was largely responsible for getting physical education into schools and says in her role she has actively "encouraged women to exercise in public. I've been telling women they don't need permission to exercise in public, they don't need permission to activate their own sports programs. And more and more they are doing it." The federation is now setting up a women's cycling team, which represents significant progress. Fatimah has benefited from the culture change at this level. She has been sent on courses so she can teach others to ride bikes and has attended training camps with the idea that at some stage there could be women cycling for the Kingdom in the Olympic Games and other international competitions.

Nadima Abu El-Einein has also benefited from and contributed to the slight relaxing in attitudes toward women cycling in Saudi Arabia. In her hometown of Jeddah on the Red Sea coast, she has become involved in encouraging and teaching women to cycle. In 2018 she organized the country's first bike race for women, its second ever women's sports race. Before this, she hadn't been immune to the negative cultural attitude to women on bikes, and had stopped cycling when she became a teenager. When her sister and mother encouraged her to take it up again in 2015, she started sharing photos of her rides on Instagram and, like Fatimah, was soon inundated with messages from other women. That same year, at the age of sixteen, she set up Bisklita, the country's first women-only cycling club which has grown from six members to five hundred and includes a wide range of ages and abilities—not least one member who, after suffering a brain injury which left her less able to balance, joins in on a trike.

Nadima had been taught to ride by her mother, so it seems natural to her to be supporting other girls and women to do the same. She is confident that there is nothing in Islam that prohibits them from doing so. When they first started going out together, when women on bikes in the city were still a rare occurrence, they would have people shout and even occasionally throw things at them. But they continued regardless and have become increasingly accepted—like the cyclists in Bamiyan—by people in the city.

The change has yet to filter through to the rest of the country, and in many cities and rural areas, women still don't feel comfortable getting on a bike. Even Fatimah's group is still occasionally stopped by the police, though now she can wave her SA cycling federation membership at them even though it's not a legal requirement. Nadima's group has also been stopped in some areas by police requesting to see permits, which led her to write to Princess Reema to ask for one from the cycling federation. In the interim the princess organized the use of a local stadium for their weekly meetups where they wouldn't be hassled so Nadima can teach her students to ride in peace.

It's difficult to say how long it will take for the situation to improve, when the time will come that any woman can just jump on a bike and pedal off. The increased encouragement of women's participation in sports is part of an initiative known as the King's Vision 2030 program—which also aims to get more women into the workforce to help boost the country's economy. But equality and full social and political enfranchisement for women, in what is one of the most gender-segregated countries in the world, is still far from a reality. This has led many to label the recent developments as window dressing rather than anything more meaningful.

The regime does not tolerate dissent, not least from women's rights activists such as the ones who fought for the end of the driving ban and who have remained in prison, even been tortured, despite the ban ending. A repressive guardianship system requires each female citizen to obtain permission from an assigned male relative before they are permitted to marry, obtain a passport, travel abroad, get released from prison or state care, apply for a life-saving abortion, or enter a shelter for victims of domestic abuse.

There are also few protections for women who suffer abuse at the hands of their guardians, which is largely why in that same poll that listed Afghanistan as the second-worst place in the world to be a woman, Saudi Arabia came fifth. There have been numerous high-profile cases of women fleeing the country to escape this oppressive system, risking imprisonment, torture or even death if they are caught.* One who succeeded and was granted asylum in Canada described the joy of no longer having to ask permission to leave the house, to wear what she wants, and countless other things many of us take for granted. She too is now learning to ride a bike, as well as swim and ice-skate, activities that her guardian would not have permitted.

At the time of writing, it has been rumored the Kingdom is planning to relax some of its guardianship rules, suggesting women will soon be able to obtain passports and travel abroad without the consent of a guardian. There is no commitment to dismantling the guardianship system completely, so it's unclear what impact this will have on women's rights and freedom of movement.

Meanwhile, at a grassroots level, women like Fatimah and Nadima are able to enjoy an activity that would have been out of

---

* One was eighteen-year-old Rahaf Mohammed al-Qunun, who absconded to Thailand in 2019 to escape her allegedly abusive family. She locked herself in a hotel room and refused to leave until eventually she was offered asylum in Canada.

bounds less than a decade ago. They are inspiring other women to take up something which is so much about freedom, movement and physicality, with Fatimah telling me how she wants to "empower Saudi women" and that getting them on bikes is part of that.

Nadima says it "fills my heart with joy" to teach other women to ride, so they too can get out of their homes and reap the physical benefits as well as "break free from the fear of social boundaries." She is convinced that there has been a positive change in attitude in the country about the idea of women and what they can do, and women out cycling is part of that shift.

CHAPTER SIX

"RISE UP, WOMEN!"

Pedal-Powering a Revolution

On February 13, as Parliament prepares to open for the formal start of the 1907 parliamentary year, over four hundred women gather at three p.m. in London's Caxton Hall for a "Women's Parliament." All are members of the Women's Social and Political Union (WSPU)—suffragettes. They are here to protest the omission, yet again, of women's suffrage from the king's speech of the previous day, and plan to march to Parliament to deliver a petition to the prime minister demanding the issue be debated.

When WSPU leader Emmeline Pankhurst commands "Rise up, Women!" the hall erupts with cries of "Now!" as the delegation divides into groups to cover the half mile along Victoria Street to the Houses of Parliament. The rational dress advocate and cyclist Lady Florence Harberton leads one of the groups, along with other high-profile WSPU activists.

On reaching Westminster Abbey, a line of police blocks their way. Instead of turning back, the marchers try to force their way through to reach the entrance to Parliament. Police on foot and horseback respond violently trying to disperse the crowd by laying into them with their batons. Most continue to push through the police cordon in what one newspaper later describes as something akin to a "football scrummage," a struggle that lasts until ten p.m., with many women physically hurt and assaulted in the brutal fray.

Some women defiantly shout, "We will not go away, we will see the prime minister." Fifteen manage to break through the line and reach the entrance, only to be arrested. Fifty-one women are taken to Scotland Yard—including WSPU leaders Emmeline, Sylvia and Christabel Pankhurst—the majority of whom are sentenced the following day to two weeks in Holloway prison, the judge sending them down declaring his determination to put an end to their "disorderly and disgusting proceedings."

Among those arrested was Alice Hawkins, a factory worker from Leicester. Alice worked as a machinist for the Equity Boot and Shoe factory, a cooperative that nurtured her deep-seated concerns for social justice. She had long believed that women should receive the same pay as men for doing the same work and that they should be granted the most fundamental of democratic rights—the right to vote.

Along with her husband, Alfred, Alice was an active campaigner, believing that women of all social classes needed a stake in the political system. The Equity was encouraging about its workers being politically engaged and supported her trip to London for the march. This was quite a contrast to most factories, where workers would have been fired for taking time off to attend a protest, let alone serve time inside. The prison sentence didn't end her activism but instead strengthened her commitment to the cause. In her account of her time in Holloway, true to her compassionate nature and commitment to social justice, she decried how badly the other non-suffragette women prisoners were treated, particularly those sentenced to hard labor. She would be arrested and imprisoned a further four times over the next seven years.

On returning to Leicester after her first Holloway incarceration, even more fired up about the injustices of the political system, Alice established the Leicester branch of the WSPU and campaigned hard to recruit fellow working women from the many factories in the city. Their first meeting was held at the Boot and Shoe Hall: Sylvia Pankhurst spoke about the suffrage cause and Alice shared her experience of her time in Holloway. Soon her Leicester WSPU had opened a Votes for Women shop, which sold their newspaper and other WSPU literature to raise money for the cause. It also served as a meeting point for fellow members, though its windows were often broken by local men who opposed their campaign. Despite this, it was the beating heart of what had become an active women's suffrage movement in the city thanks to Alice.

What has all this got to do with a book about women and cycling? Alice's campaign was built on pedal power. The bicycle was a tool she successfully employed in her fight for women's enfranchisement. While twenty years before it might have been political for a woman to just get on a bicycle, for Alice the bicycle could be used to actively advance the struggle for women's emancipation and resist the patriarchy.

Alice would cycle around the streets of Leicester holding rallies at factory gates and promoting upcoming WSPU meetings, and her influence went far beyond Leicester. Crucially, with two wheels she was able to spread the word beyond her home city and into the surrounding villages and towns in the East Midlands, some as far as thirty miles away, places where news reports of protests and arrests in London might have felt remote, irrelevant or alienating. Alice wanted to connect with working-class women like her whom the largely middle- and upper-class WSPU might not have reached, and her bicycle was the way to get to them.

Every Sunday, Alice—alongside fellow Leicester WSPU organizer Dorothy Pethick—would take her message about votes for women to nearby village greens and market squares, holding talks and rallies and distributing campaign literature such as the *Votes for Women* newspaper. They often met resistance from the authorities and local men, but they continued undeterred.

As a result of their cycling campaigning, Loughborough, fourteen miles from Leicester, soon established its own branch of the WSPU. Alice has since gone down in history as one of many women who has used her "freedom-machine" in the fight against powers that have sought to restrict people's liberty and human rights.

Clarionettes to Cycling Scouts

Alice was far from the only cycling suffragette: bicycling was in the DNA of the WSPU and many of its members were keen cyclists. Fittingly, the architects of the suffragette movement, the Pankhursts, led the way, with Christabel, daughter of Emmeline and sister to Sylvia, keenest of all.

From the age of thirteen, Christabel had petitioned her barrister father for a bicycle. At first he was apprehensive about the busy roads of their hometown of Manchester, but he finally gave in to her relentless badgering in 1896, when she was sixteen. Despite the family experiencing financial pressures, she was bought a top-of-the-range Rudge-Whitworth bicycle. Sylvia, perhaps because her pleas for a bicycle were lukewarm compared to her sister's, and possibly because she was two years younger, was given a distinctly inferior bike that a "comrade" in the local Independent Labour Party had made from bits of gas piping. This may explain why Sylvia didn't fall in love with cycling to the extent her sister did; it seems her pipe contraption was "a considerable handicap" when trying to keep up with her older and fitter sister. Despite this, and testament to Sylvia's remarkable comradeship and commitment to sisterhood, every available day was spent cycling.

Christabel didn't seem so understanding of her sister's handicap and would regularly sprint off without looking back: according to Sylvia, "She would disappear from me, climbing some hill, and arrive home sometimes an hour before me. I remember being thrown over the handle-bars and rising up so shaken that I had to walk for some distance before I could re-mount." Sylvia describes riding with her sister as a "veritable torture" and how she would be red-faced and gasping for oxygen while Christabel impatiently urged her to "Come on!" as she struggled to catch up until "it seemed my heart would burst." It's no wonder Sylvia was pleased when they joined a local Manchester cycling club, the Clarion Cycling Club, where she had the company of other riders who wouldn't abandon her at the bottom of a hill: "There were usually some slow women riders among the company, and the men were kind in helping to push one up the steepest hills." Fittingly, the club's motto was "fellowship is life." Soon the women were joining their fellow members, Clarionettes, every week for their Sunday runs into the countryside, away from the "grime" of industrial Manchester. Even Sylvia, the youngest member of the club, was won over by the camaraderie of these weekly jaunts, especially with the number of willing hands to help mend her constant punctures.

Always a politically active family, in these pre-WSPU days

they were heavily involved with the Independent Labour Party, so it's not coincidental that they chose to join a left-wing cycle club. Their club, Clarion CC, was a cycling offshoot of a socialist weekly newspaper of the same name, founded in 1891 by Robert Blatchford, who had been fired from his previous paper for writing uncompromising features about the terrible living conditions endured by Manchester's factory workers. He started *The Clarion* to continue reporting on political injustices and the realities of life for impoverished workers.

This being the cycle-crazed 1890s, *The Clarion* established its first cycle club in Birmingham in 1894. By 1897, there were seventy clubs around the U.K. Unlike many clubs, it admitted women members almost from the start, and supported rational dress. In addition to social rides each Sunday, Clarion CC's activities included picnics, cycle tours and even camping trips.

The summer camps were so popular that hundreds of Clarionettes would attend, with even Labour leader Keir Hardie staying a night at the 1896 camp and helping with the washing up. A horse-drawn caravan would transport equipment to the campsite, including a large tent which doubled as a dining and entertainment hall. As well as fresh air, exercise and socialism, it was also an opportunity, as noted by Sylvia, for the younger members to indulge in holiday romances and flirtations. Clarion CC's gender equality didn't quite extend to all areas of club life: the women members were left largely responsible for the catering at these gatherings.

In 1897, a year after Sylvia and Christabel joined, an "experimental, co-operative cottage" was leased in Bucklow Hill in the Cheshire countryside to serve as a clubhouse for nearby members. Emmeline Pankhurst was one of the people who helped financially support the cottage. Sixty people could be accommodated in its dormitories, and others could camp in the grounds.

Alice Foley, a weaver's assistant in a Bolton cotton mill, was also a member of the Manchester CC, saving some of her wages each week so she could purchase a bicycle and ride with the club to get away from the smoke and dirt of the inner city. The camp holidays for members like Alice were an affordable escape from the grind of working life at a time when holidays were financially out of reach to most workers. Children from inner-city slums were also invited, a temporary release from the poverty of their existence. It was a poverty that Sylvia describes as the reason for the early death of the most beautiful and popular girl member of the club, "the common tragedy of pinching scarcity in a working-class home where wages are small and life hard, as it was in those days."

Despite the sisters' devotion to the club, their lives were to be overtaken by events in 1898 when their father died suddenly. Manchester CC members joined the funeral procession on their bikes. For the Pankhurst girls, the Sunday rides and summer camps would soon be a thing of the past as they began to devote all their energies to women's emancipation, founding the WSPU in 1903 and moving to London. Christabel and Sylvia would regularly write features for *The Clarion* about the suffragette cause, helping it become one of the most widely read newspapers covering the issue. The sisters' time as Clarionettes would also have a lasting impact, most notably on how they spread word of the suffragette cause and recruited new members. Though the cycling club rides were an opportunity for respite and freedom for the overworked and underpaid, they were also a means to spread the socialist message by distributing *The Clarion* newspaper and holding talks in villages and towns they passed through. Alice Hawkins, a member of the Leicester Clarion CC, would use these tactics campaigning around the East Midlands from 1909.

Many WSPU members listed cycling as one of their favorite leisure activities and women on decorated bikes could be seen taking part in their processions, with others cycling around with signs emblazoned with suffragette slogans to raise awareness of the cause. However, in 1907, bicycling became part of the organization's concentrated national campaign drive under the direction of Scottish suffragette Flora Drummond.

As the person responsible for orchestrating the WSPU's marches and processionals, Flora understood the importance of visual impact. Known as "the General" for her habit of attending marches on horseback dressed in a military-style uniform, she recognized bicycles were a more practical way of taking the suffragettes' message to women in harder-to-reach areas outside of London and other major cities, and in 1907, she put together a brigade of cycling suffragettes in London. They became known as the WSPU Cycling Scouts, with Flora as their "Captain." Every Saturday the Scouts would meet outside the Court Theatre in London's Sloane Square before making their way to nearby country towns and villages, all dressed in the purple, white and green livery of the suffragette movement, their bikes decorated with WSPU flags. Some may even have ridden a WSPU bicycle, a model especially made by the Elswick Cycle manufacturing company in collaboration with the Women's Press and sold at the Women's Exhibition in 1909. Painted in the suffragette colors, the bicycle featured a badge with the union's motif designed by Sylvia—the angel of freedom, a winged female figure sounding a trumpet. The suffragettes' steed had a drop frame to accommodate long skirts and came with a cushioned sprung seat, a wheel guard to prevent skirts getting caught, and elegant curved handlebars.

Like the Clarionettes, the Cycling Scouts would hold impromptu meetings in the provincial places they passed through, ringing their bells to signal their arrival, with one member of the group standing on a box to give a talk. The scouts distributed *Votes for Women* and other pamphlets, singing suffragette songs as they cycled to the next stop on their itinerary.

Other branches around the country were encouraged to start their own bicycle brigades. One member in the Lake District offered an all-expenses-paid cycling holiday in the area for any keen suffragettes who wanted to combine a cycle tour with campaigning. As a mountainous and extremely rural region, with many difficult-to-reach villages, this was the perfect opportunity for anyone wanting to combine advancing the cause with exploring a beautiful part of the country with their girlfriends.

As the suffragettes' campaigning became increasingly militant in the face of the government's continued rejection of their demands, the bicycle continued to prove a useful tool in the struggle, most notably as a getaway vehicle, including for a spate of so-called "pillar-box outrages," where suffragettes poured corrosive substances—sometimes using an inner tube—into Royal Mail postboxes before cycling off. They were also frequently used to flee the scene of some of the more headline-grabbing WSPU actions.

On March 19, 1913, two women were seen by a policeman just before one a.m. cycling fast through the dark lanes of Egham, Surrey. Another policeman stopped them a few miles away on Staines Railway Bridge to reprimand them for not having a front light. The offender gave her name as Phyllis Brady and after relighting her lamp they continued on their way.

Phyllis was in fact Olive Beamish, and she would later be arrested and sent to prison for having done much more than failing to keep her bicycle lamp lit. The reason Olive and her friend, Elsie Duval, were cycling fast through Surrey under cover of darkness was because they had just set fire to Trevethan, a mansion belonging to Lady White, the widow of a decorated British Army officer. The house had been empty for three years, ensuring no one would get hurt, a prerequisite for all suffragette arson attacks. In their front baskets they had carried the petrol used to set alight Trevethan's grand staircase. They had also opened all the windows so the flames would get the oxygen needed to ensure maximum damage. In the garden they had left handwritten signs: "Votes for Women" and "Stop torturing our comrades in prison."

Elsie and Olive were arrested two weeks later after they were discovered carrying flammable material in leather cases at one a.m., twenty-five miles away in Croydon. Both were to abscond a few weeks later after being temporarily released from Holloway prison to recover from their hunger striking. Elsie fled the country, not returning until after the outbreak of World War I, while Olive carried on her militant activities, evading capture until the following year.

That same year, suffragette Edith Rigby, a deeply committed women's rights activist, also made an escape while on temporary release from prison in Liverpool. Like Elsie and Olive, she had been let out to recover from her hunger strike. This system of releasing suffragettes who refused to eat was called the "Cat and Mouse" act, with police tailing the women for information and re-arresting them once they had recovered their strength.

Edith had been sent to Walton Jail for nine months' hard labor after planting a bomb in the basement of the Liverpool Cotton Exchange and later setting fire to Lord Leverhulme's country residence. She was reputedly the first woman to ride a bicycle in her hometown of Preston in the 1890s, wearing bloomers and being pelted with eggs and old vegetables for doing so, so it's fitting she absconded on a bicycle. She had dressed in workmen's clothes to avoid detection. She cycled to the Liverpool docks to board a ferry to Ireland and got as far as Galway. Even her husband had no idea where she had gone. It is believed she spent many months on the run, most likely until World War I broke out in July and the government announced an amnesty on all suffragette prisoners.

In April of the following year, a few months before the outbreak of war, two young women arrived at a Suffolk boarding house on their bicycles for a holiday by the sea. It just so happened that during the time of their Suffolk sojourn there were some local arson attacks that had all the signature markings of the WSPU, not least the notes left in the wreckage of each site that read, "There can be no peace until women get the vote." Shortly after they arrived in Lowestoft, the pavilion on the Britannia Pier in nearby Great Yarmouth was burned to the ground. A large explosion, heard throughout the town, occurred at four a.m. on April 14 and the building—which had only just been rebuilt after a previous fire—was soon engulfed in flames, destroying everything but the iron girders. The incident happened to be on the same night the two women told the owner of their guesthouse that they would be staying with friends instead of returning to their room.

Their accommodation bookings were made under the name Hilda Byron, but the two women were in fact WSPU members Hilda Burkitt and Florence Tunks. For a fortnight, the two had been cycling around the area, moving between lodgings to be closer to their different targets, planning out their attacks and setting fire to haystacks in farmers' fields along the way. Their dramatic last act was the torching of the Bath Hotel in Felixstowe on April 28, which was closed for refurbishment at the time. The cycling arsonists were arrested the following day, with Hilda sentenced to two years, and the younger Florence to nine months. They were both released in the amnesty given to imprisoned suffragettes when war broke out at the end of July that year.

With the start of World War I, the WSPU suspended all militant activities in order to focus on women joining the war effort, requiring them to take on men's work that would make it even harder to continue to deny women's suffrage. Which indeed was the case when the 1918 Representation of the People Act granted the vote to women over the age of thirty who met the property qualifications, which included around 40 percent of women in the U.K., before universal suffrage was granted a decade later.

Vive la Résistance

That wasn't the end of the bicycle's role in women's active resistance to oppression. In World War II, it would become a useful tool for fighting for freedom in not dissimilar ways to how it had aided those militant suffragettes.

In the cycle-centric Netherlands, bikes were commonly employed in the covert struggle against the Nazi occupation, which is both ironic and fitting since Hitler wasn't a fan, after his experience as a bicycle messenger in World War I had left him with a hatred of cycling. He had already banned them from most German roads. Dutch cyclists living under Nazi rule were soon required to abide by strict new anti-cycling laws, such as giving way to any passing German vehicles, with many citizens deliberately flouting the new legislation as part of their own small daily resistance. Despite Hitler's distaste for bikes, he passed an official order to confiscate a large number of them from the

Dutch—as well as the Danes—to use them for the German military after fuel became scarce. This followed a 1942 decree that demanded all Jewish people hand over their bicycles to the authorities. The Dutch did their best to thwart them, hiding their bikes anywhere they could, including burying them in their gardens, and a few citizens were even shot for not giving them up.

It's estimated occupying forces managed to take ownership of around two million of the four million bicycles in the country during the war, depriving owners of their most practical means of getting around at a time when public transportation was barely operating. Many Dutch also used their bicycles to travel out to the countryside to forage when food was in short supply under rationing. This would have been particularly devastating during the Dutch famine in the winter of 1944–45, when the Germans blockaded food supplies to the major cities, resulting in the deaths of eighteen thousand people.

Even when the Allies liberated the Netherlands in 1945, many German soldiers stole bicycles to escape back to Germany to avoid becoming prisoners of war. The confiscations and thefts were so controversial that for decades the Dutch chanted "Give us back our bicycles" whenever their team played Germany at soccer, and in 2009, one former soldier tried to locate the Dutch owners of the bike he had stolen so he could repay them.

Despite bicycles being difficult to hold on to during wartime, two Dutch teenage sisters did manage, and those bikes were pivotal in their dangerous work fighting the Nazi occupation of the Netherlands, and not just in flagrantly disregarding the new anti-cycling laws.

Freddie and Truus Oversteegen were fourteen and sixteen respectively when Germany invaded their country in 1940. Raised in Haarlem, twenty kilometers north of Amsterdam, they had been brought up by their communist mother to "stand up for the oppressed and fight injustice." They helped the local Communist party distribute anti-Nazi leaflets, storing the contraband literature in their bicycle baskets, as well as defacing Nazi propaganda posters before quickly pedaling away from the scene. Soon they were hiding Dutch and German Jewish families in their small apartment. The refugees couldn't stay for long, since the family's well-known left-wing sympathies made their home too obvious a hiding place. The following year, the commander of Haarlem's underground resistance cell asked their mother if he could involve the girls in their covert and highly dangerous work against the Nazis and their Dutch collaborators. Only once the Oversteegen sisters' training was underway did they find out the shocking nature of the missions they would undertake.

There were other women involved in resistance work at this time, but most were restricted to working as couriers or circulating anti-Nazi propaganda. Even pre-Hollywood Audrey Hepburn was reputedly delivering resistance leaflets on her bike in Arnhem, seventy-five miles to the east of Haarlem, where she was living and attending school at that time. This type of resistance activity wasn't exactly safe, with many couriers killed, including Annick van Hardeveld, who was shot in Amsterdam in May 1945. Annick had been on a mission to deliver a message to four resistance fighters about a meeting they were required to attend. There is now a memorial on the spot where she died.

British record-breaking competitive cyclist Evelyn Hamilton also claimed that she had used her cycling prowess to transport messages for the resistance when she ended up in Paris during the Occupation, much as Giro d'Italia and Tour de France winner Gino Bartali had famously used his training rides as a cover to carry messages that would help many Jews escape Italy. However, Evelyn was renowned for spinning some tall stories in her later years, and while her competitive cycling records can be verified, sadly it's less easy to do so with her wartime claims. There were, though, many women—as well as men—in the resistance, pedaling all over France transporting forbidden documents, with some tragically sent to Auschwitz for their activities.

For the commander of the Haarlem resistance, the Oversteegen sisters' youth and gender was their greatest asset. What could seem more innocuous than two teen schoolgirls in plaits riding their bicycles around the streets of Haarlem? No one would guess that they were carrying firearms in their front baskets, but that's exactly what they were doing. Their seemingly youthful innocence is doubtless what helped keep them alive throughout the war despite the perilous work they were carrying out. Soon they were sabotaging railway lines and bridges with dynamite, again transporting their equipment in their baskets before speeding away from the scene. They were also taught how to fire a gun—the group required them to carry out assassinations of Nazis and their Dutch collaborators. They would shoot at their targets as they cycled past, Truus pedaling while Freddie took aim. Truus would also do her share, including seducing a Nazi officer in a bar, suggesting a romantic walk in nearby woods where she then shot him dead.

The sisters also helped transport Jewish children across the country to designated safe houses on the back of their bicycles. They would often dress in Red Cross uniforms, since the organization's nurses were allowed greater freedom to move around— much as nurses like Friedel Bohny-Reiter in France used her bike to take sick Jewish babies from a prison camp to receive hospital treatment. In one instance the Oversteegens even opted for the uniform of a female German soldier in order to remove a Jewish child from a Dutch camp. Their missions, though, weren't always successful: in 1944, a Jewish child seated on the back of

Truus's bike was accidentally shot by a British plane as they cycled past a group of German soldiers. She had to continue cycling with the child until she could safely bury him at a farm.

Somehow, they managed to keep their bicycles operational. No small feat when there were no inner tubes—or other cycle parts—available for much of the war. Dutch cyclists resorted to using items like garden hoses in lieu of tires or simply riding on the metal rims. Remarkably, the two women also survived the war, despite the Nazis offering a large reward for their capture. Sadly, their comrade in the resistance, Hannie Schaft, was executed a few weeks before liberation—the roots of her famous red hair, which she had dyed black to disguise it, had betrayed her identity.

Freddie and Truus were awarded the Mobilization War Cross in 2014 for their work saving lives and helping defeat the enemy.

"A Bicycle of My Own"

Meanwhile, in France, another teenage resistance fighter had taken up arms against Nazi occupation. Eighteen-year-old Simone Segouin was from a village near Chartres, fifty miles southwest of Paris. In 1944, she joined the *Francs-tireurs et partisans*, a communist resistance organization, and was given the nom de guerre, and all-important false identity papers, of Nicole Minet. Her first task for the group was to steal a bicycle belonging to a German military administrator—perhaps one that had been stolen from the Netherlands. After disguising it with a new paint job, it became her reconnaissance vehicle, enabling her to work as a courier for the group and conduct stakeouts. In August, Simone was part of the successful operation to capture twenty-five soldiers and liberate Chartres. She was spotted during the celebrations that followed by war photographer Robert

Capa, who took a series of iconic photographs of Simone with her Schmeisser MP-40 gun that were published in *Life* magazine the following month.

A few days after their success in Chartres, she went on to assist in the liberation of Paris, the city where another French woman, also named Simone, had been riding a stolen, repainted bicycle throughout the war as part of her own personal resistance against the Nazi occupation. She wasn't involved in any combat, but her bicycle was her personal "freedom-machine," when liberation seemed an impossibility.

Before the Nazis took control of Paris in June 1940, the writer and philosopher Simone de Beauvoir had never ridden a bicycle, as her mother had deemed it unseemly for someone of her class. By the end of the war, it had become a lifeline. Simone had initially fled the city ahead of the imminent invasion as part of the great exodus of Parisians on June 10, but had returned by the end of the month, opting to try to live a life as close as was possible to her prewar existence of teaching, writing and socializing with the other artists and intellectuals who also stayed on in the capital. Her close friend—and possibly sometime lover—Natalie Sorokin, gifted her a bicycle not long after her return. Natalie had become a bicycle thief to survive the privations of wartime, with the money she made from her larceny enabling her to buy food—when available—on the black market.

Bicycles were valuable in occupied Paris. The Nazis had requisitioned all the cars and had suspended most of the public transport system, and even taxis at this time had turned into "vélos-taxis," makeshift rickshaws with bicycles pulling covered boxes on wheels to accommodate passengers. Natalie used the artist Alberto Giacometti's courtyard to repaint her purloined wheels before she sold them on, and she taught Simone how to ride on one of them.

Natalie was either a good teacher or her pupil a fast learner, as Simone wrote in her diary that by the end of the first lesson she could balance, mount by herself and turn corners. By her third lesson she was boasting of taking "real rides" to parks around Paris, though not completely without incident: "Once I ran into a dog, and another time into two good ladies—who were very indignant about it—but for the most part it was a glorious performance."

During this period of struggling to adapt to the grim realities of life under occupation—and longing for the return of her lover and "soul-partner" Jean-Paul Sartre, who had been drafted into the army before becoming a prisoner of war—Simone's accounts of her bicycling adventures in her diaries and letters sing with excitement. She writes to Jean-Paul to tell him that exploring Paris on her bicycle is "absolutely delightful," just as reading Hegel in the library also has a soothing effect at this fraught time. By August, she is covering more and more miles alongside Natalie, taking in the forests and chateaux beyond the city, even going as far as Normandy—"I pedaled on, and the sheer physical exertion kept me occupied." Relations between the two women were not always as blissful as their rides, though, with Simone describing Natalie's desire to "court scandal" wherever they went—indulging in stunts such as washing her hands in a holy font—testing Simone's customary indifference to public opinion. However, Simone's desire to ride was at this point seemingly insatiable: "I only wanted to eat up the kilometers on my bicycle. It's a new joy in life that I've discovered and, instead of wishing for a car, my desires will henceforth be limited to a bicycle of my own." Thanks to Natalie's bicycle thievery, that "bicycle of my own" was soon a reality, and Simone had no qualms about accepting it.

As the woman who would go on to write the feminist classic

The Second Sex, in which she described femininity as a social construct, it's unsurprising that Simone so enthusiastically rebelled against the bourgeois and patriarchal childhood which had dictated that "good" girls don't cycle. She described her cycling self as a "lusty wench," which may have been poking fun at the conservative belief of those like her mother that women on bikes are on a slippery slope to promiscuity—though it could also have meant she felt healthy and vigorous. For someone who would write about how women are not free, it's understandable she delighted in the sensations of weightlessness, physical freedom and independence she experienced as she spun through the streets of Paris. Cycling was also a personal resistance against, and temporary escape from, an oppressive occupying regime that sought to limit freedoms wherever it could.

This is not to say that the rest of her wartime experience was unendurable: it was certainly a lot less stressful than that of Truus and Freddie. In fact, Simone would emerge as an international literary star from the novels she wrote during this time. Despite living in a war zone, she was still able to write most days at her favorite table at Café de Flore, teaching at the lycée and studying philosophy in the library. In the evenings she would dance and drink at parties with other left-wing luminaries such as Picasso and Dora Maar, Georges Bataille and Jean Cocteau. She would watch films at the cinema, attend plays and even go on ski trips, all activities that offered a temporary escape and a means of staying sane during the wartime strictures.

Nevertheless, Paris under the Occupation was a very different place from what it had been before the war. Her diaries and letters are full of details of the terrible conditions she and other Parisians had to endure, which worsened as the war progressed, from near starvation, power cuts, rat-infested accommodations and arctic temperatures, as well as the constant threat of violence and the devastation of friends, and so many others, whose lives were cut short by war. Cycling was her temporary escape from the horror, particularly when pedaling outside the occupied zone.

I wonder how much it contributed to her intellectual thinking and writing. There is a long history of writers and artists who connect the activity of walking with creativity, such as Henry David Thoreau, who stated that "the moment my legs begin to move, my thoughts begin to flow." Scientific research seems to back this up too, with a study conducted on students at Stanford University showing that those who went out for a walk came up with far more original ideas than those who stayed seated at a desk.* Some argue cycling doesn't have the same effect because it's that much faster, that it's out of sync with our natural thinking flow, and that it's too physical to allow for more creative thought. I disagree. I frequently find that if I'm in the process of dealing with a knotty problem and take a break to go for a ride, new and better solutions arise despite me not actively looking for them. Even if I'm not consciously thinking about work, ideas and connections often pop into my head that make me see something more clearly than I have previously. I sometimes have to pull up at the side of the road to note these thoughts down before I forget them. It's as if the distance from my desk allows for a more expansive way of thinking, and there is something about the repetitive motion of legs turning pedals, combined with being outdoors, that enables my thoughts to percolate and order

---

* Four experiments carried out at Stanford in 2014 by Dr. Marily Oppezzo and Professor Daniel Schwartz showed that a person's ability to produce creative ideas increased by up to 60 percent during or just after walking. The participants didn't even have to walk outside to perform better; walking on a treadmill produced the same results.

themselves—though being denied the ability to scroll dementedly through social media posts on my smartphone also helps. As Virginia Woolf said of her walks on the South Downs, "I like to have space to spread my mind out in," and when I'm in a smooth rhythm on a quiet road, that's exactly how I feel too.

The war years were an intellectually productive time for Simone, and coincidentally the time she was doing the most cycling; and I like to think the latter contributed to the former. Perhaps it was also how she got to grips with Hegel's notoriously opaque *Phenomenology of Mind*, which she started studying in 1940, around the time she started cycling. Initially she said she could "scarcely make head nor tail of it," but after many hours in the library, and hundreds of miles covered on her bicycle, she said she understood "rather better."

In September 1940, Simone escaped to Brittany for a cycling holiday with her friend Bianca. They explored its sunny pine forests and sand dunes, gorging on lobster and pancakes. She was elated at not meeting any Germans during their two-week trip, which made them temporarily forget their wartime existence. This pedal-powered escape from life under occupation was to become a regular fixture for Simone for the rest of the war, a "delicious form of freedom."

The following August she took another cycling holiday, this time with Jean-Paul. This vacation was originally intended to be more political. The two had recently formed what would be a relatively short-lived and ineffectual resistance group, "Socialism and Liberty," with a number of their Parisian intellectual friends—though the group spent more time debating and discussing philosophy than doing active resistance work, which left its members unclear about their actual purpose and strategies. Nor were they as clandestine as they could have been, with Natalie throwing their leaflets indiscriminately out of her bicycle basket as she cycled through Paris and another member leaving a suitcase on the Métro which held sensitive documents that identified the group.

Despite the chaotic approach, Jean-Paul hoped to recruit more friends to the cause who were living in the south under the collaborationist Vichy government, in the so-called "Free Zone." To get there wasn't a straightforward affair. To avoid attracting attention, they sent their bicycles and tents ahead, before taking a train southeast out of Paris to Montceau-les-Mines in Burgundy, on the border between the Occupied and Free Zones. There they paid a woman who worked as a *passeur* to help them across to the other side. The crossing had to be done under cover of darkness, with the three creeping through moonlit fields and woods. Once safely over, they stopped at the first inn and found it full of clandestine border crossers like themselves. This was to be the first of repeated covert crossings into Vichy France that the couple would take over the next few years. And each trip was an act of defiance against the German authorities, which made Simone feel she had regained a little of her liberty.

Reunited with the bicycles in Roanne on the Loire River, they set out with their luggage strapped to their frames, toward the vineyards and olive groves, mountains and Mediterranean Sea to the south. When Jean-Paul's already heavily patched tires got a puncture not long into the journey, neither of them knew how to fix it. They were saved by a passing mechanic who showed Simone how it was done, and soon she became adept at fixing their worn tires.

While Jean-Paul would often sprint ahead on the hills, she was critical of his erratic approach to cycling, accusing him of "pedaling so indolently" on the flat, his mind wandering, that he would frequently career into a ditch at the side of the road. He would claim he was too busy thinking. Both shared a love of "whizzing" downhill at speed. They pedaled hundreds of miles—many mountainous—on this first trip along the Rhône River, through the forested mountains of the Cévennes and Ardèche, and down into sun-drenched Provence, "intoxicated by the swift transformation of the landscape" compared to walking. Each evening, after a long day in the saddle, they pitched their tent, Simone feeling carefree and happy in a way that she hadn't felt since the start of the war.

Their resistance work was less rewarding. None of the friends they visited were willing to sign up to their group. The writer Colette Audry, a member of her local resistance group in Grenoble, suggested wisely that they should "leave espionage to those who know how to do it." It was on the return journey north, passing over the steep climbs of the Maritime Alps to stay with Colette, that Simone had an accident so disastrous it might have deterred a less devoted cyclist from getting into the saddle again.

Their route over the Alps to Grenoble, which included the 7,382-foot-high Col d'Allos, a Tour de France staple, would challenge most relatively fit cyclists, even with the advantages of today's lightweight cycles. Simone and Jean-Paul had much heavier bicycles, not to mention their luggage, and far fewer gears. The ascent wasn't the problem for Simone—it was the descent. After stopping for some lunch and a few glasses of wine, they began an exhilarating freewheel down toward Grenoble. However, the alcohol had gone to Simone's head and on encountering two cyclists coming the other way, she swerved in the wrong direction and, thanks to her deficient brakes, soon found herself skidding on gravel and headed toward the precipice. When she eventually came to, she discovered that she had somehow managed to avoid flying over the edge, but she felt more than a little bruised and shaken. Once the effects of her concussion had worn off, she quite understandably insisted they take a train the rest of the way down. When Simone was finally able to survey the damage in a mirror, she could see why Colette had not recognized her when they had arrived: "I had lost a tooth, one of my eyes was closed, my face had swollen up to twice its normal size, and the skin was all scraped raw. I couldn't get so much as a grape between my lips." It also explained why her fellow train passengers had appeared so startled. What's unclear is why Jean-Paul hadn't mentioned any of this to her. The missing tooth was to make a miraculous reappearance a few weeks later, back in Paris, when it emerged from a boil she squeezed on her chin.

Such a terrifying brush with mortality, and by her own admission looking "hideous," wasn't enough to put her off getting back in the saddle the next day to complete the last few hundred miles before recrossing the border. She describes the final days of their journey in tones as rapturous as those before her accident, particularly the views of the Burgundy vineyards in their autumn colors. The sight of the sun breaking through the autumn mists filled her with "a childish sense of well-being." Even running out of money, and therefore food, wasn't enough to dampen her enthusiasm. The traumatic experience on the Col had far from diminished her appetite for touring by bike; instead, it was now a much treasured and longed-for annual event during wartime for the writer.

After the return crossing over the border with twenty other cyclists led by another *passeur*, the couple returned to a Paris, which, that autumn, was even more tense and repressive. While they were away, among other atrocities, a series of communist uprisings had been violently quashed by the Germans, with the accused killed or sent to concentration camps. Simone describes how during this time she felt like she was "reduced to a condition of total impotence" and didn't even allow herself to dream that defeat of Hitler's Reich might be possible. It would have been a stark contrast to those sunny days of relatively carefree pedal-powered exhilaration. Understandably, by the following summer they were itching to get back to those long days in the saddle, as far away from German soldiers as possible in the middle of wartime. They were also keen to celebrate the news that French publisher Gallimard wanted to publish the novel she had been working on.

This time their starting point was the Basque region of the Pyrenees, and they crossed the border into the Free Zone at a point that was renowned for being more permeable. The inn just on the other side was heaving, this time largely with Jews who were hoping to escape on into Spain, out of necessity rather than choice. Like the Alps, the Pyrenees aren't without their challenges for the cyclist. Even Simone admitted this trip, in which they were to travel from the mountains of the eastern Pyrenees all the way to Marseille—around four hundred miles if you are going a direct route, and they weren't—and then part of the way back again, was "pretty tiring." Even more so if you are half starved. She recounts in her diaries how lunch would generally consist of no more than fruit and tomatoes, with dinner usually a clear soup and unappetizing vegetables. Not exactly the fuel needed for powering over mountains and cols. Most cyclists today wouldn't dream of attempting even part of a journey like this without saddlebags stuffed with energy gels and protein bars, and the assurance of a large meal at the end of each day.

En route to Marseille they pedaled through the *départements* of Aude and the Ariège, a region I've lived in. Simone and Jean-Paul had fallen in love with the place on the eve of war, where in the walled city of Carcassonne—already filling with French troops—they had wandered its medieval streets and drunk wine under arbors. They had also explored its Cathar castles and the beautiful villages nestled in the foothills of the Pyrenees, delaying their return to Paris and what lay ahead, all the while trying to reassure each other that this bucolic region would remain untouched by the war. Knowing they would return after it was all over would help sustain them throughout.

I've cycled through those same quiet towns and villages, which I doubt have changed much since they were here. I can imagine them pulled up at the side of the road, grabbing handfuls of grapes from the many vineyards which she says "saved us from literally starving," bunking up in hay barns for the night or Simone bent over by the side of the road to fix yet another puncture in their well-worn inner tubes. Despite their hunger, which she describes as becoming, understandably, an "obsession," there was no question of cutting the ride short. So single-minded was she about continuing the journey that despite their lack of nutrition, Jean-Paul raised no objections, which she put down to not wanting to "deprive me of my pleasure."

The situation got properly sticky when they ran out of money a few days before recrossing the border and weren't able to purchase the meager rations they had been just about surviving on until this point. When they finally reached the house of a friend, emaciated and exhausted, just three spoons of soup caused Jean-Paul to faint, after which he was confined to bed for three days. Simone noted that she had lost sixteen pounds over the course of the trip and so they stayed on for another month to recover their strength.

The winter of 1942–43 was particularly bleak: when they returned from their rehabilitation in the country, they discovered all their possessions had been thrown away by the hotel where they had been staying. Then the temperature dropped to a record low, with fuel for heating extremely scarce and with Simone now having to live in the most unimaginably squalid hotel. Food was even thinner on the ground, and often infested with maggots and weevils. Despite this, she writes that she could endure any austerity apart from having to give up her travels, and the following summer, just after she had been suspended from her job teaching at the lycée for her allegedly inappropriate relationship with Natalie Sorokin, she was off again with her tent and bicycle, this time alone.

In *The Second Sex*, de Beauvoir writes of T. E. Lawrence's tour through France by bicycle as a teenager, and how a young girl generally wouldn't have been allowed to go on such an adventure. She describes his trip as one defined by the "headiness of freedom and discovery," one in which he "learns to look at the entire world as his fief."* In 1943, at the age of thirty-five, she was doing just that, returning to Roanne, where she and Jean-Paul had begun their first summer cycle adventure. Each day she was on the road by six a.m., making her way over mountains, plagued as ever by constantly failing inner tubes. Food was a lot easier to come by on this trip, and her letters and diary are crammed with details of all the delicious meals and non-rationed food she consumed.

She enjoyed this solo adventure, but she also missed Jean-Paul, who had promised to join her en route. In a letter to him she writes that the thought of once more seeing his "back on the road in front" makes her heart "burst with joy." Three weeks later, and several hundred miles from her start, they were reunited in

---

* In 1908, nineteen-year-old student Thomas Edward Lawrence cycled around two thousand miles through France with the objective of visiting as many important medieval sites as he could manage.

Uzerche. Descriptions of them seeking cover from thunderstorms in their matching yellow rain capes, with Jean-Paul wiping water off his spectacles, are particularly enjoyable. In one torrential downpour the pages of his manuscript for *The Reprieve* escape from his bicycle bag, floating off in muddy puddles, ink running, before they are recaptured. For the most part, the trip is sunny and filled with good food and scenery, a stark contrast to the previous winter.

Their return to Paris was a lot less painful than the last time. The autumn of 1943 saw the publication of her novel *She Came to Stay*, which was a critical and commercial success, but being a celebrated novelist wasn't enough to put food on the table in wartime. In early 1944, when the Allies were carrying out sustained bombardments on occupied Paris, food in the city was scarcer than ever. Simone often resorted to cycling around the countryside to forage and barter for provisions. This was not without its risks, despite much of the area surrounding Paris being now out of Nazi control. She frequently heard explosions as she cycled along the rural roads, and in one instance, on hearing the air-raid siren as she passed through the bombed-out remains of Creil, north of Paris, she was so spooked that she "pedaled across the railway bridge at breakneck speed: the silence and solitude of the place was terrifying." The Normandy landings in June 1944 indicated the German occupation was finally coming to an end and by August 25, 1944, the Germans had surrendered Paris, but not without a bloody fight in which random civilians, including housewives doing their shopping, were shot dead in the streets. Finally Simone and her fellow Parisians had their beloved city back.

The following summer, a few months after V-E Day, Simone was setting off "on a little journey all alone" with a new bicycle given to her by Jean-Paul, this time in the direction of the

Cévennes hills, full of the same "headiness of freedom and discovery" as T. E. Lawrence before her and with the horrors of war ebbing away. This was also the year women in France were given the right to vote, over twenty-five years after the U.K. and U.S.

I don't know if Simone did much cycling after this; I have found no mention of it, and it wasn't long before her literary stardom took her to the United States on a long lecture tour. What I do know is that during some very dark times, when freedom often felt like a distant memory, it was a way for her to experience a sense of release and liberation, whether it was during the hundreds of miles she cycled across the country or even on her brief rides across Paris between the library or lycée and her table at her favorite café. As her legs turned the pedals it may also have helped spark ideas that contributed to her writings on feminism and existentialism which have made her one of the greatest thinkers of the twentieth century.

PART III

THE OPEN ROAD

CHAPTER SEVEN

THE GREAT ESCAPE

Wanderlust

"What would become of us, if we walked only in a garden or a mall?" was a question posed in 1862 by poet, philosopher and keen walker Henry David Thoreau, which could also have been asked of cyclists a few decades later. As we know, they didn't just keep to their local parks and streets. Instead, during the nineteenth-century boom in travel and tourism—particularly in affluent Western Europe and North America—using a bike to explore destinations further afield became increasingly common.

Cycling holidays abroad became so popular that travel company Thomas Cook started offering bike tours, though more intrepid cyclists preferred to go it alone off the beaten track. In the 1890s, the U.K. Cyclists' Touring Club (CTC) membership quadrupled, with many members traveling to places they otherwise might never have reached. The club's gazette was packed with their stories of travels at home and abroad, inspiring others to follow their example, each account illustrated with black-and-white photography or sketches.

The editor of the "Ladies" page of the CTC's *Gazette*, Lillias Campbell Davidson, knew from personal experience that women who learned to ride would "thirst for longer flights; for the pleasure of going on and on, and never turning back" and in so doing would feel like "an explorer venturing for the first time into a new country and discovering a world for herself." And so increasing numbers of those who had the luxury of both time and money were opting to spend a few days, weeks or even months pedaling from place to place, through landscapes—and countries—that were hitherto unknown to them except through books and paintings. Some became pioneers as the first women to cycle through certain countries or regions, and one undertook a solo around-the-world pedal in 1894, though most didn't feel they needed to venture quite so far to feel like adventurers.

Today, the relative cheapness and availability of mass and private transport has made the world more accessible, but a long bike journey remains an adventure, enabling the exploration of new areas in ways that can't be replicated from behind the window of a vehicle. While cycling around one's city is too often about getting from A to B by the most efficient and safest route, on a longer trip, it is all about the journey.

Cycle trips across continents or around the world for months or even years have become a popular antidote to the pressures of busy, technology-driven modern lives, a way to feel more alive and in the moment by stripping things back down to the basics of just turning the pedals along the open road to see how far you can go and where it will take you. Some want the challenge, others are looking for escape or hoping to find themselves along the way. A few even hope to set new records or test the limits of their physical endurance.

Juliana Buhring became the first woman to hold the record for fastest circumnavigation of the world by bike. You might think she wouldn't have much time to take things in, but in her account of her race against the clock, she wrote that being on the bike is like being "*inside* the movie, an essential part of it. Completely reliant on your environment, you observe and absorb every sensation around you."

When I travel by bike, I might not take in absolutely everything, but I do need to be alert and responsive in ways I'm not required to be on public transport, which gives me a heightened awareness of my surroundings. Even on routes I know well, like the one I sometimes take from London to see my family in Somerset, through the quiet lanes of Berkshire and Wiltshire where I now recognize every turn in the road, anticipating certain landmarks along the way, like the bronze-age white horse carved into the hill, there is always something new to observe. Sometimes it's just about taking in the changing of the seasons from one month to the next—the bright bluebells spiking the woodlands in April and the hawthorn blossom and cowslips bursting from the hedgerows in May. These are things I would miss if— were I able to drive—I had taken the M4 motorway instead. I am moving through the landscape in a way that feels more intimate and responsive, even if it sometimes means having to endure the worst that the weather throws at me or mechanical faults. Though if the weather does happen to be foul, then a hot bath, enormous meal or reviving drink at the end is more delicious and earned than it ever would have been otherwise.

Had I lived in France in the 1890s and wanted to join the French equivalent of the Cyclists' Touring Club, I would have needed my husband's permission. However, since women started cycling, they had been getting out and exploring the world around them—with or without permission.

Not all of them were ready to set off entirely on their own at a time when women doing anything unchaperoned still wasn't the norm, and particularly when they were being told that dangers lurked around every corner for lone women. One Victorian writer and cyclist Mrs. Harcourt Williamson felt that women cycling alone were in "some considerable peril," particularly from "tramps"—the bogeymen of the day—who may be "desperate with hunger or naturally vicious." Seeking strength in numbers, some hired cyclist chaperones. These female cycling guides handled all aspects of the trip from route planning to accommodation, as well as basic mechanics, leading their charges through picturesque scenery and taking in historic sites. Others joined the Lady Cyclists' Association to connect with other enthusiasts who might want to join them on some cycling adventures, using their LCA handbook of approved inns to find accommodation en route run by landlords or landladies who wouldn't blink when women arrived a-wheel.

When American cyclist Martha set out with four of her girlfriends to tour Germany in 1892, they didn't seem to need such a handbook. When they disembarked in Hamburg, they were met by incredulous customs officers who took some persuading that they were really the owners of the bicycles that had emerged from the ship's hold. After a few days reassembling their steel steeds in their hotel, they started out on the road to Leipzig, carrying their luggage in canvas rolls attached to their handlebars. Their packing was light—a change of underwear, combs, cosmetics, German-English dictionary and map. They must have read Maria Ward's *Bicycling for Ladies* since they were unflustered mending punctures and a broken chain.

It wasn't only the customs officers who were astonished by five women pedaling through Germany, with Martha describing how they immediately became "the observed of all observers" when "business men, errand boys, bakers, butchers, fruit women and all sizes of children gazed at us with open-eyed, and, in many cases, often open-mouthed, astonishment." Another member of the party wondered whether "they think I am going to fly over their heads." Luckily the crowd wasn't planning a witch hunt and eventually parted to let the women on their way. During their journey they did not see a single other woman riding a bicycle. When they told one innkeeper that they were American, "all seemed explained—Americans dare anything." The Germans they met were welcoming, providing them with shelter from the rain, offering them beds for the night and plying them with food and drink. The group made the most of the country's beer halls and inns, refueling with wine and wurst before pedaling on to Leipzig.

Not all women felt they needed to travel with companions. Lillias Campbell Davidson in her 1896 *Handbook for Lady Cyclists* was confident that in the U.K. and much of Europe, it was "quite safe for a lady to ride alone without any fear of molestation or annoyance"—a statement that many would have found difficult to believe having been told the exact opposite for so long. Lillias had been encouraging women to travel solo, to take trains and even scale mountains, since she published *Hints for Lady Travellers* in 1889—a book aimed at women whose lives she described as having hitherto been "unnaturally cramped and contracted within doors." She was a great advocate for venturing out into the wider world, though admits that women earlier in the decade, those pioneers of cycling such as herself, had often encountered some "annoyance, unpleasant comment, and rudeness" when they traveled the country by bicycle. However, she felt that by the mid-1890s, the peak of the cycle craze, things had improved. Women solo tourers would "probably receive nothing but kindness and courtesy from one end of their journey to the other . . . even if they are attired in rational dress." Though she too warned that tramps on the big roads into cities might cause problems.

For Lillias, the main danger for women cyclists in rural areas was not people, but animals, with even hens "a great affliction to the lady cyclist." To combat the problem of dogs running after cyclists, she recommended her readers pack a long whip to scare them off. As someone who is frequently chased by dogs when cycling through the countryside, and once a flock of angry geese, I can understand why she felt this was such a pressing issue. But since I can usually outpace geese and dogs, I haven't resorted to carrying a whip.

When more fearsome animals like bears and wolves were a possibility, some cycle tourers opted for a more deadly weapon. In 1897, Margaret Valentine Le Long packed a borrowed pistol for her solo cycle from Chicago to San Francisco. She was an unwilling firearms user, packing it in her tool bag to make it hard to get at.

Margaret's friends and family had tried to dissuade her from attempting such a journey, and hoped to scare her out of it with "prophecies of broken limbs, starvation, death from thirst, abduction by cowboys and scalping by Indians." Her account of the ups and downs of her journey in *Outing* magazine tell how, undeterred, she set off westward from Chicago in May, battling the strong winds of Midwestern Illinois and Iowa before hitting the mountains of Colorado and Wyoming and the deserts of Utah and Nevada. Passing through places with such evocative names as Medicine Bow Crossing, Rattlesnake Pass, Devil's Gate and Dirty Woman's Ranch, as well as the eerie ghost towns left behind by emigrant settlers. She begged food and a bed for the night at remote farms and sometimes had to drag her bicycle over rocks and through rivers. She avoided dehydration in the desert by drinking from barrels of water buried by railway workers. Elsewhere she dined on trout with fishermen, antelope steak with hunters. She also went the wrong way—a lot.

The gun did get some use when a herd of cattle gathered on the path in front of her, pawing the ground and bellowing before putting their heads down and charging. She fired five shots with her eyes shut. She opened them to discover the herd had thankfully turned heel and dispersed.

While she may have had a uniquely adventurous journey, Margaret was less open-minded when it came to her clothes, opting for a slightly shortened skirt instead of bloomers. She credited this outfit with eliciting the courtesy and kindness she encountered nearly everywhere she went. Though she admits that by the time she reached San Francisco she was in a somewhat disheveled state and looked not unlike the tramps of whom she too was so fearful.

Lillias would have sympathized; she was only too aware of the emphasis and expectations placed on women's appearance. She recommended that since lady tourers wouldn't have much room in their handlebar bags other than for toiletries and a few other essentials, they post spare clothes ahead of them. She describes how one woman she knew managed this: "She has two spare frocks and dispatches them alternately, so that every evening, when she halts at a new place, she is able to shed her riding costume." She also advised carrying a needle, thread—including glove silk—and a supply of buttons, hooks and eyes for any repairs.

Thankfully, attitudes to clothing have generally become more relaxed. We don't need to ship long dresses around the country in order to look "civilized," with most women free to opt for modern cycling wear, which is lightweight and low maintenance. I find there is a certain satisfaction in carrying everything I need with me, packing only the essentials into my bike bags. It's a salutary exercise in the benefits of minimalism—useful for someone whose wardrobe is probably more expansive than it should be and whose standard approach to packing a suitcase is to always fill it to bursting. Although sometimes I do wish I had room for just one more pair of shoes . . .

The Grand Bicycle Tour

Elizabeth Robins Pennell, the American biographer and art critic, didn't bother to send spare dresses ahead of her during her long cycle journeys in the 1880s and 1890s. Instead, she opted for an adjustable skirt, hooking it up when she rode and letting it down again when she dismounted, to avoid "being stared at as a 'Freak' escaped from the sideshow." In fact, it was her husband's cycling outfit of stockings and knee-length breeches that attracted attention wherever they went. She wrote about their trips for magazines and published them as books, all illustrated with charming pen-and-ink drawings by her husband, the artist Joseph Pennell. Elizabeth was a keen advocate of touring, which she considered a liberating travel experience, particularly for women: "Hers is all the joy of motion, not to be under-estimated, and of long days in the open air; all the joy of adventure and change. Hers is the delightful sense of independence and power, the charm of seeing the country in the only way in which it can be seen; instead of being carried at lightning speed from one town to another." Instead of the sickliness of a stifling life indoors, the female cycle tourer experiences "a perfect state of physical well-being."

Very much classed a "New Woman," the former convent schoolgirl didn't want to play homemaker. Instead, she opted to "relieve the dullness" of her existence by traveling and making a living by writing about her many interests. As someone who also became a celebrated food writer, despite confessing to not even being able to boil an egg, she wasn't one to let much get in the way of her ambitions. As soon as she married Joseph, they bid adieu to the United States and set off for Europe. They were to live there for over three decades, splitting their time between France and London, and traveling whenever and wherever they could, with Elizabeth publishing twenty-five books on art, literature and food.

The Pennells' first bicycle tour was published as *A Canterbury Pilgrimage* in 1885, an account of following the ancient pilgrim route as depicted by Chaucer, from London to Canterbury Cathedral, on their tandem tricycle, with its wheels replacing the walking of the countless travelers who had preceded them. They had both been tricycling since acquiring one in Philadelphia in the 1870s, but this was the first in what would turn out to be a series of increasingly adventurous and physically demanding tricycle and then bicycle trips. Elizabeth was intoxicated by wanderlust, and the bicycle was the perfect mode of transport to satisfy it: "The world is our great book of beauty and romance, and on your cycle you can gradually master it, chapter by chapter, volume by volume." She would later dedicate one of her travelogues to the Alpine Club, hoping to convince them that cycling was the superior way to see the world.

Their second tandem tricycle trip, a few years later, was also inspired by literature. This time they followed the route the author Laurence Sterne made in the 1770s by horse and carriage and later fictionalized in his final novel, *A Sentimental Journey through France and Italy*. Like Sterne's book, their account ends before they reach Italy.

In the tradition of the grand tours of the seventeenth and eighteenth centuries, their journey was focused on taking in important architectural sights and artworks. These grand tours were experiences that had previously been restricted to the aristocracy, with the sons, and sometimes daughters, of the upper echelons of society touring Europe for a few months to several years to learn about classical art and culture to complete their rarefied education, a journey that would usually culminate in Rome. This was the only way, apart from books and art, for the elite to experience those exalted emblems of European culture at the time. Travel then was limited and slow, with the only option horseback, private carriage or public stagecoach over poor roads. Distances that might be a ten-minute car journey today likely would have been quite an arduous and lengthy undertaking, a reality that meant the average person would not have gone more than fifteen miles from their home in their lifetime.

The arrival of mass transport in the nineteenth century—railways and passenger steamships, as well as smoother roads—helped define that latter part of the century as one of movement and change. It also brought traveling abroad within the reach of the wealthy middle class and, like Elizabeth, they were clamoring to see sights that they previously could only have read and dreamed about. Publishers were soon producing guidebooks with suggested routes and must-see sights to cater to these new tourists. While these travelers weren't necessarily aristocracy, they were still the moneyed elite, since most working people would not have had any paid holidays and instead were restricted to day trips on bank holidays or Sundays.

Freelance and independently wealthy, the Pennells had the freedom to spend several months at a time pedaling through Europe. Their class privilege did occasionally lead them to act with a certain entitlement, and they also weren't averse to a bit of national stereotyping. They may have exclaimed much about the beauty of the places they passed through, but they also exhibited a low tolerance for many things, such as the state of the roads and towns that didn't meet their expectations, as well as the behavior of the French, including continually suspecting they were being overcharged.

They felt they were often treated as lower-class citizens on account of their chosen form of transport. In one hotel they were given a bowl of water in their room to wash with, whereas the carriage party had a private dressing room. Their dinner was an omelet in the kitchen while the others feasted in the dining room. They were, though, the subject of great interest everywhere they passed through, with crowds gathering around their tricycle, which the Pennells tended to find more of an irritation than a compliment. While they set out to write the nineteenth-century cycling equivalent of Laurence Sterne, they were in fact far less interested in the other people they encountered than the great novelist had been.

A few years ago, I spent a week cycling along part of the route they followed on their way to Italy—the section following the Seine from Paris, through the forests of Sénart and Fontainebleau and down through the Loire valley toward Lyon. Just as Elizabeth and Joseph followed the carriage tracks of Sterne, I was following their 130-year-old tricycle grooves. Unlike them, I had to share the way with motor traffic, though thankfully the road surfaces had greatly improved. In fact a lot of my journey was on bike paths that followed the same rivers and canals the Pennells had.

The pace of our journeys was different, though, thanks to the advantages of twenty-first-century bike design, and not being weighed down by Victorian skirts. I covered the kind of distances in one day that took them many.

We did, however, both have issues with our luggage. When the bag the Pennells had strapped to their tricycle came apart, the only option was to fix it on a blacksmith's forge. When a bolt snapped on my partner's bag rack, I had to cycle to the nearest village to find the modern equivalent to make the repair. This turned out to be an old Peugeot garage where, after much confusion due to language difficulties—and it being a workshop for cars—I was eventually able to procure a replacement to get us on the road again.

Farther along the route, Elizabeth exclaims over the beauty of Nemours, though in typically haughty fashion, she was far less complimentary about its inhabitants: "The less, I think, we say of them the better . . . The people were disagreeable, that was all." She bemoaned that the restaurants inexplicably refused to serve them, though it being France, with its notoriously strict restaurant hours, they were probably just too late. In contrast, when we went through the town, a stallholder refused to let us pay for our drinks after hearing how far we were cycling that day. Unlike theirs, our journey didn't end with us being arrested for "furious riding" and refusing to stop, as the Pennells had been in Rome, which resulted in them having to sell their tricycle to pay the fine.

By the early 1890s, the Pennells had moved on from tricycles to two-wheeled Safety bicycles—a relief for Joseph, who had accused Elizabeth of not pulling her weight. Their first journey on their new wheels was to Hungary, which they would later publish as *To Gipsyland*. This time the purpose of their trip was not to take in the highlights of western culture, but to find what they defined as a true Romany gypsy. With their bicycles they were able to access all the "remote, unknown, unpronounceable villages far from railways" and travel high up into the mountains of Transylvania, "over the wild passes where we met no one but the shepherd with his black-faced sheep." Despite their exhaustive search, they returned disappointed, their much-fetishized traveling gypsy somewhat elusive. They no longer seemed to be living a nomadic life but had settled in towns and villages to work as farm laborers, which led the Pennells to wonder, in their overly romanticized and unreflective way, if it is they with their bicycles who are now the only ones who are truly "free as the deer in the forest / As the fish where the river flows / Free as the bird in the air!"

Their next trip was to be an even more energy-intensive five-week tour crossing nine Swiss alpine peaks. Elizabeth thought she might have been the first woman to have done such a thing: "I am told I made a record. I think I have, and one to be proud of. I went over nine passes—six in less than a week. I worked at times as hard as a dock laborer . . . Any woman who rides—and knows how to ride . . . and who is not afraid of work, may learn what pleasure there is in the exploit." Whether she did break a record I'm not able to verify, though according to her account, she didn't see any other women cyclists when slogging up the various mountain passes.

The only women cyclists Elizabeth encountered were on a boat crossing Lake Como in Italy, and she was quick to judge they were no match for her athleticism. The first she described as "a big German frau in knickerbockers and many bangles." Elizabeth seemed doubtful that the woman was capable of cycling at all. Based on what, I'm not sure, except as someone who cycled in skirts, it seems she disapproved of the German's appearance and what she describes as her "swagger"—and that was enough for Elizabeth to make up her mind that she had no substance as a cyclist. The other tourers were two Americans who told her, possibly to Elizabeth's relief, that they had put their bikes on a train up the passes. They weren't going to be challenging her record. Instead they flattered her ego when they told her they recognized her from her previous book. While Elizabeth encountered numerous male cyclists, including Americans, she noted that none were English, something she found amusingly ironic since she thought they were always crowing about their athletic prowess.

She was certainly no shrinking violet about her own athleticism, boasting that on one day they ascended two passes before lunch, declaring that she was willing to die in the attempt rather than give up—"People may object that I rode too fast. But I had not come out to play the enthusiast and record my emotions on postcards; I had come to ride over the Alps on a bicycle." Personality and prejudices aside, her desire to "immortalize the name and adventures of the first woman" to climb the Alps by bicycle— i.e., herself—is to be applauded at a time when adventuring, and the stories told about it, had been—and largely still are—such a male occupation. Not least considering the bikes they were riding. Their weighty machines would have had no gears despite all the climbing they had to do, with Elizabeth's lady's drop-frame weighing even more than Joseph's. She had to push her bike up the steeper climbs, making for very long days on the endlessly zigzagging roads into the clouds. It's no wonder some of the other cyclists hired carriages to get their bikes up the mountains.

The descents were no less problematic, with a deficient braking system in which a leather strap was used to pull a brake to the tire, instead of the wheel rim like many of today's bikes— which also relied heavily on backpedaling. Not to mention that Elizabeth did all this in her long skirts. She admits her temper did fray frequently due to the physical exertion, but nothing was going to deter her from achieving her goal. Snow and wind, icy precipices and hairpin bends—with wooden crosses marking the sites where previous travelers had perished—didn't put her off her pedal strokes, even if her heart was in her mouth on the downhills. All the time disproving, as women had been told for so long, that they were the "weaker sex." On St. Gotthard, a 6,909-foot peak they tackled in the worst weather, where Joseph admitted he was never so close to giving up, she refused a lift from a passing cart—"I was doing this thing myself; I had not come to have it done for me."

Despite not approving of bicycle racing, Elizabeth wasn't keen on any other cyclists passing her. She even took a certain pleasure in seeing a Swiss cyclist fall off after overtaking her on a descent. When he called out for help, she cycled straight past him. Similarly, after speaking at length with a Parisian who was part of the delegation responsible for gifting the Statue of Liberty to the United States on behalf of the French, they left him floundering in the mud after a fall without a backward glance.

Switzerland, thanks to steam trains and Thomas Cook's tours, was one of the most visited places in Europe at this time, with the moneyed middle class making a beeline to see the awe-inspiring alpine peaks that the likes of Jean-Jacques Rousseau and William Wordsworth had made so famous the previous century. Elizabeth describes these tourists as having turned it into the "playground of Europe," as they "swarmed" over its majestic mountains and formed a "constant procession" on horseback, in carriages, on foot and on bike.

Much to her annoyance, they were also constantly ambling in her way. The Pennells did their best to avoid fraternizing with the masses: Elizabeth stated she would rather have a modest meal with the monks on the Simplon Pass than "dine with the fifty or sixty tourists that you find any summer evening at the St. Bernard, all eating and drinking like pigs." In her opinion, the German tourists were a "public nuisance" when traveling. As for the Swiss, she doesn't have too many kind words to say about them either, describing the "petty persecutions" of their customs officials and generally feeling exploited by their rapacious tourism industry.

While she may be a bit of a snob, she's often witty and acerbic, such as her observation that the tour groups who had once "wept over the sublimities of nature which they could not see for their tears," now barely glance at the landscape and "let their feelings loose upon illustrated postcards" instead. I dread to think what she would have made of twenty-first-century selfie culture.

Perhaps, after this remarkable journey, Elizabeth felt she had nothing more to prove, as this was the last cycling travelogue she published. It may also have been deemed uncommercial by her publishers, since the craze for cycle touring began to subside in the early part of the twentieth century. I do know that they continued to enjoy cycling even if they weren't writing about it.

Off the Beaten Track

With the nineteenth-century tourism boom going largely to countries formerly on the grand tour itinerary, some intrepid travelers decided they wanted to go further afield—particularly the wealthy upper class, people who had the time and money to spend months and even sometimes years abroad. Some of these were wealthy society women—mostly from the U.K. and U.S.— making the most of the global transport revolution and greater social freedoms, traveling as far afield as Africa, Asia and the Middle East. In this age of exploration, women were going on adventures—sometimes solo—that were redefining what they could do. Many also wanted to contribute to our understanding of the world through their exploration, studying the archeology, the social customs or the flora and fauna of the places they visited, though some of them were more colonial in their approach than others.

Isabella Lucy Bird, the British naturalist, photographer and writer, was one such intrepid explorer. Despite frequent ill health, she traveled unchaperoned to the United States, Hawaii and Australia, before moving on to Asia, the Middle East and North Africa. She practiced medicine as a missionary, refused to ride sidesaddle and became the first woman member of the Royal Geographical Society in 1892. She was also very put out when *The Times* newspaper wrongly claimed she wore trousers during her 800-mile journey across Colorado's Rockies in 1873.

Mary Kingsley, the British explorer and ethnographer, traveled unaccompanied to Africa, living with locals to gain an insight into how to survive in the remote and wild places she would then explore. She collected rare wildlife specimens and wrote about the practices of the local tribes in the many books she published. Mary wasn't so keen to be labeled a "New Woman," however, deeming the question of women's suffrage of minor importance and making her way through the jungle in the traditional nineteenth-century English attire of long dress, hat and umbrella.

By contrast, Swiss traveler Isabelle Eberhardt adopted the clothing of a male Berber to move around more freely and avoid unwanted attention in 1890s Islamic Algeria.

Against this background of nineteenth-century female adventuring, Fanny Bullock Workman was someone who wanted to make important discoveries and contribute to the growing literature about less-traveled parts of the globe. Born into one of the richest families in Massachusetts in 1859, she was educated at an elite U.S. school before attending finishing schools in Europe. The stories she penned as a teen about girls running away to become mountaineers and explorers were a precursor to the life she would eventually lead. By her twenties, she was climbing the highest peaks of the northeastern U.S., where she benefited from the more progressive attitude of most American mountaineering clubs which, unlike the European ones, allowed women members. But this wasn't enough to keep her restless desire to explore at bay, and in 1889, she and her GP husband, William Hunter Workman, set off for Europe to tour Germany and Scandinavia, the first of a series of extensive journeys that would come to define their lives.

They had both received substantial family inheritances, which meant they had the luxury of being able to devote their entire lives to traveling the globe, becoming world-famous cyclists as well as mountaineers. Like those of Isabella Bird before her, Fanny's travels would result in her being welcomed into the sacred, hallowed and overwhelmingly male ranks of the Royal Geographical Society. Fanny wanted to make history as an adventurer equal to any man and to be acknowledged for her contributions to science through her travel writing. Playing the Victorian domestic goddess was not her idea of a fulfilling life and it certainly helped that they could pay others to look after their children, far from an option for all women at the time, even if they'd had similar ambitions.

In his dedication to Fanny in one of their bicycle travelogues, William praised her "courage, endurance and enthusiasm, often under circumstances of hardship and sometimes of danger" which "have never failed." Since she was the prime instigator, there is no question that she was his equal as an adventurer. Despite this, she never exchanged her long skirts in favor of something more suitable for the often very wild places they visited and the physically arduous journeys they undertook.

Fanny's cycle touring era began in Germany when they acquired two Rover Safety bicycles. They used them to explore the neighboring countries of France, Italy and Switzerland before moving farther off the beaten track. After their four-year-old son died of pneumonia, they left their daughter in the care of nursemaids and governesses and set off in 1895 on the first of their lengthy bicycle tours—a year they would spend almost entirely on the road, biking 2,800 miles across Spain, and 1,500 miles around Algeria. They would later publish accounts of these trips, largely written by Fanny.

Like Elizabeth Robins Pennell before her, Fanny was also achieving a first for her sex, as—reputedly—the first woman to cycle around Spain, and presumably Algeria as well. It was also allegedly the most extensive bike tour anyone had undertaken in either country. Fanny had already become the first woman to climb Mont Blanc by this point—competition wasn't something she ever shied away from.

On their tour around Spain, their "Don Quixotian days on the turnpike," they averaged around forty-five miles a day, sometimes racking up as many as eighty in order to find a bed for the night. The terrain was also mountainous, which they struggled over on heavy Safety bicycles weighed down with luggage. Despite the effort involved—and the almost daily punctures—they too felt the bicycle was the ideal mode of transport "enabling us an entire independence of the usual hindrances of the traveler, to pass through the country at leisure, stopping where and when we pleased." They weren't just trying to get from A to B, they wanted to experience the landscape and history, its people and culture, up close, even if at times they were rather judgmental and less open to the locals than they perhaps thought they were.

Spain enabled them to live up to their image of themselves as adventurers, since they perceived it to be "not so far advanced in civilization," a comment which speaks volumes about their Waspish American privilege and prevailing attitudes of the day. The tone of their accounts is quite different from the Pennells'— there are fewer capers and literary references and more detailed accounts of what they encountered, from archeological sites to the customs of the locals, evidence of Fanny wanting to be accepted into the ranks of serious travelers and geographers.

There was so much interest about their trip in Spain that the country's newspapers frequently reported on their progress. The couple, for reasons unclear, held their cards close to their chests in the interviews they gave, however, despite claiming to speak the language well. Consequently, journalists resorted to speculation. The Spanish were intrigued by this American couple on their bicycles, and the Workmans felt they were observed "with much the same awe-inspired expression as might have been called forth had we been inhabitants of one of the heavenly bodies," though it's possible they enjoyed this more than they were willing to let on.

While they did meet some Spaniards who cycled, the couple found the activity to be popular exclusively among "the better classes." Rich people like themselves, in other words, since it's likely they were the only ones who could afford to buy a bicycle. Members of cycling clubs would often meet them en route and escort them into their city. They would take them into their homes, refuse to let them pay for anything and ride with them for a time the following day. No wonder they were more willing to share details of their itinerary with these clubs than the press.

Not everyone was so pleased to see them. They complained of being chased out of villages by children who threw stones, and as their journey progressed, it was animals who caused more of a problem. It became increasingly apparent the further south they went that bicycles were not a common sight on the roads. While the locals may have been intrigued by the couple on their wheels, the animals were often terrified. Cart-pulling mules would go into meltdown at the sight of them, and on one occasion a mule bolted, throwing his passenger into the road who, in his anger, picked up his long-bladed farm tool and charged toward the Workmans. They quickly pulled out their revolvers, stopping him in his tracks so they could make their getaway.

During their travels through Valencia, they were threatened for causing a mule fracas on the road several times. At one point a disgruntled driver pulled a 12-inch knife on them and at that moment "there seemed to be no chance of escape. The stab of the gleaming blade could almost be felt." Fortunately the man's companion pulled him back just in time and they escaped. They were so shaken they considered giving up the journey entirely. This close shave, though, ended up being the last of its kind, which they put down to the people of Valencia being "the most ill-disposed and revengeful of any in Spain."

These weren't the last Spaniards they judged so harshly, however, with the cyclists accusing locals elsewhere of "backwardness," not least in Aragon where they describe how "the women stared like cattle" while "the men and boys could not keep their hands off our bicycles, ringing the bells, feeling the tires, and pressing the saddles as if these vehicles were on exhibition for their particular entertainment and instruction."

Not that they were too keen on the other foreign tourists either, particularly those in Granada's Alhambra, whom they describe as "philistines," people who they presumably thought were insufficiently cultured to appreciate this architectural wonder of Moorish Spain.

In Barcelona, Fanny found herself subjected to unwanted attention. Despite her modest long dress, she was hassled by men on the street, leading them to warn their readers that it is "not a pleasant place for a woman to visit with a bicycle." In Algeria, she thought it was the animals who took particular offense to a woman on a bike, believing it was she, not her husband, who caused horses and mules to take fright. Even the dogs—"gaunt, wolfish-looking beasts"—were more liable to chase her: "It may be that dogs, which seem to regard themselves as a sort of special police, consider women out of place on a wheel, and in need of correction."

As befitted a woman who would be photographed in 1912 in the Himalayas holding a copy of the WSPU's *Votes for Women* newspaper, the condition of women in the countries they cycled through attracted Fanny's attention. When French colonialists told them the Kabylie women in Northern Algeria were relatively free, Fanny was convinced they only had a superficial understanding of their lives. Instead, she told the reader that "one must look deeper than this and see how man regards woman, and how woman regards herself in Kabylie land." The conclusion she came to, which may not have been based on any deeper analysis, contradicted the French view, something she saw as represented most starkly by the law that permits men to murder their wives if it is deemed "necessary."

In addition, she reported that the Kabylie women were often denied education and routinely sold into marriage, and "a life of continued drudgery," starting from the age of twelve. This would have been unfathomable to the highly educated Fanny, who had the means to reject domesticity or manual labor in favor of a lifetime of adventuring and learning. She concluded that the women of Algeria look upon European women with a combination of "envy and hopelessness."

She might not have been qualified to cast judgment on the circumstances of these women's lives, but there is not a question that Fanny was committed to women's rights and education. So much so that she used that image of her with the suffragette newspaper on the cover of a book about her climbing feats. She also became the first woman to lecture at Paris's Sorbonne University and left money in her will to four U.S. women's colleges.

A few years after their tours of Algeria and Spain, the couple were off on an even more epic journey. Departing in November 1897, they spent the next two and a half years cycling 14,000 miles across Southeast Asia, through Myanmar, Sri Lanka, Java and India. On this expedition, they visited the region's famed, and at that time little explored, archeological sites and temples, traveling by steamships between countries and resorting to trains when roads became impassable.

The book they wrote about this trip focused exclusively on the Indian leg of the journey. Again, she contemplates the lives of women in the country, such as those in purdah confined to their women-only quarters whom Fanny spends time with in Hyderabad. These wives of local rulers had, in her eyes, little physical, economic or social freedom—something that was anathema to Fanny's western feminist ideology and as someone so defined by movement and independence. She viewed their condition as a product of the general inequality between men and women and hoped that "light may fall upon the souls of the men, that they may realize the great injustice practiced on the weaker sex, and that a day of awakening may come, when the latter may be free to develop as their nature demands."

For such a taxing journey, the Workmans remained largely

unfazed by any hardships they endured, like having to sleep on wooden benches in railway stations or on porches for want of any other bed for the night. The assistance of a servant, who traveled by train to meet them every few days, certainly helped lighten the load. This luxury allowed them to carry just the essentials, including a few days' worth of food in their tiffin tins which they ate each day beneath flocks of wild parakeets and under the watchful gaze of monkeys. On the days they met up with their servant, he was required to cook their meals and find accommodation, much like a valet. Even then, things didn't always go according to plan, with the couple sometimes arriving at their destination with no evidence of a meal or a bed, which led them to behave with their servant in a way that seems decidedly imperious and mistrustful, to say the least.

Despite the advantages afforded by their class and wealth, the trip itself was still an arduous one, with many long days in the saddle in hot and humid conditions, often with little food and water—not to mention a plague of punctures, sometimes as many as forty a day. On routes through remote regions off the railway network, where their servant wasn't able to meet them for many days, they had to carry everything they would need, as much as a hundred pounds of supplies between them strapped to their bikes. They were frequently warned by various officials to steer clear of certain places, such as an area afflicted by famine where they were told the starving people might be dangerous. But they took no heed. Similarly, they didn't worry about rumors of elephants on the road ahead, despite their previous history with bikes and animals. The rifles in their saddlebags remained unused.

The end of this journey in northern India was the start of a new phase in Fanny's career as an explorer. To escape the heat of summer, they left their bikes and headed up to the high passes of the Himalayas, an area they were so taken with that they returned eight times over the next fourteen years. Here Fanny revived her first love, mountaineering, making increasingly challenging and dangerous ascents and breaking several female altitude records. She wasn't only the first woman to climb many of these mountains; they were often the first westerners to make the attempt. They even named one of the mountains they conquered, a peak over 19,000 feet in the Karakoram, Mount Bullock Workman. Another they christened Siegfriedhorn after the son who had died, though the mountains have both long since been renamed.

Despite their remarkable records and their reputation as possibly the most accomplished mountaineers of their day, the couple were accused of treating the numerous local porters they relied on to carry the equipment needed for many months at high altitude with a lack of empathy or understanding. What Fanny achieved as a climber, though, was remarkable, a product of the same grit and determination that had powered her through her long cycle tours. Not least of her exploits was the expedition to the Rose and Siachen Glaciers in Karakoram, the most inaccessible and unexplored in the world at that time. Fanny was the one responsible for leading the two-month-long trek, which was spent entirely above 14,700 feet in altitude. The trip made them miss their daughter's wedding and resulted in the death of one of their guides who was killed by falling into a crevasse—an accident that Fanny only narrowly survived.

It was during this expedition that the photo of Fanny with her *Votes for Women* newspaper on the top of a 21,000-foot peak, wearing her favored outfit of hobnailed boots and long skirt, was taken by William. Her passionate support of women's rights didn't extend to her applauding the feats of other female mountaineers, though. When, in 1909, fellow American Annie Smith

Peck claimed to have climbed 23,000 feet in Peru, Fanny hired a team of French surveyors at a cost of $13,000 to confirm that the Peruvian peak wasn't as high as that. It took them four months to reach this conclusion, leaving Fanny's own altitude record of 22,736 feet untouched until 1934.

Competitiveness aside, she was undoubtedly one of the most intrepid and indefatigable explorers of her time, someone who trampled and cycled over all prevailing prejudices about what women were or were not capable of achieving.

CHAPTER EIGHT

GOING THE DISTANCE

The Great Outdoors

Marylou Jackson, Velma Jackson, Ethyl Miller, Leolya Nelson and Constance White were met by reporters when they wheeled into Washington, D.C., on Easter Sunday, 1928, dressed in bloomers and caps. The five African-American cyclists from New York City had spent the last three days pedaling from their home city to the capital, covering 250 miles via Philadelphia and Wilmington, Delaware. Each night of the trip they had stayed at a YWCA hostel before arriving in D.C., where they found time to fit in a bit of sightseeing despite having cycled a hundred miles that day.

Two of the women worked in sports—one was the physical education director of the Harlem YWCA—and it's likely that they were members of cycling clubs in the city. They told a reporter their "love of the great-out-of-doors" had motivated them to set out on this journey and they hoped other women would try to better their distance record. The following day, Easter

Monday, they boarded the train home to their lives and work in New York City. Constance White, filled with wanderlust, would soon leave Harlem for travels farther afield. First for Russia and then to journey through Europe, where she stayed for some time after falling in love with a woman there before they settled together in the United States.

I don't know how many other women back then followed their lead, but over eighty years later their ride continues to inspire people to get on their bikes: in 2013, a black cyclists' collective completed the women's route in reverse as part of their ambition to diversify the image of cyclists in the United States and encourage others to join them.

Despite popular accounts by the likes of Elizabeth Robins Pennell and Fanny Bullock Workman that were all about the excitement and adventure of a long-distance cycle trip, holding the bike up as the perfect form of transport to see the world, by the early twentieth century cycle touring had largely fallen out of fashion among the wealthy middle and upper classes, who had moved on to the car instead.* This trend was reflected by the cycling section of *The Outing Magazine*, which had once been full of accounts of incredible worldwide journeys on two wheels; by the turn of the new century, it had disappeared. It was replaced by a motoring section.

Constance and her friends proved that there were still people—including many women—who were continuing to clock up the miles under their own steam. They were part of a new generation eager to explore the world at a time when travel, tour-

---

* Cars were increasingly affordable by this point: in 1909, the average price of a Ford Model T was $850; by the early 1920s, it was $260.

ism and even leisure time were no longer the preserve of the rich and privileged. For them the bicycle was an enduring symbol of the romance of the open road, one of the best ways to truly travel. In fact, it became such a popular pastime again in Europe from the 1920s to the late 1950s that it is now seen as the golden age of bicycle touring.

This time it was a lot more egalitarian. In the 1890s, the average workweek in Europe had been over sixty hours; by 1910, in the U.K., it was around fifty-three hours; and by the 1930s, it had gone down to forty-three hours. Many of these workers were women; in the U.K., for instance, they made up a third of the workforce by the mid-1930s. While there was a stark gender pay gap and many lingering inequalities, they had the vote and more freedoms than previous generations, not least the benefit of more relaxed attitudes toward what they could wear, even if it took another world war for trousers to become fully accepted attire for women.

Most, even with their jobs, couldn't dream of affording a car at this time, especially with the global economic downturn of the late 1920s and '30s, with only one family in ten in the U.K. owning one in 1931. Many could stretch to a bicycle, though, and for some it was more than just a cheap way to get to work. Mrs. Cattaneo, who worked in a factory in York in the 1930s, described the weekend rides with her cycle club as the highlight of her life: "I had never known holidays or been anywhere until we got this bike and went all over . . . I didn't want money then 'cos I had this bike. We would pack up on a Sunday and we would call anywhere at these cafés, and they would give you as much tea as you wanted to drink for fourpence . . . I loved that cycle and I loved every Sunday."

There were countless others too, with increasing leisure time and a limited budget, who shared Constance's love of the out-doors. Jumping into the saddle for a few hours, days or longer offered an escape from the grind of work and daily life in the city. Some would cover astonishing—even record-breaking—distances on their machines, going far off the beaten track.

The renewed interest in touring the countryside on a bike in Europe, and to a lesser extent the United States, became part of a general outdoors movement in the interwar period. Youth hostels began opening, offering cheap accommodation in scenic locations for walkers and cyclists. With increasing numbers living in urban areas, not least having gone through a devastating war, more and more were craving just such an escape. The countryside became hip again for a time, just as it had when the Romantic poets were writing about it at the end of the eighteenth century and as it is again today, with the Instagram generation posing for selfies in scenic spots. Indeed, weekend touring became so popular in the U.K. that in 1937, a reader wrote to *Cycling* magazine to complain that it was *too* popular, with "hordes" of cyclists ruining every good view.

It helped that bikes were more affordable and that this new generation of long-distance cyclists could benefit from more lightweight machines designed specifically for comfortably covering many miles on what would have been—largely—greatly improved road surfaces. They also had a range of gears to tackle hills and even mountains, a welcome evolution after those heavy Safety bicycles on which the Pennells and Workmans had valiantly slogged through their epic journeys. Perversely, in the United States, bicycles were getting heavier and slower, with a trend for new cruiser styles that looked more like motorcycles, complete with balloon tires. Many models weighed over forty-five pounds, more than double the weight of European bikes, which might explain why cycle touring didn't take off again in the States to the same extent.

The membership of the U.K.'s Cyclists' Touring Club (CTC) began to swell once more, as did that of its European counterparts. CTC members even benefited from special trains for cyclists so they could enjoy a day of cycling in the countryside before returning home. People might have been inspired by artist Frank Patterson's line drawings of cycle tourers exploring an idealized English countryside that filled the pages of the U.K.'s cycling magazines at this time. Such scenes were a long way from modernity and war, and suggestive of more innocent times, something many people were understandably nostalgic for, even if those times had never existed.

As social codes became more relaxed, it became a lot less controversial than it had been in Victorian and Edwardian times for an unmarried couple to go out together unchaperoned, and young people made the most of it. Bike ads at the time reflected this, with a large number featuring white, heterosexual young couples having fun on their touring cycles. An ad for a Hercules bike in 1934 depicts a teenage couple in a passionate embrace above a picture of a bicycle, the accompanying text suggesting that a day out on a Hercules with your love interest, followed by "that glorious moonlight ride home," inevitably ends the same way: buy this bike and you will get the girl. Though laughably, "Joan" is still expected to pour the tea when they stop for lunch. In other ads, they cycle along lanes holding hands or sit on beaches looking at their maps with their bicycles beside them.

The 1949 British romantic comedy film *A Boy, a Girl and a Bike* features a Yorkshire cycling club whose members' social lives are centered around their weekly rides in the Yorkshire Dales and summer camps on the moors, starring the glamorous

Honor Blackman and a teenage Diana Dors, the U.K.'s Marilyn Monroe.*

Bicycles made for two were surging in popularity, with one magazine mentioning a tandem race from Birmingham to Gretna Green, the U.K.'s premiere elopement destination, to be the first to arrive and get married. The cycling press regularly included photographs from cycling-themed weddings, with guests holding bicycles aloft over the bride and groom as they exit the church, couples who had presumably met through their cycling club.

If the newly married cyclists went on to have children, it didn't necessarily mean an end to those carefree days in the saddle. Increasingly families were taking their kids along for the ride. Cycle-mad parents got inventive, with couples on tandems pulling trailers or sidecars loaded up with toddlers and babies too young to cycle, much like the cargo bikes used today to do the school run in cities like Amsterdam and Copenhagen, and increasingly in London. I've even seen a picture of a pram mounted to a bicycle (not a trend that stood the test of time it seems, and probably for a good reason). Those with older children could opt for a triplet bike so the family could ride on one machine. A quad tandem bike was possible for larger families and there is a British Pathé film from 1961, *Cycling Family*, which features the Fosters, a family of ten from Lincolnshire, who ride with one parent pulling a trailer filled with two of the youngest children and camping equipment. Their other children bring up the rear on tandems and ordinary bikes.

---

* It's telling how much the upper classes had fallen out of love with cycling by this point, that when a wealthy young man falls in love with Honor Blackman's character and joins the club, his family is horrified that he's taking up what they see as a working-class activity.

Keep Fit, Girls

In 1938, twenty-four-year-old Billie Fleming (née Dovey), a secretary and typist, was a keen cyclist who wanted to inspire more women to take it up, and in so doing became a household name for her long-distance achievements. Billie had been taught to ride by a boyfriend when she was eighteen and quickly became "besotted." So much so that she decided she would cycle around the U.K. every day for a year, so she didn't have to stop. She wrote to Rudge-Whitworth asking for sponsorship and they promptly agreed, appointing her their "Keep-Fit Girl" and giving her a bicycle and the necessary financial backing to stay on the road for 365 days straight. That year she racked up 29,603.4 miles on a bike with just three gears—more than the circumference of the Earth and a world record for women's long-distance cycling. This achievement Billie put down to being "young and fit and ready to take on anything." Amazingly, she only had one puncture.

Her routine was to ride every day of the year, regardless of weather. Her evenings were spent giving talks to promote the health benefits of cycling. She carried only a change of clothes and some tools in a small saddlebag. Cadbury sent her chocolate every month and in return she appeared in some ads. Her distances were confirmed through a system of checking cards signed by witnesses which were then verified by *Cycling* magazine. What they show is that she averaged eighty-one miles a day and the farthest she cycled in one day was 186 miles, when she decided she wanted to spend the night in her own bed. The magazine regularly checked her cyclometer to ensure nothing was amiss.

Billie lived to a hundred, so she was clearly right about the health benefits. She has remained an inspiration, with many attempting to beat her record. In 1942, Australia's Pat Hawkins claimed to have cycled over 54,000 miles. The cycling authorities threw the claim out when they scrutinized her records and found they didn't add up. Remarkably, it took until 2016 for Billie's record to be beaten, when Swedish-born Kajsa Tylen took on the challenge and clocked up 32,326 miles between New Year's Day and the following New Year's Eve.

Had World War II not broken out, Billie would have cycled across the United States as her next challenge. She may have seen more women on bikes there than a decade before, even if they weren't quite matching her miles. The Great Depression had boosted bicycle sales as many opted to bike to work—or to look for a job—during this time of extreme austerity, and soon the industry decided it would specifically target women by encouraging them to take up cycling for fitness.

Hollywood lent a hand when, in 1934, the actor Joan Crawford was snapped for the cover of a magazine in trousers and a sweater, riding a man's bicycle on rollers—the indoor trainer of the 1930s. She told the magazine that she and her then husband, Douglas Fairbanks Jr., had started cycling to keep in shape. Twelve years later, she was photographed with a U.S.-made Schwinn bike, again eulogizing about the health benefits of the activity: "I recommend bicycling on a Schwinn to anyone who seeks exercise for good health, a good figure, and good fun."

Other actresses were photographed throughout the 1930s and '40s on bikes, including Katharine Hepburn. She had been riding a bicycle since she was three and a half, so didn't need a sponsorship deal to encourage her to ride around the Warner Bros. lot or when taking a break from filming on location, something she would continue to do for decades. With this stamp of Hollywood approval, women were soon keen to be seen on two wheels, and as a result they went from 10 percent to 33 percent of the market in the 1930s. Department stores began stocking the latest cycling fashions which were sported by these new cyclists in cities across the United States. At coastal resorts they could hire bikes to ride up and down the boardwalks, à la Joan in Venice Beach, Los Angeles. As a trend it was short-lived, and it wasn't long before most bikes manufactured in the country were made for children.

Cycling remained popular during the war, often out of necessity since gasoline was so scarce. Postwar austerity made cycle touring popular in Europe again as people looked for an economical break. However, its days as a mass activity were numbered, since by the mid-1950s there were three times more cars on the road in Europe than there had been the previous decade. In 1960 in the United States, there was one car for every three people; by 1970, it was one for every two.

Cycle touring and cycling in general—apart from racing—was falling out of favor, something reflected in the CTC's membership figures, which halved between 1939 and 1969. Soon it largely became seen as something you did because you couldn't afford a car, a stigma that would stick for decades except in countries like the Netherlands and Denmark, where cycling remains an essential component of daily life, as a result of an infrastructure that makes it as easy as walking. Elsewhere, those who continued to ride had to battle a lot more traffic than they had a decade before, something not everyone was willing to face.

While most western countries fell out of love with cycling, by the 1960s a cycling boom was happening in other parts of the world, most significantly in Asia. There were so many bikes on the streets in China it became known as the "Bicycle Kingdom." Between 1948 and 1958, the number of bikes in the country doubled to one million. By the 1990s, it peaked at around 670 million before nose-diving as cars became more affordable for its population, a boom-and-bust that the West had already experienced.

Dunkirk to Delhi

In 1963, just as cycle touring was falling out of fashion, a thirty-one-year-old woman from rural Ireland set out to cycle alone from Dunkirk to Delhi, a six-month journey of around three thousand miles through Europe, Iran, Afghanistan, Pakistan and India. Dervla Murphy decided on this specific destination, and the general route she would follow, shortly after being gifted an atlas and a secondhand bicycle for her tenth birthday. She had homed in on India after a pen pal in the Punjab had awakened her interest in this "wondrous land."

What particularly appealed to Dervla was the idea of traveling independently—fitting for someone who was already climbing mountains, swimming in the nearby Blackwater river, and cycling increasingly long distances in her home county of Waterford, all unaccompanied. She would go on to spend her life exploring the world on foot and cycle, mostly solo. As she looked down at her feet powering the pedals of her new bike, the thought came to her that "If I went on doing this for long enough, I could get to India," a plan which she had to put on hold for over two decades, but she never lost sight of it. Just as some people see their future marked out by events such as going to university or getting married and having kids, for Dervla biking to India was part of her life plan, even if at times it felt increasingly elusive.

Four years after making her decision, Dervla had to leave

school to look after her mother, who had become all but paralyzed by rheumatoid arthritis. The former child adventurer would be her main caregiver for over eighteen years, trapped in what she describes in her memoirs as a "domestic cage." For much of that time she was unable to leave the house since her mother couldn't be left alone for any length of time. For someone who had thrived on immersing herself in the outdoors, roaming wherever she fancied, it's understandable that this drastic change in her routine, and the overwhelming weight of her new responsibilities, made her feel "completely trapped and miserable," and that she "just wanted to be free."

As her mother's health continued to deteriorate, those precious moments of liberty were gradually "whittled away," leaving her longing for the kind of freedoms taken for granted by her peers. This situation became even more of a struggle when her father died suddenly, leaving her as the sole caregiver. She survived with the support of friends and by escaping on her bike whenever she got the chance.

When she had the occasional break she was encouraged to travel, particularly by her mother, who had also traveled alone before her marriage and now recognized her daughter needed to experience the same sense of freedom and opportunity. Dervla's cycle tours became lifelines during these years of diminishing personal freedom. The first trip was three weeks in the summer of 1951, which she spent cycling around Wales and the south of England, staying in youth hostels. This was a seminal trip for someone who had spent most of her life within a thirty-mile radius of her hometown of Lismore.

Some of the neighbors back home were "aghast" that she was making such a trip on her own. For many in rural Ireland in the 1950s, this just wasn't something girls did. When daughters in what was then a predominantly conservative Catholic country were largely expected to be self-sacrificing, it's perhaps unsurprising that the idea of a young woman going on a solo cycling holiday was viewed by some as more shocking than giving up an education to care for her mother. Among many things, the trip proved she could pedal a hundred miles a day without undue effort, further evidence that her longed-for 3,000-mile journey was in reach.

The following year she escaped for five weeks to cycle through Belgium, Germany and France, another restorative trip, though on the way home she narrowly escaped being kidnapped by a couple in Paris who she believed were planning to force her into sex work. Undeterred, two years later she set off for Spain on a trip that was further off the beaten track than any she had done before. She managed 120 miles a day on a heavy bike loaded with large panniers over mountainous terrain. The following year she returned, having fallen in love with Spain. On her way home she crossed the Pyrenees loaded with twelve large bottles of brandy rolled up in her sleeping bags as a souvenir—a weight that eventually buckled a wheel beyond repair, but a useful lesson in packing economically.

Dervla's trips served to further fan the flames of her desire to get to India. And lacking that one essential component—the freedom to do so—was to torment her for the remaining years as her mother's caregiver. During this time she would spiral into periods of depression, when some days even being outdoors in daylight was an impossibility, and instead she was confined to the "suffocating monotony" of her routine, particularly when her mother's health disintegrated to the point that Dervla had to sleep in her room so as to be on hand at all times. When her mother died in 1962, thirty-year-old Dervla mourned her loss but was also understandably "exalted by the realization of freedom." She describes currents of liberty running through her like "mild electric shocks." If her confinement had continued, she felt it would eventually have destroyed her.

Finally, in January 1963, one of the coldest winters in living memory, Dervla set off east on her bicycle, on an icy road out of Dunkirk—at last realizing the plan she had made as a ten-year-old on a hilltop in Lismore. Her bicycle was a men's Armstrong Cadet she had bought a few years before and named Roz, after Don Quixote's long-suffering horse, Rocinante. *Rocin* means workhorse—apt for a bike that would diligently carry its rider through many miles and adventures. Roz would take such a hammering over numerous bad or nonexistent roads that at times he had to be held together with wire and string. Weighing a not insignificant thirty-five pounds, Roz was loaded down with another twenty-six pounds in luggage. Dervla would feel every ounce during the times she had no choice but to carry it—sometimes for miles—over difficult terrain.

Before she left, she spent a month studying road maps to plan the best route to Delhi and mailing spare tires to consulates in cities she would pass through—three thousand miles would wear through a lot of rubber. She also had Roz's gears removed, since she thought they wouldn't survive the bad roads through Asia, rendering it a single speed, despite the fact she would be going over a lot of mountains. She also practiced firing the .25-caliber pistol that she had decided to carry with her and which, not long after setting out, she would be extremely grateful to have packed.

After waiting twenty-one years to start her journey, she was forced to delay setting off for yet another week because Europe was going through its coldest winter in eighty years. When the thaw didn't come, she continued with her plans regardless. This was something she came close to regretting over the next few weeks of arctic temperatures through France, Italy and what was then Yugoslavia. She endured frostbitten hands and feet as she cycled through blizzards and floods, as well as gales that knocked her off Roz, while trying to follow roads hidden below drifts of snow and black ice. Her delight about finally being on her way to India was severely impeded by conditions that were so challenging that it was more about survival than the carefree days she'd hoped for, pedaling east as far as her legs would take her. But no matter how close to unendurable it felt at times, this would be a story worth telling when she was finally through it.

Even Dervla had to admit she wasn't invincible at this point, despite her winter armor of ski cap, balaclava and fur-lined mittens. She eventually resorted to taking a train over the Alps into Italy, since they were completely impassable by bike, as well as having to "ignominiously" accept lifts on the snowbound mountain roads through large swaths of Eastern Europe, where it was too icy to cycle without risk of skidding straight off the edge. This was all incredibly frustrating for someone more than capable of making her way independently in ordinary circumstances, and who now, for very different reasons than before, did not have the freedom to do so.

Not that being in a motor vehicle in this environment was any guarantee of safety either. One truck she traveled in through Serbia (then Yugoslavia) slipped right off the road and hit a tree. Though she suffered a minor head injury in the collision, Dervla left the driver to go in search of help from the nearest village. On the way there she was jumped on by what she believed to be three emaciated wolves, with one taking purchase on the shoulder of her jacket, another her trouser leg and the third preparing to pounce. Her time spent practicing whipping her .25 from her pocket and taking aim paid off, as she swiftly shot the two that were on her while the other scarpered. All the while she was wondering if she was dreaming, which could have been very possible with the head injury she'd sustained. The police later told her that the "wolves" may well have been wild dogs. Regardless, this terrifying incident in a remote snowy forest, like something out of a Grimm's fairy tale, was certainly a story worth repeating, the first of many that would make it into *Full Tilt*, her account of this remarkable ride, where it was always about the journey rather than the end point.

It's All about the Journey

I was reminded of those wolves when in late December 2018 I spent a few days cycling from the ferry in Rosslare through southeast Ireland to visit Dervla, then eighty-seven, at her home in Lismore. Not that there are any wolves in Ireland, but there are lots of dogs, particularly little yapping ones that love to chase cyclists passing through their territory. A nuisance, but there was no danger of being mauled to death. More of a problem was my lack of preparation for what I had seen as a few days of relatively easy cycling of around 180 miles there and back.

Unlike Dervla, I had not paid due diligence to the journey ahead. Instead I had opted to take a bike I'd never done any touring on before, on the basis that its mudguards and more robust tires would be better suited to Irish rural roads in winter. The first rule of cycling anywhere of any distance, though, is to make sure your mount is in good working order. Mine had done hundreds of wet miles around London since it was last serviced and was in dire need of some TLC. It's a good thing I wasn't cycling to India, because when I tried to attach my bag rack after wheeling off the ferry, it wouldn't fit on the saddle unless I moved it into a position which wasn't comfortable to ride on.

Twenty-five miles into the journey, after a second puncture, I realized that the tires were going to be my downfall. They were more worn than I realized, and little tears were likely harboring small bits of stone or glass that were piercing each fresh inner tube. A plague of punctures on the first day made me lose so much precious midwinter daylight that I had to complete the last twenty-five miles of my ride, thankfully along the car-free Waterford Greenway, entirely in the dark. What should have been a speedy, stress-free section was made painfully slow by not having lights designed for dark country roads, so I couldn't see more than a few feet in front of me. Needless to say, this is not cycle-touring best practice. Though at least it didn't rain, which is unusual for Ireland in December. On the return journey I took a detour to a bike shop for a replacement tire and had a blissfully puncture-free final leg.

The experience reminded me of Lillias Campbell Davidson's advice from 1896 that women should make sure they can mend a puncture before they head out on a tour. This was knowledge that she thought was worth risking breaking a nail to acquire, even if she thought it generally "a hideous bit of business" and couldn't imagine why anyone would do it if a willing man was available. Something Dervla, despite her thousands of miles or perhaps because of them, agrees with. She joked with me that "that's what men are for."

In the most remote places on that first long journey, and the ones that followed, someone would usually come past to whom she could hand over the inner tube. On my journey to Lismore I let an eager local man who was walking his dog help fix one of my punctures; by that point I was thoroughly bored of doing it myself. In extremis though, such as the middle of the desert in Afghanistan, Dervla was able to get back on the road herself; she just chose not to if she didn't absolutely have to. A surprising insight into someone whose life has largely been defined by independence and self-sufficiency.

Involving someone in fixing a puncture is of course a good way to engage with people as you pass through their country. My puncture-mender was keen to chat, telling me about local landmarks and his own cycling. As I sat with Dervla in her study—one of a series of ancient stone buildings that had been part of the old market in Lismore—warmed by the wood burner, and with her dogs snoring at our feet, she tells me that her way of traveling was entirely dependent on the locals since she was so far from the tourist trail. They would often invite her into their homes, give her a bed for the night, feed her and recommend places to visit or what to avoid, which was particularly welcome so far off the beaten track.

This was what Dervla wanted to experience: getting to know a country through its people, something that's possible when traveling by bike and not so easy when speeding through in a car, train or coach. The writer and activist Rebecca Solnit has described how modern life is increasingly a "series of interiors," which has made us disconnected from the world around us and other people. She is passionate about walking, which, like cycling, is about being in a public space, where the "random, the unscreened, allows you to find what you don't know you are looking for, and you don't know a place until it surprises you." In her view, our reliance on technology is making us miss out, and she describes how walking can be a way of being, rather than just a way to get from A to B. For Dervla too, travel—on bike or foot—is all about the journey, which in her way is full of the unplanned and unexpected, free from schedules and time constraints.

With Roz she could cover good distances—she was doing around eighty miles a day on the India trip—but she was also immersed in the fabric of the countries she passed through, soaking up the environment around her and interacting with the people she encountered. Equally important for Dervla was that the journey was on her terms: as a solo traveler she could stop or detour whenever or wherever she liked. Independence as well as openness to new experiences and cultures is core to Dervla's nature. When someone once asked her if she'd been to Central America, she told them she hadn't. She'd forgotten that she had been through on the way back from Peru, but as she hadn't been on bike or on foot, she didn't count it as travel and it may as well have not happened.

The cycle tourer and writer Anne Mustoe came to the same conclusion in 1983 when traveling by bus across India. She had looked out of the window and seen a man cycling across the Thar Desert and was "seized with sudden envy . . . I wanted to be out there myself on that road on a bicycle, alone and free, feeling the reality of India, not gazing at it through a pane of glass." Two years later, the fifty-four-year-old headmistress was still so certain that this was the best way to travel, one that would allow her time to think, observe and travel at her own pace, that she set off to cycle around the world from west to east. As with Dervla, Anne felt the richest experiences often came through her interactions with strangers and she felt that the bicycle has a "classlessness" which allowed her to meet anyone on "a level of mutual trust." After that first journey of twelve thousand miles in fifteen months, Anne was such a convert to cycle touring that she devoted the rest of her life to exploring the world on two wheels, including another round-the-world trip, this time from east to west. She died aged seventy-six after falling ill in Syria in 2009, her final bicycle trip.

For Dervla, a journey is something that doesn't just happen to you—it is active, not passive. This idea of travel aligns more closely to its etymological origin from the Middle Ages of *travailen*, which stems from *travail*, meaning to work, toil or suffer, from a time when traveling was always an arduous undertaking. Though in Dervla's case it's less about suffering and more about effort, and the enrichment that comes with it. At times she pushed herself to the limits of her physical endurance, though even then she derived a sense of elation from the experience. Fleas, bedbugs, sand flies, mosquitoes, stings from scorpions and hornets, dehydration, sunstroke, dysentery and broken ribs were minor inconveniences in comparison. She once tried to convey this to an American engineer when she was pedaling Roz toward Afghanistan along a desert road in Iran. He had stopped his jeep to ask, "What the hell are you doing on this goddammed road?" and insist she sling her bike in the back so she could be driven over the border. She refused, explaining that cycling was her preferred way to travel, that Roz, the sky and earth were enough for total happiness. He eventually drove off calling her a "nutcase."

Nevertheless, a woman cycling alone through countries like Iran, Afghanistan, Pakistan and India was not a common occurrence in the early 1960s. This was several years before it became part of the hippy trail, and even then, I don't think many—if any—were doing it on a bike. In many less accessible places, such as the high mountain passes of Kashmir, the same mountains where earlier that century Fanny Bullock Workman had carried out her pioneering mountaineering expeditions, Dervla was possibly the first woman to have cycled through. Some of the more remote communities had never seen a bicycle, let alone a woman riding one, and she was repeatedly called upon to give demonstrations and let locals have a go.

So unusual was the idea of a lone woman making this kind of journey that the Afghan embassy in Iran refused to grant her the visa she needed to travel, on the grounds they deemed it unsafe. Instead they offered her free transport to Kabul, assuming she was cycling because she couldn't afford to travel any other way. They had in fact banned all solo women travelers after a Swedish woman on a motorcycle had been murdered. Dervla was undeterred, telling them that women get murdered in Europe too. She eventually persuaded a senior official at the U.S. embassy to ask them to grant her a visa on the grounds she was entering the country at her own risk.

When she finally entered Afghanistan, it was the country she would fall in love with more than any other on her trip, a country that was, sadly, already in a tug-of-war between Russia and the United States, causing her to change her route to avoid conflict zones, and where she was constantly told about foreigners who had been murdered. She found the people were welcoming and kind. Though they had very little, they went out of their way to share what they did have with her. Not even the broken ribs she acquired after being accidentally hit by a rifle butt belonging to a fellow bus passenger, after a bad road destroyed Roz's tires and forced her to take public transport, dented her enthusiasm for the country.

Women solo travelers today are constantly asked if they are afraid and told what they are doing isn't safe, the suggestion being that they are more vulnerable and thus reckless, alone and lonely. Men, on the other hand, are adventurous. The endurance athlete and adventurer Jenny Tough has spent a lot of time cycling and running alone in remote and inaccessible places and has been repeatedly asked if she's fearful for her safety. Running over four hundred miles across the Bolivian Andes, she was told by people in villages that what she was doing was dangerous, that she could be killed. The more people told her to be afraid, she felt, "the more that doubt creeps in," but each day she got up and kept going, proving that fear isn't a useful response.

When she ran across the Atlas Mountains in Morocco, she was followed almost daily by police who kept telling her it wasn't safe. Just as the Afghan embassy had tried to prevent Dervla from entering the country on the grounds of the perceived risk to her personal safety, the police tried to dissuade Jenny from following her route, offering her lifts and insisting she stay each night in villages to keep her "safe." In the land of the Berbers, the self-described "free people," she says she never felt less free. She was physically and mentally stressed by the constant watchful gaze she was under.

When I type "women solo travel" into Google, "Is solo female travel safe?" is one of the first things that comes up under the "People also ask" section. Yet the idea of men going it alone in the wilderness has always been accepted and celebrated as a masculine rite of passage, the rugged frozen-beard archetypes who resort to eating their dogs as they cross Antarctica or the intrepid adventurers getting lost in the Amazon and living with an undiscovered tribe. Their stories are embedded in our history, with accounts by women who've done similar journeys often forgotten and overlooked. The writer Kate Harris, who has cycled the length of the Silk Road, observed that women explorers are too often bracketed as making such journeys as a way to "find themselves," in response to an emotional crisis of some kind. Such an outlook restricts female adventuring to an *Eat*

Pray Love self-discovery narrative, and a way of feminizing their experience. They aren't seen as exploring for the sake of adventure, but rather fleeing from something.

It's also true that while men are free to be rugged, fearless and independent explorers, women who want to do the same regularly complain that they are subjected to interrogations about their plans, a list of risks they could encounter and moral judgments if they have children. Dervla has no time for that, telling me that it's "ridiculous" that people see that first journey as a great achievement, that "there's just nothing to getting on a bicycle and going to India." That's not to say that she didn't find herself in difficult or threatening situations. (Somewhat ironically, on the India trip, some of the only instances of threats specific to being a woman traveling alone happened before she even got to Afghanistan, the one country they tried to stop her entering because of the potential risks.) The first was in Turkey, on the border with Iran, when she woke in the middle of the night in the flea-filled bed of her lodgings to find her covers removed and a six-foot Kurdish man standing over her. Once again, her lightning-fast reflexes were tested as she grabbed her gun from under her pillow and fired into the ceiling, causing the man to flee. No one came to find out why a gun had been fired in the middle of the night.

In Azerbaijan, on the border with Iran, she was to have an even closer shave and considered it then the only place she wouldn't return to on her own. First, bandits armed with shovels had tried to steal Roz, but a few rounds from her gun fired into the air soon sent them running. The second was a policeman who locked her inside a compound with him while he attempted to sexually assault her. In her book she says the tactics she used to temporarily paralyze him with pain, so she could grab the keys from his discarded trousers and escape, were "unprintable."

Despite these instances, Dervla balks at the idea of being called courageous for choosing to travel alone, arguing that it's self-preservation rather than courage that gets her through any difficult situations. It also helps that she is not a pessimist, refusing to believe in disaster until it's happening.

She has never believed anything is out of bounds to her as a female traveler, taking inspiration from those too-often forgotten Victorian women pioneers of exploration. She tells me she feels closest to Isabella Bird Bishop, who she thought traveled for the "hell of it, to enjoy traveling." Though when Dervla traveled through the Middle East and India, as Isabella had done nearly a hundred years before, many people in the region still found the concept of a lone woman traveler an alien one—as some do today. So much so that in Iran, for instance, Dervla found that people generally just assumed she was a man and so she would be given a bed in men's dormitories. Her short haircut, utilitarian boots and shirt donated by the U.S. Army may have helped with that misconception. She found this ambiguity liberating, being seen as "merely a human being" by the people she passed on Roz freed her from the judgments that come with the identification of gender, nationality and class. The Belgian-French explorer Alexandra David-Néel similarly found freedom in her disguise as a beggar and Buddhist monk when in the winter of 1924 she made her extraordinary journey, crossing the Himalayas to enter the forbidden Tibetan city of Lhasa, something that would have been impossible had her identity been revealed.

For Dervla, an androgynous appearance came in handy in areas of the country where anti-women's-emancipation riots were taking place and women had been murdered after the religious leaders rejected the then Shah's plans to modernize Iran. In a country where women were, and largely still are, less free, being mistaken for a man could sometimes be an asset.

Even when she was recognized as a woman, as a foreigner she was mostly exempt from the restrictions, particularly on movement, placed on women in some of the more conservative areas she traveled through. Her position as an outsider was unique in that she could talk to men and women, including those who were obliged to observe strict purdah customs and remain indoors. When U.S. writer and activist Shannon Galpin biked in Afghanistan over forty years later, she described how being a foreign woman meant she was seen as more akin to a "hybrid gender" or "an honorary man." Though there were occasions where Afghan men tried to flirt with her—or in one instance grope her, assuming that as a western woman she must be promiscuous—most of the time it meant she could talk to men more or less as their equal, as well as the women, giving her a deeper insight into the country.

Back in the early 1960s, many people Dervla met during her travels as well as back home in Ireland may have wondered why a woman in her early thirties wasn't at home, married with children, the specter of the spinster looming large. Since she was in her teens, she had known that she didn't want that kind of life, describing it as the "antithesis of my ideal unplanned existence."

When she did get pregnant in her late thirties, she traveled through Turkey up until the end of her second trimester and raised her daughter alone, which is unsurprising for someone who describes herself as "solitary" by nature. She didn't care what people thought and tells me that motherhood didn't change her; she still wanted to spend her life traveling and writing. When her daughter, Rachel, was old enough, they traveled together: around southern India when Rachel was five; walking 1,600 miles across the high Peruvian Andes when she was nine; then around Madagascar when she was fourteen, something that sent minor ripples of shock around her hometown.

Once Rachel was an adult, Dervla packed up her panniers again for more long solo journeys, including a 3,000-mile ride from Kenya to Zimbabwe on a mountain bike. Yet despite being a woman in her sixties by that point, her plans were still a source of concern. A worried-looking airport official in Nairobi questioned her about her bicycle, telling her that "old people" should be traveling in vehicles. In this instance, Dervla was happy to put his misplaced concern down to the African custom of cherishing the elders in society.

While osteoarthritis has sadly now put an end to Dervla's years in the saddle, she tells me that she still receives letters from women—and men—telling her that *Full Tilt* has inspired them to go on their own long cycle trip. Technology has changed the way we make such journeys today. While Dervla was relaxed—happy even—when there was no way to get in touch with people back home when she was away, it is rare for travelers these days to go for longer than a few hours without being able to connect with friends and family. In fact, it's expected. And instead of the series of paper maps that Dervla planned her routes with, most of us would be lost without our GPS. She also thinks that her style of travel, which relied so much on strangers welcoming her into their homes, is less possible now, though there are people who do still travel in a similar way, with apps like Couchsurfing connecting travelers with hosts around the world who are willing to put them up for the night for free. Technology makes it easy, if a lot less spontaneous, to facilitate meaningful interactions between relative strangers.

Travel—particularly on a bike or on foot—is still full of unexpected and meaningful encounters; my relatively short journey to Lismore provided me with some memorable ones. Before I headed back onto the road toward the ferry, Dervla invited me to lunch with Rachel and her granddaughter. While she prepared the soup, she recommended I bike up the hill outside the town to take in the view. It is indeed a good vantage point to look out over the green rolling hills of Waterford and the Blackwater river. Sadly, I forgot to ask if it was the same hill where she had made that decision to cycle to India all those years ago.

CHAPTER NINE

AROUND THE WORLD

A Race against the Clock

Crowds lined the streets of Naples as a motorcade drove through the city toward Piazza del Plebiscito on December 22, 2012. People weren't gathered to see the men on their Harleys; they were here to see the woman on her bicycle following behind—the exhausted but elated cyclist who was about to cross the finish line to become the first woman to hold a Guinness World Record for circumnavigating the globe on a bicycle. A journey which, unlike Dervla Murphy's, is very much about getting to that end point, and within a punishing time frame. The world's press was there to capture the historic moment.

When the cyclist Juliana Buhring had left her home city on her record-breaking journey 152 days before, few had taken her attempt seriously. Her trainer had told her she needed at least another year of putting the miles in before undertaking such an audacious endeavor. No sponsors had been willing to fund the attempt, even though men had been breaking the record for decades. They may or may not have had reservations about a woman being able to do such a thing, but it's likely they had doubts that this particular thirty-one-year-old, who had only started cycling eight months before, could pull it off. Apart from the support of friends, Juliana was on her own when she cycled out of Naples, heading west first to Lisbon and then on to America, for over five months of life on the road.

Juliana may be the first female record holder for cycling around the world, but she wasn't the first to attempt to do so. Almost exactly 118 years before Juliana pedaled out of the Piazza del Plebiscito, a twenty-four-year-old woman was being waved off by a crowd in Boston, which included suffragists and Woman's Christian Temperance Union members, as she pedaled off in June 1894 toward New York on the first leg of her journey. Like Juliana, she wasn't an obvious contender for such a feat; Annie Kopchovsky, a Latvian-Jewish immigrant, had never even been on a bicycle until a few days before she set out.

Until then, Annie had worked for local newspapers selling advertising space while living in a tenement in Boston with her husband, Max, and their three children, all under five. Despite appearing a world away from the idea of a record-breaking cyclist, Annie told the press that she had been chosen by two wealthy Bostonian merchants who had made a wager about whether a woman could get around the world by bike within fifteen months. At the time, the record of 13,500 miles in thirty-two months was held by an Englishman, Thomas Stevens, who had done the journey the previous decade on a penny-farthing. If she succeeded, they would reward her with ten thousand dollars—a huge amount of money at a time when the average annual income was around a thousand dollars.

The Victorian era was one of invention, exploration and adventure. It was also one of competition, with people attempting to be the first or fastest to do a dizzying range of feats, such as scaling uncharted peaks and making the highest balloon flight. The idea of going around the world against the clock was particularly popular, in part because of the commercial success of Jules Verne's fictional creation Phileas Fogg. Most famously, Elizabeth Cochran, a fearless investigative journalist for the New York *World* writing under the pseudonym Nellie Bly, made it around the world in 1889 in a record-breaking seventy-two days using an array of transport from steam trains, ships, horses and rickshaws. Readers back home eagerly awaited the articles published daily about her progress. This was a symbolic moment at a point in history where mass travel was making the world smaller and more accessible than many had ever thought possible.

Annie was the first woman to attempt such a thing on a bicycle, at a time when the idea of women just cycling around the local park wasn't universally accepted. She wasn't the only one undertaking a solo global bicycle race at that time, though. U.S. adventurer Frank Lenz, the son of German immigrants, had already been on the road for two years by the time Annie pedaled out of Boston. Frank had been writing regular reports on his journey, which were published in *Outing* magazine. The month before Annie set off, he had made it to Tabriz in Iran. This was the last anyone ever heard from him; later it was confirmed that he had been killed by Kurdish bandits in Turkey after apparently insulting one of their chiefs.

According to Annie, she had fifteen months to get back to Boston to collect her prize. She also claimed that the wager required her to make five thousand dollars during her journey and not accept a single cent without having earned it—something she started working on before she even got on her bike. Knowing the power, and value, of advertising, she set about selling ad space on her bicycle and herself, in much the same way she had for her newspaper pages. The first deal was with Londonderry Lithia Spring Water; Annie agreed to hang a signboard for their product on her bike and to rename herself "Annie Londonderry." It seems that even Annie's personal identity had a price, and, in this instance, it was a hundred dollars. Along the way, she would make many similar deals, her bike weighed down with streamers and boards advertising a range of products and services. Annie became a global sensation, attracting attention in every country she passed through, and she worked hard to keep herself in the papers. She understood publicity and how to get it, even if it meant a little, and sometimes a lot, of exaggeration or invention.

Annie displayed remarkable common sense, guts and an innate flair for self-promotion, but even then it still seems quite a leap to go from a Boston tenement, caring for her children and struggling to make ends meet, to leaving home for over a year to become a worldwide phenomenon as the first round-the-world female cyclist—a scenario that sounds like a Jules Verne creation. Which makes it even harder to understand how it was all but forgotten until her great-grandnephew, Peter Zheutlin, decided to research her story and write her biography. Until the late 1990s, neither he nor most of his family members had even heard of her. It was only when a researcher who had stumbled across an archived newspaper story about Annie's journey contacted him for more information that Peter jumped on the trail to unearth her extraordinary story. What he discovered was a journey that was "audacious and unprecedented," a "tour de force of moxie, self-promotion *and* athleticism."

While he describes Annie as "the embodiment of the New

Woman" for disregarding society's expectations, one of the wild
woman pioneers who displayed chutzpah and determination to
succeed, he believes there were a fair few inconsistencies in her
account. The first was the wager itself, which he thinks never
existed—possibly explaining the riddle of how the two men
could have landed on Annie as their woman: the men didn't exist
and the whole race was Annie's own bombastic and incredible
invention. The fact she gives inconsistent accounts of the rules of
their bet in many of her interviews seems to back this up, though
in my view it serves to make the whole endeavor even more brilliant: two men didn't make her a star; instead she invented them
as part of her strategy to capture the world's attention. And it
worked.

In the absence of a real wager, Annie could afford to be a bit
flexible when it came to the rules of her fifteen-month mission,
the time limit seemed to be the only nonnegotiable condition—a
stark contrast to the terms laid down by Guinness World Records. When Juliana Buhring wrote to the organization in 2012
to inform them of her intention to attempt to become the first
woman to hold the record, they responded with the long list of
rules she needed to comply with. The first was that she had to
travel more than 24,900 miles (over the length of the equator),
18,000 of which must be completed on the bike; that the route
must be continuous in either an east-to-west or west-to-east direction, passing two antipodal points, and a GPS spot tracker
must be attached to the bike so her progress could be followed at
all times. In addition, Juliana, like Billie Fleming in her record
attempt in 1938 for most miles in one year, had to get signatures
from people along the way as further proof.

A few weeks before Juliana started, Guinness informed her
they had changed the rules and the clock would no longer stop
when she was traveling off the bike. Now when she took a flight,

that time would be included in her final total, which meant she would need to get through airports and set off again in the shortest time possible. They had also decided to set a time limit of 150 days for both men *and* women, an oddly punishing decision when no man had yet made that time, despite multiple record attempts. This time frame would require her to cycle around 125 miles a day—more than she had been doing during her training—and allowed for no rest days. When she queried why they had landed on this particular number, they didn't seem able to explain. However, five days before she was due to depart, they contacted her again to say they had decided to change the women's maximum time to 175 days. Juliana decided to go for the men's record anyway.

At this point, Juliana made the decision to swap her comfortable touring bike for a nippy carbon road bike weighing under sixteen pounds, which she named Pegasus after the mythical winged horse that Greek hero Bellerophon rode to defeat the monstrous Chimera. She stripped her luggage down to the minimum, with just a change of cycle clothing and some other essentials.

Annie wasn't traveling so light and free. Her Columbia lady's bicycle, most likely given to her as a promotional exercise by the Boston-based Pope company, weighed a hefty forty-four pounds. Its drop frame meant she could wear her regular outfit of long skirts and corsets, but the combined weight of the bike and clothing made long days in the saddle rather more arduous than they might have been. Apart from her pearl-handled revolver, she packed light, sending trunks with spare clothes on ahead of her. Her first destination was New York City where, seemingly unfazed by the clock ticking, she stayed for an entire month, giving interviews to raise further awareness of her endeavor.

In late September, a thousand miles and three months in, she arrived in Chicago. Annie wasn't feeling so gung-ho about her plans as she wheeled into the Windy City. The immensity of the remaining journey, and the utter exhaustion of life on the road on her heavy bike, resulted in her announcing she was abandoning her endeavor. Instead she would settle for setting a new record cycling back to New York City. That was until another company, Sterling Bicycles, stepped into the breach to help resuscitate her ambitious plans. They offered her a man's bicycle that weighed half as much as her Columbia in exchange for promoting their brand. Like Juliana's upgrade, it would make the miles go that much faster and easier. She also abandoned the skirts and corsets in favor of bloomers. She became such a convert that she often eulogized to the press about the benefits of rational dress.

Annie had another problem that wasn't quite so easy to fix. It dawned on her that her planned route west was flawed: she wouldn't make it across the mountains to reach San Francisco before the winter snows. The only option was to head back east, retracing her route nearly a thousand miles, to New York City to catch a boat to Europe instead of to the West Coast and then on to Asia. One consolation was that her Sterling meant the return journey wasn't going to be quite so tiring.

For any cyclist, weather can be a challenging adversary. When you are on a strict schedule, it can send the best laid plans into disarray. In Annie's case, it was poor planning, not unexpected weather. Of the riders hoping to achieve a record for around-the-world cycling, the majority head east since this is viewed as a better direction for prevailing winds. Juliana, departing in midsummer in Europe, calculated that if she headed east she would hit the monsoons in Asia, so she opted to battle the headwinds and pedal westward. She rode from southern Italy into France, through 104-degree heat and the devastation wrought by forest fires in Spain, and on to Lisbon to catch her flight to America. Once there, leaving Annie's home city of Boston, she felt the full force of the winds she'd been warned about, along with rain, hills and countless punctures.

As she crossed America, people told her she was heading the wrong way, not helpful advice since a change of direction was out of the question. She describes riding constantly into wind as something that "drains your morale, saps your energy and makes you want to scream, weep and beat the handlebars in frustration." I know this feeling well and I've never tried to cycle around the world: I have lived in the windiest *département* in France and there were days when it felt like pedaling on a spin bike on the high setting. When the wind's in the right direction, though, it can feel closer to flying. By the time Juliana reached the flat Midwest, the wind had become so unbearable that she opted to reroute, adding more miles to her journey by zigzagging in an effort to avoid the continual full-frontal assault.

All this and she still didn't escape the rain in Asia; a typhoon landed right in the middle of her route through India. She spent days cycling through wind and rain on roads that had turned into a mud bath mixed with rubbish and—more unpleasantly— excrement that covered her and Pegasus from head to pedal. Again she was forced into an urgent reroute to avoid becoming seriously unwell.

Annie's change of route didn't entirely avoid inclement weather either. When she reached France, it was early December and she headed south out of Paris in freezing rain that had turned to snow by the time she hit the Loire. She didn't have to brave the elements alone though: she had a relay team of fans to cycle with her all the way from Paris to Marseille. She had spent several weeks in Paris, giving interviews and lectures, attending a bicycle exhibition to help promote various products, and generally building hype. By the time she left, it's likely there wasn't a single person in the country who didn't know about this American woman making her way south on her Sterling, and many cyclists were keen to accompany her for part of the way. She arrived in Marseille to a hero's welcome; crowds lined the streets eager to greet the woman they had read so much about. Annie was a cycling celebrity.

In France, where women riding bikes in bloomers raised fewer eyebrows than in most countries at that time, they couldn't get enough of this globe-circling cyclist. Despite the elation she must have felt, by this point she was looking and feeling like she'd gone through quite an ordeal. As she wheeled into Marseille flanked by riders from a local cycling club, she was pedaling one-legged, the other leg bandaged and propped up on her handlebars. She told the press it had been damaged when highwaymen tried to rob her near Avignon. Peter, her great-grandnephew, concluded this was unlikely. The injury possibly resulted from a far more mundane accident near Lyon.

Annie basked in the attention; it must have felt a million miles from her anonymous life in Boston. With her new name, she had created a new persona, and the stories she spun were an important part of that. The fiction was financially rewarding too. Her celebrity status meant she could sell autographed photos and promote products from perfume to tires, appearing in ads and adding more banners to her bike. People paid to hear her talk about her travels, and to keep the crowd's attention she was inclined to let her storytelling run away with her.

Even if, unlike Annie, you don't need to earn today's equivalent of five thousand dollars while also cycling around the world, it doesn't come without its costs. Although Juliana hadn't managed to secure a brand sponsor before she left, she had hoped that once she had covered a bit of ground, and people saw how determined she was, someone might come onboard with much-needed funds, but it didn't happen. She was running out of money by the time she crossed New Zealand. This was a low point in the journey in other respects too: a nonfunctioning GPS meant she had gone miles off route and over unnecessary mountains, while being battered by cold, rain and gale-force winds.

She was on the verge of giving up and heading back home when the internet became her salvation. Just as people had followed Annie's journey from Boston through stories and interviews in the press, in 2012, increasing numbers had been monitoring Juliana's GPS tracker online and her messages and videos on Facebook. When they heard she might have to abandon the attempt, many dug deep to keep Juliana on the road, crowdfunding her journey. Others, many of them women, met her en route, buying her food and drinks. Friends, and friends of friends, put her up for the night, doing everything they could to keep her on track. Unlike Annie, Juliana didn't have to weave fiction into her account; there was enough drama in her journey without having to invent anything.

She certainly couldn't have misled anyone about the route she took and how far she cycled since all eyes, including those of Guinness, were on her GPS SPOT tracker. Such technology wasn't available to track Annie's journey, though she did have a cyclometer which notched up her miles on the bike. When she got back to Boston, she claimed she had cycled over nine thousand miles. She had of course covered a lot of ground on her way east back to Boston, not least in the seven weeks from leaving Marseille on January 20 and arriving in Japan, a journey she said had taken her through North Africa and the Middle East, over the Himalayas and across China. Among other tales of adventure, she told reporters and audiences in packed lecture halls that she went to the front line of the Sino-Japanese War and was imprisoned, hunted tigers in Bengal, witnessed the Russian prison camps in Siberia and was shot in the shoulder, all during the journey east.

After examining reams of press coverage, Peter Zheutlin concluded that much of her journey from France to Japan was pure fantasy. It would have been impossible to cycle all that way on her Sterling, while fitting in the many scrapes and adventures she claimed, in such a short space of time. No wonder her accounts tended to contradict each other, with each interviewer getting a different version.

There is no question the steamer ship she boarded in Marseille was the same one she disembarked from in Yokohama in March. Despite the tall stories, though, her boat trip wasn't in fact negating the conditions of her attempt. In all of Annie's explanations of the wager, she made no mention of any rule stipulating the number of miles she had to cover on her bicycle. In France, while it's incontrovertible she cycled many hundreds of miles across the country, since for most of the way she was accompanied by other cyclists, she jumped on a few trains too. It's also possible she got off the steamship and cycled around the many ports where it docked along the way. But by the time she disembarked in San Francisco after leaving Japan, her entertaining but tellingly conflicting stories had begun to catch up with her. The press were no longer ready to believe everything she threw at them.

On the final stretch of her journey back to Boston, increasingly reporters cast doubt on her accounts of her adventures. Her final leg was a challenging and indirect route of thousands of miles that went south down the California coast, then east across Arizona and New Mexico, before heading back up north to Chicago, crossing arid deserts and mountains—along the way pulling in huge audiences who paid to hear this remarkable and gutsy woman. In El Paso, they couldn't get enough of her wild tales, though the press reported she arrived and left on a train.

While she undoubtedly hopped on some trains, she also cycled at least some of the way and had a broken wrist to show for it after a collision with some pigs, or a farmer, depending on the account you read. When she arrived back in Boston, fifteen months to the day of her departure, her arm was encased in plaster. Broken limbs aside, this young mother had made history as the first woman to get around the world on—and sometimes with—a bike, making herself a star in the process. Whether the wager existed or not, Annie was triumphant. Her journey showed that women need not be defined solely as wives and mothers.

It's notable that when she changed her name, she created a new identity for herself. As Annie Londonderry she never mentioned her marital status or the children she had left behind. A wise tactic to avoid castigation for leaving her family for such a long time. Had it been her husband, Max, setting off to cycle the world, I doubt he would have been criticized for his dereliction of fatherly duties—just a man heading off on his adventures, a double standard that still persists to this day.

We can only guess at Annie's motivation and her feelings about being so far from her family for such a long time. There can be no doubt, however, that at a time when women's choices were limited, particularly regarding family planning, Annie made an active choice to have her own independent adventure that far exceeded the expectations of a working-class Jewish mother of three in Boston in the late nineteenth century. It's significant that she chose to do this on a bicycle, a symbol of the great disruption of strict Victorian gender codes and the wider push toward greater freedom for women. It's just a shame her story was forgotten for so long.

Throwing Down the Gauntlet

Perhaps if Annie's journey hadn't faded from the history books, it wouldn't have taken until 2012 for someone to attempt an official women's record for circumnavigating the globe by bike.

Juliana admits that because she had never previously shown any interest in sports, there "was nothing to qualify me for such a huge undertaking." Instead it was "willpower and the determination to finish, no matter what" that kept her on the road, as well as the desire to prove that "anything is possible." A bereavement had initially pushed her to attempt such a seemingly impossible feat, but in the process, it changed her. She had grown up in a repressive religious cult, separated from her parents for most of her formative years, until she finally escaped at twenty-three. An experience like that would have put the grueling hours in the saddle into perspective. She thinks her eight-year-old self would never have believed she would one day take on such a challenge, let alone succeed.

Juliana believes her childhood experience made her tough, able to endure higher levels of physical and mental pain, and more equipped to deal with the worst of what the trip threw at her. Her traits of independence, self-reliance and adaptability came to the forefront during the long, lonely days on the road in often tough conditions.

Arguably one of the greatest female endurance athletes in the world, she puts her success down to stubbornness rather than strength. Nor does she think her achievements—which have since included the 2013 inaugural Transcontinental Race, the toughest unsupported race across Europe, starting in Belgium and ending in Istanbul, where she was the only woman in the race, finishing ninth overall; and also the 4,200-mile Trans Am Bike Race, where she was the first woman over the line and fourth competitor to finish—make her extraordinary. Where other people might give up and go home, she refuses to quit. On her bike she becomes "another being, I just lose all sense of identity and even of sex—as in being feminine—I just become an animal, and I just go, it's like a horse smelling that finish line." Though her achievements are exceptional, she sees herself as entirely ordinary, believing that many people possess untapped potential.

There is something undeniably epic about a person alone on a bike battling against the clock, the weather, the environment and countless other obstacles; it inevitably turns them into heroes of that particular story. One such person is Jenny Graham, who in 2018, aged thirty-eight, set a new record for fastest woman to circumnavigate the globe on a bike. She was only the third to do so, the second being Italian Paola Gianotti in 2014, whose record attempt of 144 days was upheld by Guinness despite having had to stop the clock for four months after she fractured a vertebra in a road accident. Jenny covered 18,428 miles in just 124 days. Going east from Berlin, she has followed a similar route to Mark Beaumont, who, in 2017, had set a new men's record of 79 days, smashing his previous 2008 record of 194 days. Clearly it was a good route.

I met Jenny in a café in North London five months after she

claimed the world record. Like Juliana, she also believes that we can often achieve much more than we think, with her journey to world record–breaker a case in point. She tells me she never previously would have believed herself capable of such a thing. At eighteen she had a baby, and such an idea would have seemed impossible and remote. When she saw people like Mark Beaumont talking about their achievements and adventures, she never believed she could do something similar.

She admits that she had never been into sports at school, skipping lessons whenever she could. But as her son grew older, she started getting into mountain biking in the hills around her hometown of Inverness in Scotland. Being a young mom with little free time motivated her to use every opportunity she had to get out there. For parents—or those responsible for someone's care—free time is a luxury in scarce supply, particularly for women, who still tend to be the main caregivers. Research shows that women who parent are less likely to spend any free time they have doing something for themselves, like physical activity. They report feeling guilty and self-indulgent if they do. It might explain why there are lots of men in my cycling club with young children who still manage to get out on a Sunday morning for a club run, while there are far fewer women doing the same. Jenny believes the lack of time made her feel motivated to use the few hours she did manage to snatch here and there in a more focused way. When her son started going to after-school clubs, she would grab the opportunity to jump on her bike and go. As her son got older, she had more free time to spend cycling so she started covering longer and longer distances and competing in increasingly tough challenges.

Jenny never thought she fit into the mold of adventurer before she decided to push herself further and further. Men had been setting round-the-world cycling records for decades before Juliana made her attempt. The fact there were no women doing the same suggests they lacked the belief they could do it. A legacy of being told women aren't physically capable of such things. Even in the run-up to her departure, Jenny says she felt like an "imposter." She tells me that it was the "hardest part of the whole thing, getting to the start line and working through all those doubts," particularly the thought of "failing spectacularly" with so many eyes on her.

Whatever her doubts, she had a strong support network who believed she could do it. Not least was the Adventure Syndicate, a global collective of women endurance bike riders whose aim is to inspire others—particularly women and girls—through their stories and group rides, to go out on their own cycle adventures, changing the narrative about what is possible. Before deciding on her round-the-world challenge, Jenny had borrowed money from her son, now an adult, to get to one of their camps. It was worth it: after she got back to Scotland, the camp's coach offered to train her for free for a year. She recognized this as a "life-changing" opportunity, though it wasn't until a few months later, having read about Juliana's round-the-world ride, that Jenny decided what her next challenge would be. Soon brands came onboard to sponsor.

Once Jenny crossed the start line she had set for herself in Berlin, heading east through Poland, Latvia, Lithuania, Russia, Mongolia and to Beijing before hopping on a flight to Australia, all the doubts lifted. Instead, she was filled with a sense of contentment that "I was born to be here, this is what I was made for, this is what I should be doing right here, right now." Embarking on a race against the clock, spending an average of sixteen hours a day on the bike to cover around 180 miles daily, she was living in the moment in a way that is hard to do in our normal lives. Juliana too described her ride as "a kind of meditation. A complete stillness," which shows that even on a journey like this it's still possible to be immersed in the here and now and not just focused on the next food or sleep stop, or indeed the finish line.

Unlike Dervla Murphy on her leisurely travels, Jenny didn't have the luxury of stopping and spending time in places that took her fancy. Nevertheless, she experienced what she describes as "gorgeous interactions with people" along the way that felt all the more meaningful knowing that she would never see them again. There were challenges en route, but she didn't allow them to disturb the general sense of contentment she felt.

In person, Jenny is brimming with energy and positivity which I'm sure went a long way to push her through the tough times—lack of sleep and exhaustion, freezing cold temperatures, or having to ride at night to avoid getting mown over by trucks on the roads through Russia. The type of challenges that I wonder if I, or others, might decide were too much. She makes sleeping in drainage ditches under the road sound as comfortable as a night in a well-appointed hotel.

To fill the lonely hours, she would sing along to playlists friends had compiled for her. She also listened to audiobooks, including Apsley Cherry-Garrard's *The Worst Journey in the World*. This gripping account of the disastrous 1910–13 Terra Nova Antarctic expedition, in which explorer Robert Falcon Scott and several others froze to death on the way back from the South Pole, helped keep Jenny from falling asleep on the road and put her own trials into perspective. Women were excluded from Scott's party because they weren't deemed capable of taking on such a challenge—an erroneous assumption as it has since been proven that women are better able to cope in the harsh polar environment. In 1937, over a thousand women applied to be part of another Antarctic expedition but not one was accepted. For decades the United States enforced a ban on women going to the area. It's a recent development that women have been accepted—as scientists and explorers—in what had been historically demarcated as an exclusively male—also western and white—territory.

While women are now gaining ground in Antarctica, and people like Jenny are redefining what female adventurers and athletes are capable of elsewhere, women are statistically still less likely to attempt such challenges, particularly solo ones. As we have seen, this is in part a result of the history of adventuring having been so male dominated: women haven't felt welcome or qualified to join in. With the likes of Jenny and Juliana showing that women are capable of such feats, hopefully that will change.

That said, there are other factors standing in the way of female participation in adventuring and exploration. A recent Gallup survey revealed that 34 percent of women in the United States worry about being sexually assaulted, compared to only 5 percent of men. Many are afraid to walk in their own neighborhoods alone after dark, let alone cycle around the world. Just as Victorian clothing made women immobile, the perceived or real threat of sexual violence or harassment stops many women from moving freely.

Jenny tells me that she didn't feel vulnerable as a solo female traveler. She researched women's rights in the countries she would be traveling through to try to prepare herself for how a solo female cyclist might be received. She occasionally took precautions, adapting her behavior to avoid any potentially threatening situations, steering clear of Russian truck stops, not wanting to alert the large numbers of men there to the fact there was a woman cycling through the night alone. Her tactic was to make herself "an invisible person, so not a male or a female, non-threatening, just a silhouette, just passing through not drawing attention to yourself." Something I doubt Mark Beaumont gave much thought to on his round-the-world cycle.

She describes a handful of incidents which she deemed "inappropriate," instances where truckers followed or waited for her on the road and she had to keep cycling to shake them off. She never felt it was something she couldn't handle, and the uncomfortable moments were outweighed by the positive interactions with strangers she had on her journey. What concerned her more was how to not get run over by those same truckers where there was no room for them to pass her safely, which is why she had switched to cycling through the night in the first place.

A 2018 Thomson Reuters poll of experts listed India as the most dangerous country for women, due to its high rates of sexual violence and slave labor. The statistics are appalling, with an estimated four rapes taking place every hour. Perpetrators are seldom convicted, and there are multiple barriers to women reporting the crime or being taken seriously if they do. India was the place Juliana felt most uncomfortable as a lone female cyclist. In addition to dealing with severe stomach problems and sickness, dodgy roads and dangerous traffic, she would frequently draw crowds of "circus freak show proportions," and she decided she wouldn't risk cycling after dark. She describes how, particularly on the eastern coast, she would often become surrounded by "hordes of silent, staring men." On one occasion, the police had to disperse the crowd with their batons. In other instances, she was followed for miles by men on scooters, something she understandably found threatening. She developed a technique of shouting aggressively and waving her fists, which did eventually disperse them—a "highly effective weapon in a lone female's arsenal."

While developing countries make up most of the Thomson Reuters top ten list of most dangerous countries for women, it's a misconception that sexual violence is less of an issue in western countries. In the same poll, the United States was listed jointly with Syria as the third most dangerous country for women. Cindy Southworth, executive vice president of the Washington-based National Network to End Domestic Violence, commented "people want to think income means you're protected from misogyny, and sadly that's not the case."

It may come as a shock that Sweden is cited as having one of the highest incidences of rape in the world. The statistics may be skewed by the fact in some countries women are too fearful or ashamed to report sexual assault and definitions vary. It is also true that women, wherever they live, are much more likely to suffer physical and sexual violence at the hands of someone they know, so the idea that a lone woman traveler is a lot less safe in non-western countries isn't necessarily the case. A 2018 University of Glasgow study of rape and sexual assault victims in Scotland showed that 90 percent knew their attacker.

That's not to say terrible things don't happen. But they occur less often than we are led to believe by stories that exploit women's fear of violent assault by a stranger, and disproportionately represent the risk they face. In fact, when Juliana was riding through Australia, she was repeatedly warned what she was doing was dangerous. The horror film *Wolf Creek*, about two female backpackers kidnapped in the outback, tortured and killed was frequently cited. The marketing for the film was purposely misleading, claiming it was based on real-life events, and so adding to a mythology about the disproportionate dangers lurking in the Australian outback for lone women travelers.

Juliana hadn't seen the film, but she decided to heed the advice of numerous Australian women—as I'm sure I would too—who told her to never ride at night through the remoter parts of the country and one who advised she avoid the sparsely populated coast road and take the busier inland route instead.

Despite the cautions, she experienced nothing but generosity and kindness, much as Dervla Murphy had in Afghanistan after being warned to the contrary. As women traveling alone, or going about our daily lives, we're constantly adapting our behavior to avoid certain hazardous situations, or not draw attention to ourselves, in ways that are automatic and deep-rooted—as a result of both experience and narratives that purposely inflate risk. So much so that we sometimes don't even realize we are doing it.

The biggest threat Jenny faced in Australia was nature, first the rain and freezing cold winter temperatures and then the animals, specifically the kangaroos. Cycling through the dark, she would see these huge mammals, sometimes as tall as six feet, looming at the side of the road. Though they seldom attack humans unless provoked—unlike the magpies that tormented Juliana by dive-bombing her—they are a terrifying sight when you are alone on the road at night.

When she was cycling through Alaska, sleeping in a bivvy bag at the side of the road most nights, the locals were astonished she wasn't carrying a gun in case of a bear attack since she was passing through during the period they stockpile food to prepare for winter hibernation. Jenny thinks that sheer exhaustion at this point escalated the potential threat in her head. As a precaution she armed herself with bear spray and attached a bell to her handlebars to warn unsuspecting bears she was approaching. She would also sing loudly when she was on the road in the dark so there was no possibility of her startling them.

Down through the Yukon she added bison to the list. The huge herds she passed in the dark did not distract from the beauty of the vast and wild landscape and the wonder of the northern lights.

Jenny tells me that the hardest part of the journey was the last leg through Europe, where she found herself having frequent mini–emotional breakdowns at the side of the road. She felt "so overwhelmed, it all came crashing down on me," the immensity of what she was doing finally catching up with her. The closer she got to the finish line, the more and more people got involved, until she felt like she was no longer in control of the decisions anymore. It was a culture shock after thousands of miles pedaling away on her own. For Jenny had chosen to do her trip, like Juliana, entirely self-supported, which—unlike some round-the-world attempts, including Mark Beaumont's—meant she had no one following her in a van and providing food, a place to sleep, emotional support, massages; there was no one sorting out crucial logistics like flights and border crossings. Strangely, Guinness makes no distinction between supported and unsupported record attempts.

Jenny carried everything she needed with her and was entirely self-reliant, cycling in the way she has always done and enjoys the most. When Lee Craigie from the Adventure Syndicate joined her for the final leg through Spain and France, Jenny insisted on strict rules to ensure the ride would remain solo. Lee could only ride with her for a few hours here and there. The only rule Lee broke was giving an exhausted Jenny a hug at three a.m. in a McDonald's on the final day. In Jenny's rulebook even cuddles were out unless she definitely needed one, and in this instance she really did.

After 124 days on the road, she found herself craving home and normality. But instead of resuming her old life, Jenny decided to give up her job and join Lee as codirector of the Adventure Syndicate, to continue helping inspire others to go on adventures—schoolgirls who hate sports and young moms who would never previously have thought themselves capable. When we met, she had just arrived back in the U.K. from guiding a group of female cyclists—perhaps some who might go on to challenge Jenny's own record—for a week through the Sierra Nevada mountains in Spain, her bike parked outside the café loaded down with all her kit. While she was still on the round-the-world ride, she had started to receive messages from people telling her they had been motivated to try to make their own attempt. Women now know that such a thing is entirely possible thanks to Juliana, Jenny and Paola, as well as the intrepid and indefatigable Annie Kopchovsky, who have rewritten the rules for what women can do, helping open a world that many may have been wrongly led to believe was a boys-only club.

PART IV

QUEENS OF
TRACK, ROAD
AND MOUNTAIN

CHAPTER TEN

TO RACE IS LIFE

Interlopers

At a golf course on the shores of Lake Michigan, around seventy-five men gathered in its clubhouse in September 1941 to reminisce about their sporting glory days. They weren't talking about golf tournaments, but their time as some of the country's best bicycle racers at the tail end of the previous century. Several had competed on high-wheels, others had been champions on the then new Safety bicycles of the 1890s, and many had taken part in six-day races. This popular format was the ultimate test of endurance and stamina, requiring cycling laps around a track for sometimes as much as twenty hours a day, grabbing a few hours' sleep when they could no longer turn the pedals and had begun hallucinating or raving from exhaustion. The winner was the one who racked up the greatest distance before the clock stopped.

They might have relied on drugs supplied by their soigneur to do so: strychnine, trimethyl, heroin, cocaine and morphine, all then legal and permissible on the track. Sometimes they competed against horses, in cowboy versus bicycle races. While the horsemen—including Buffalo Bill Cody no less—were allowed to change their mounts when they tired, the cyclists had to carry on regardless. Thousands turned out to watch and there was a lot of money to be won. The men had been national, in some cases international, stars, when bike racing was the most popular spectator sport of the era. They had pushed their bodies to the limits and broken records previously thought unbreakable. Here was an opportunity to bask in the memories of those golden years, when they had been at the peak of physical fitness and life was all about the bike. What they hadn't expected from this nostalgia fest was that there would be an interloper who would disrupt the proceedings and crush the idea that the world of nineteenth-century racing was just a boys' club.

As the afternoon progressed and the men each took to the stand to reminisce about the good old days, a woman in her sixties crossed the pristine lawn and made straight for the party. When she introduced herself, they knew why she had come—it was Tillie Anderson, one of the greatest women bicycle racers of the 1890s. She had records to match most—and even surpass some—of those gathered, from her time spent spinning around tracks across the United States in front of huge crowds. Despite this, Tillie hadn't been invited to this "stars of the nineteenth century" event because women's cycle racing wasn't considered part of the official story of the sport. Tillie's achievements, along with those of her female contemporaries and many who came after, had been pushed to the margins, forgotten and overlooked.

Female bicycle races had once brought in huge crowds—and their money—and helped sell newspapers, but once their novelty had run its course, they were no longer of value to the sport and the overwhelmingly male image it wanted to present. It seems Tillie was warmly received by her male contemporaries gathered at the golf course, but she had to force her way into the men's party to take up her rightful place. One in a long line of women throughout the history of cycle racing who had to fight to be recognized in what former Olympic and all-round superstar cyclist Nicole Cooke described in 2017 as "a sport run by men, for men."

Women's racing is now officially recognized by the Union Cycliste Internationale (UCI), the sport's global governing body, but there remains some way to go before we achieve parity with the men. Ever since Tillie's day, women have been fighting for recognition, equal pay, opportunities and to be taken seriously in the sport. Progress has been slow. Women's track racing became part of the Olympic Games in 1988, though women had been racing on the track for more than a hundred years by that point. In fact, there was no women's cycling whatsoever at the Olympics until 1984, while men have competed since 1896. Only since 2012 have there been an equal number of men's and women's cycling events.

Cycling has a long history of sidelining female participants, from Tillie right up to today's professional riders. Flick through Olympian and Tour de France winner Bradley Wiggins's 2018 book *Icons*, in which he writes about twenty-one of his cycling heroes, and you'll see that not one of them is a woman.

Back in the 1940s, Tillie was adamant that she too should be acknowledged as a "star" and attended every subsequent annual gathering until her death at age eighty-eight.

Strongwomen and High-Wheels

My great-grandfather, Samuel Moss, won many medals at London's Herne Hill Velodrome in the 1890s and 1900s. Built in

1891, it is one of the oldest and most famous remaining outdoor tracks, one of the few to survive the end of the cycling boom. During the era when Samuel was pedaling around the track, its legendary Good Friday races would attract upward of ten thousand spectators. When Frank Shortland, one of the era's most successful cyclists in the U.K., took to the track in 1894 for a twenty-four-hour race, twenty thousand turned out to watch him, many of whom had broken through the barricades to see his triumphant ride. Police served as bodyguards to prevent him from being mobbed when he left the stadium.

The huge popularity of these events made me wonder if there were women's races too, but a book of Herne Hill's history makes no mention of any during this period. I initially assumed they weren't happening anywhere else either. Since women had encountered great resistance to just sedately getting around on a bicycle at this time, I thought perhaps women going as far as to compete on bikes was outright banned. It turns out this wasn't the case. While they struggled to be recognized by the cycling authorities, that didn't stop them. In fact, cycling was one of the first competitive sports that women participated in—which makes the decades of marginalization bitterly ironic.

It is generally agreed that the first ever women's cycle race took place in November 1868 at the Parc Bordelais in Bordeaux, where four women competed on velocipedes or "boneshakers." This was only a few months after the first ever recorded men's race. The event was won by Mademoiselle Julie, narrowly beating a Mademoiselle Louise, who had led the pack for most of the race, with their efforts watched by thousands of spectators. In an illustration of the event, the "vélocipediennes" are shown dressed in mid-length skirts that flow out behind, their stockinged, or possibly even bare, legs thrust out in front, turning the pedals attached to their front wheels. In the United States, the image was censored for inclusion in *Harper's* magazine, with decency preserved by the addition of billowy bloomers underneath the women's skirts to cover their legs.

The following year, at another French event, it was reported that at least three women competed among a field of around 120 men in the first long-distance road race. Only thirty-three entrants managed to finish the 76-mile course from Paris to Rouen. Twenty-ninth across the line was a woman from Lyon riding under the name "Miss America." Her husband apparently came thirtieth. She soon became a fixture in races around France throughout the velocipede craze.

When the high-wheel won people's hearts in the 1880s, a handful of women, mostly in North America, were determined to make their mark in the racing world. They would challenge other women, men and sometimes horses to see who was fastest. In 1881, Elsa von Blumen, born Caroline Wilhelmina Kiner in 1859 to German immigrant parents in Kansas, took on a horse named Hattie R on her high-wheel in front of 2,500 spectators at Driving Park in Rochester, New York. As a teen, Elsa had been diagnosed with consumption and had taken up walking to regain her health. She quickly discovered she had remarkable endurance, and by 1879 she was a champion competitive walker, the "Queen of Lady Pedestriennes."

At that time, walking races were as popular a spectator sport as baseball, though its hard to fathom the appeal of watching someone walk around and around a small track for hours, sometimes days, with only short breaks for food. Elsa regularly took part in 100-mile events on specially built indoor tracks or sawdust loops on music hall stages, completing the distance in twenty-seven hours. By 1880, she had moved on to the high-wheel, which was a lot faster and decidedly more dangerous. After her contest with the horse, she pedaled a thousand miles in six days on a course in Pittsburgh. One picture shows Elsa wearing buttoned-up leather ankle boots, a peaked hat, and neatly fitting bloomers and jacket, with a little fringed skirt over the top; no female high-wheeler would have risked a long skirt.

Elsa often competed against men, but her main female rival was French-Canadian Louise Armaindo, who had also come to cycling through the competitive-walking route. The daughter of a strongwoman, Louise had started out as a trapeze artist and strongwoman in a Chicago circus. She boasted that her mother could lift nearly nine hundred pounds in her prime, so notions of female frailty were utter nonsense in Louise's experience. In 1882, Louise and Elsa raced each other in the first recorded women-only high-wheel race, consisting of five-mile heats over six days. Louise won and held the crown of women's champion high-wheeler for most of the decade.

Like Elsa, Louise regularly competed against men. In 1883, she took on U.S. champions William M. Woodside and William J. Morgan in a six-day race on a makeshift cinder track in the armory near the waterfront in Chicago. The three flew around the track for twelve hours a day in front of an audience of two thousand, with adjudicators carefully counting the laps of each rider. Taking a break would have allowed the other riders to make gains, so they avoided stopping as much as possible. By the end of the first day there wasn't much between the three, but by the fourth, Louise had started to overtake the men. She increased her lead still further over the final two days, ending the seventy-second hour triumphant, with 843 miles compared to Morgan's 820 and Woodside's meager 723. She told a journalist that "No one can have any idea how I had to punish myself to hold to the end; but I had determined to beat those two men, and I did it."

Unhappy about being beaten by a girl, William Woodside challenged her to a 120-mile race spread across three evenings the following week in Wisconsin. Again, she beat both men. William didn't leave it there: the three came together again in Milwaukee for a three-hour-a-night, six-day race. He was so confident he would win this time that he gave Louise a thirty-mile advantage and William Morgan twelve miles. Once again Louise won, with 294 miles to Morgan and Woodside's 285 and 277 respectively. By the end of the year she is alleged to have earned the equivalent of around $100,000 in today's money for her remarkable racing prowess.

For the next few years, there was no other female bike racer to contest Queen Louise, but by the end of the decade her crown was slipping. A new crop of young riders in their teens and early twenties had entered the scene—perhaps having been inspired by Louise—and were testing their mettle on cinder tracks all over the United States, bringing her reign to an end. Before she retired from her life on the road, taking on whoever would challenge her at track after track, Louise joined a touring troupe of female high-wheelers who traveled the country racing each other, sometimes for eight hours a day, six days a week, in packed stadiums like Madison Square Garden in New York. Some of them, including Louise, even traveled across the Atlantic for a tour of the U.K. from September 1889 to January 1890, competing against each other in towns such as Grimsby, North Shields, Long Eaton, Sheffield and Northampton. Thousands came to watch, most of whom would never have seen a woman race a bike before. The women worked hard, competing in everything from a twenty-hour race over six days to 100-mile competitions, as well as taking on male challengers.

Louise never managed to claw her way back to the top against her stronger new rivals. One of these was Lottie Stanley, who stayed on in the U.K. to continue to race against men, such was the novelty of a woman cycle racer. One of her events, at Wolverhampton Wanderers Football Club, attracted around seventeen thousand spectators.

Tillie the Terrible and Mademoiselle Lisette

While Louise's star had waned, she had been a remarkable rider in her prime and would have been entirely justified, were she still alive, in attending that celebratory event alongside Tillie. Sadly, fate dealt her rather a cruel hand: a hotel fire left her with such severe injuries in 1896 that she could never race again, and in 1900, she died in what seems to be obscurity.

In her final decade, she would have seen great changes to the world which had made her a star and it's likely she would have been aware of Tillie Anderson's meteoric rise to be crowned the new queen of U.S. bike racing. It was also the end of the high-wheel's domination, and Tillie and her contemporaries were competing on the new, more practical Safety bicycles. Bicycle racing was also now an official sport. In the United States it was regulated by the League of American Wheelmen (LAW), which acted as an advocate for cyclists in general, ran races and kept records. High-wheel racing had been a relative sporting Wild West, where anyone could take on anyone or anything. But those days were gone, and what the LAW particularly objected to was the idea of women racing anyone at all, just as in 1894 they banned nonwhite members from joining the organization. Instead, Tillie and her contemporaries were pushed to the margins to compete in a world outside of the men's "official" one. None of their races were included in the LAW's records and velodromes that ran women's cycling events were liable to be blacklisted.

Despite the fact that riders like Louise had been proving that they were strong and fearless and could take on, and even beat, men, it's likely the LAW had a view similar to many at that time: women sweating it out on the track was both unacceptable and too controversial to get involved with. At a time when women were still having to prove they had as much right to ride a bike as men, even many of those who strongly supported them to do so felt that racing was a pedal stroke too far.

Magazines and much of the cycling press at this time were full of warnings of the "scorcher," someone seen as riding fast and furiously, and for women to "scorch" was so far from the ideals of femininity that the LAW wanted no part in it. For many conservatives it was the most extreme example of the damage that could be done to a woman from riding a bike. Many in the U.K. shared these views, including *Cycling* magazine, which declared in 1894 that the sport "is not, nor can it ever be, a fit thing for ladies to indulge in. The feminine constitution was never intended to withstand the strain of such competition" and "it should be derogatory to any woman's sense of modesty." Elizabeth Robins Pennell concurred that for women, "if carried to excess, cycling becomes a positive evil."

Not everyone felt the same, and in France it was much less controversial, which considering it was the country most unfazed by women donning bloomers and had put on the first races, makes sense. In 1893, Mademoiselle de Saint-Sauveur made the first ever women's hour record (the furthest distance covered in sixty minutes) at the Vélodrome Buffalo in Paris and inspired numerous others to have a go at beating her time. There were regular women's races on road and track, as well as women competing against men. Some of these riders became international stars, like Lisette (nom de plume of Amélie Le Gall), and Belgium's Hélène Dutrieu, who was awarded a medal for her cycling achievements by King Leopold II.

In the United States, it's likely the LAW also thought that women just weren't capable of serious competition. It's certainly true that at that time women had little opportunity to prove otherwise and rarely in front of the general public. Tennis was an exception, with women taking part in Wimbledon as early as 1884, but participants would have demonstrated little of the physicality of the Williams sisters today, not least because they were still required to wear their regulation long skirts. Maud Watson, winner of the first ever Wimbledon ladies' singles title, did so wearing an all-white ensemble of woolen ankle-length skirt complete with small bustle, long-sleeved silk blouse and sailor hat. Not exactly an outfit designed to help you fly around the court returning tricky serves. Twenty-year-old Blanche Bingley competed at that same event wearing a whale-bone corset that pierced her skin as she played, resulting in her bleeding through her white blouse. Another competitor fainted, perhaps because her outfit was unsuited to the heat. When women were permitted to compete at tennis in the 1900 Olympics—as well as in the upper-class sports of sailing, croquet, equestrianism and golf—their clothing remained as impractical as ever.

Bicycle racing in regular Victorian women's wear just wasn't practical, and as the 1890s progressed and competition on the track intensified, Louise's and Elsa's bloomer costumes gave way to aero short-shorts and tights. Some of the male spectators may have been drawn to the races by the thought of all these female legs, normally swathed in layers of fabric, on display. It's likely the LAW might well have felt this aspect could taint the serious image they wanted to project of the new sport, bringing in audiences more interested in sensation than true sportsmanship. The fact that several of the female riders at that time, not least Louise Armaindo, had also previously performed in the more risqué arenas of circus or music halls, so were used to flouting convention and using their bodies in ways that challenged the status quo, may have contributed to the perception of women's racing as more risqué sideshow spectacle than a serious competition between true athletes.

It's true that the sight of women on a racetrack using their bodies in such a physical way would have been a novelty, but contemporary accounts show that spectators may have recognized that these women had an objective other than titillation. A local newspaper in Sheffield acknowledged this when Louise and her high-wheel gang raced in the city in 1889, where it reported that "instead of a demonstration of limbs," the women "rode with speed and skill worthy of the best male bicycle riders."

Not that Tillie and other female racers of the 1890s, and most particularly their agents and managers, were unaware of the impact of their bodies. The press was fixated on their outfits, looks and body shapes. Then as ever, sex sells, and some of the riders exploited this to raise their profile. One of Tillie's rivals, Dottie Farnsworth, wore an eye-catching costume of scarlet satin shorts and top, which earned her the nickname "the Red Bird." She had previously worked in the theater and understood the value of making an entrance and would walk onto the track wearing a long white robe which she would then remove to reveal her sensational outfit. The press and spectators loved it.

The top riders were celebrities, interviewed in the media, and many had glamorous images taken of themselves with their bikes, like Hollywood stars the following century. They were under pressure to prove that while they may be demons on the track, they had far from turned into men. Before one race Tillie had a medical doctor, alongside a journalist, examine her legs to determine whether they had been made manly in the process of her training. It was reported that they had a "beautiful" shape, but that her veins, which they felt were too prominent, did detract rather.

Tillie's career was based on a lot more than her image. She had arrived in Chicago from Sweden in 1891 and worked in laundries and as a seamstress. Seeing women in the city on bicycles, she began to desire her own. By 1894, she had not only managed to obtain one but had discovered she possessed a natural talent. She took to training each day before work, and the following year she set a century (hundred-mile) record on the Elgin-Aurora course in Chicago, where she was spotted by a sponsor and given a better bike.

Her next challenge was a six-day race, which consisted of three hours of racing a day, with Tillie easily beating her more established rivals to scoop the $200 prize. Though women's racing was not recognized by the LAW, she realized it offered better finacial prospects, not to mention fame and adulation, if you had the talent and determination, than was possible as a lowly seamstress. In 1895, it's estimated she earned the equivalent of around $150,000 in today's money, an astonishing figure for someone who had previously been living with her parents above a meat market, struggling to make ends meet. She was a formidable athlete, training full-time and winning 123 out of 130 races between 1895 and 1902. "Tillie the Terrible," as she was dubbed in the press, was determined to test her strength against the men, but the LAW had banned this. When she was finally given a chance at an informal race in Chicago, she duly wiped the floor with her male opponent.

Despite its outsider status, from the mid to late 1890s, women's bike racing in the United States was big business, with audiences in the thousands flocking to see Tillie and others battle it out on the track. The sport thrived, and it wasn't just about legs. Some put this down to fatigue with men's six-day races, in which participants slogged around a track for up to twenty hours a day, six days straight. Instead, the women's version was limited to just three or four hours a day, which made for a faster and more gripping competition and involved far less commitment from the audience.

The ban on women competing in the same venues as the men had been overcome by canny organizers who built temporary velodromes that consisted of steep-sided wooden oval tracks, on theater and music hall stages, or wherever else would accommodate them. It was quite a skill to maneuver safely around these petite courses with their sides sloping up to as much as 45 degrees. Accidents—including broken bones and severe concussions—weren't uncommon. Those who raced deemed it more than worth the risk to earn a good living, possibly as much as, or more than, the men. Something which makes today's huge gender pay gap in much of professional cycling look like a backward step. No doubt the women's managers and agents were also making a lot of money out of their riders, and undoubtedly some women only received a small proportion of what they had earned for their efforts.

A day at the cycle races, pre-cinema, was one of the most popular attractions across Europe, North America, Australia and elsewhere, and organizers worked hard to pull in the crowds. Orchestras were hired to accompany the racing, upping the anticipation and excitement levels. Unlike the rarefied and hushed atmosphere of Wimbledon, cycle racing would have been loud and raucous, with drinking and betting, not least at the Royal Aquarium in London, which regularly put on women's six-day races, and attracted star riders from France and Belgium to compete against U.K. talent.

Organizers found including a program of women's cycling alongside the men's—in the U.K. there was no ban on women racing in the same venues as men—a highly lucrative endeavor, and they offered a panoply of other entertainments to pull in the crowds and keep them entertained during any lulls on the track—acrobats, clowns, strongmen and women, Japanese jugglers, synchronized swimmers, human cannonballs and the more morally questionable performing elephants, minstrels and a "human horse."

In November 1895, all eyes were on the track for the women's international six-day race, described by London's *Standard* newspaper as the "talk of the world." In this race, the U.K.'s Monica Harwood came from complete obscurity to win in front of a sold-out audience of thousands. A few months previously Monica had answered an ad looking for women to race across England and Scotland and soon discovered she had talent. Like Tillie that same year, she wiped the floor with the established competition, including the celebrated Clara Grace (or Mrs. Grace as she was called by the press), who came ninth after a fall on the fifth day, and who, it turns out, had helped train her new rival.

The cyclist who came second, with 368 miles and six laps to Monica's 371 and two laps, was France's Lisette, touted as the greatest female rider in the world despite there being no official way to verify this claim. That was far from the end of the track for Lisette; the following May she competed against Clara Grace on home turf, at the Vélodrome d'Hiver in Paris, beating her over a distance of 100 kilometers. That same year she set a new women's hour-paced record (where riders in front set the speed and give the competitor the advantage of drafting behind them) with 43.461 kilometers, which was unbeaten for many years. She also took on, and was beaten by, star Welsh racer Jimmy Michael in a 50-kilometer race in Paris. Then she returned once more to London's Royal Aquarium, emerging triumphant this time, pushing her rival Monica into second place in another six-day race.

Lisette was a global cycling star who worked hard to create a mythology around her origins, no doubt to keep the media and public interested. In one version, she claimed to have been a shepherdess in Brittany and after telling a passing cyclist how much she longed to give it a go, soon discovered she had a natural talent when he returned with a bike. In another, she was an orphan in Paris, working long hours in a factory which made her sickly, and so took up cycling for the sake of her health before going on to race.

Whatever her true origins, her real name was Amélie Le Gall and she was a formidable talent—though perhaps not quite the greatest in the world, as became apparent in 1898 when she set her sights on conquering America. Over the following years she took part in a series of races against the so-called "big five," which included Tillie and Dottie, "the Red Bird." Lisette didn't win a single one, but the crowd still went wild over this French legend who didn't wear shorts, just tights. She may have been handicapped by the diminutive and steep-sided U.S. tracks that

Tillie and Co. were adapted to and were a far cry from the full-sized velodromes she was used to at home. This may have contributed to the bad fall she took on the second day of her first six-day race, which was witnessed by a crowd of four thousand people. Unwilling to admit defeat, she got back on, then a few days later another crash left her with a concussion. Dottie, who had fallen in front of Lisette's path and caused the collision, claimed to have suffered a broken rib. Despite the severity of their injuries, they were both back on their bikes for the third night. In the end it was Tillie who finished triumphant, with Lisette in second place and Dottie pushed into fourth. Rather than return to France, Lisette decided to stay on in the country, perhaps because it was more lucrative to do so.

The papers and crowds loved the enigmatic French cyclist, despite her never managing to get a lead on Tillie. A report published in Chicago's *Inter Ocean* newspaper ahead of her racing in the city showed the extent to which so many had bought into Lisette's mythology. Not only did they refer to her as the "speediest of all cyclists," they also erroneously claimed she had beaten Jimmy Michael. Most of all they adored her Frenchness, which they described as a "winning 'chic' that brands the real Parisian" and praised her for following a training schedule "much less severe" than that of her U.S. and U.K. counterparts, by which I assume they meant more appropriately feminine.

No matter how "chic," Lisette couldn't stop women's racing in the United States falling out of fashion by the following year. Audiences were moving on to other spectator sports like baseball, and even the men's cycle racing in the established velodromes was attracting less attention. It wasn't long before the sport's star female riders started wheeling off the track to earn a living elsewhere. One of the first was Dottie, the Red Bird, who joined a circus troupe to perform stunts on a tiny, even steeper-sided track known as the Cycle Dazzle. Lisette also performed on occasion and continued to do so after she too stopped racing.

On one fateful night, Dottie went right over the edge and sustained injuries so serious she died just a few hours later. This terrible accident coincided with the end of the road for Tillie, Lisette and others, with the Swede retraining as a masseuse and the French racer moving into cooking, opening restaurants in New Orleans and then Miami with her husband.

The story was the same in the U.K., and even France, with enthusiasm for women's track racing evaporating with the new century. London's once famous Aquarium, where champion Lisette unexpectedly lost out to a British newcomer, was demolished in 1903. Its former stars were soon forgotten and as that generation died out, with no official records to keep alive their achievements, most descendants had no idea they had a celebrated, fearless, indefatigable and powerful "cyclienne" in their family tree.

Not the End of the Road

If women racing on track wasn't the draw it had been at the start of the twentieth century, they hadn't stopped being competitive about their cycling. Women the world over were still intent on breaking records, though this became more about notching up road miles than laps in a stadium.

German-born Margaret Gast, who had previously competed in six-day races in the United States and in 1901, at age eighteen (having told the organizers she was twenty-one so she could take part), cycled 2,000 miles in 222 hours, 5.5 minutes by riding a 25-mile circuit on Long Island built by the Vanderbilts for their new motor cars. She beat the previous men's record by three hours and one minute. Margaret had originally set out to better the 1,500-mile women's record but felt so full of energy when she reached that milestone that she decided to carry on for another five hundred miles. When she got to two thousand, with only a few hours' sleep snatched here and there, having fallen off several times from sheer exhaustion, and endured thunderstorms and torrential rain that turned the road to mud, she still wasn't done. It wasn't until she had racked up 2,600 miles, breaking a new distance record for men and women, that she stopped pedaling. Had it been up to her, she would have continued until she'd made three thousand, but the residents living on the road had her stopped.

They shared the view of a newspaper article that condemned Margaret as a "disgraceful exhibition" and told a journalist they feared for the effect the "spectacle" would have on the minds of the children. I assume they meant they wouldn't want their own daughters thinking this was an appropriate activity, and so duly made sure it couldn't happen again on their rarefied patch. Other papers, even if they thought what she'd achieved was remarkable, were keen to point out the physical toll it had taken, with one declaring that she was "far from a pleasant picture to look upon." Prioritizing her femininity over her achievements is something Margaret would have profoundly disagreed with. She would later donate a valuable puppy to an auction in New York City to raise money for women's suffrage.

After her Vanderbilt achievement she may have felt she had nothing more to prove as a cyclist. Like Dottie, she moved on to performing stunts on stage. In Margaret's case, she dropped the bicycle altogether for another invention, the motorcycle, continuing to defy expectations for her gender as the "mile a minute girl" riding a "wall of death," as well as competing with men in races. Despite several close shaves, unlike poor Dottie she survived her stunt years and excelled as a competitor. She was once asked by a journalist if she felt women needed a different type of motorbike and she responded, true to form, to say that women who race want a "machine that is just as hard to handle as the man's."

Devil in a Dress

Italy had its own cycling pioneer in Alfonsina Strada (née Morini). Born in 1891, she had learned to ride at the age of ten on her father's bike, tearing around the roads in her village near Modena. She was reportedly nicknamed the "Devil in a Dress," and won her first race at age thirteen, for which she was awarded a pig. Like Lisette before her, Alfonsina didn't discourage the press from mythologizing her rural peasant roots, but it's likely the family was grateful for the animal even if it seems they would rather she had taken up sewing as a profession.

Alfonsina was nothing if not determined, and having won many of her early races, against both girls and boys, she soon acquired a reputation as a formidable competitor. At eighteen, she traveled to St. Petersburg to compete in a Grand Prix and was awarded a medal by Tsar Nicholas II, which must have been quite an experience for the teenager at a time when few if any members of her family had traveled beyond Modena.

If that wasn't enough to convince any skeptical relatives of her career choice, then breaking the women's (still unofficial) hour record not long after at a velodrome in Turin, with 23.110 miles, a record that would hold for twenty-six years, was hopefully enough to finally convince them. Even if it didn't, it's likely that the opinion of Luigi Strada, the man she married in 1915, mattered much more. Luigi was a metalworker who raced in his spare time. Luigi was so convinced of his wife's capabilities that he put his own racing on the back burner to focus on her training instead. His wedding gift to Alfonsina was a new racing bicycle, and over the next few decades, she would pedal her way to becoming the Regina della Pedivella, the "Queen of the Cranks," a true legend in cycling history.

Alfonsina was undoubtedly frustrated by the lack of racing opportunities available to women, so when the organizer of the Giro di Lombardia, Armando Cougnet, invited her to join the race as the only woman in 1917, she didn't hesitate in taking her place on the starting line. The race had never specifically omitted women, but Italy in those days was a highly conservative Catholic country, and it's possible they assumed no woman would entertain the thought of entering. Armando was also editor of the *Gazzetta dello Sport* and understood the power of a good story. With many of their usual star riders off fighting the war, he was looking to inject some interest into the competition. That's not to say there wasn't still some fierce competition, and the Queen of the Cranks finished the 204-kilometer race last, an hour and thirty-four minutes behind the winner, though with only a few seconds between her and the two other finishers before her. Twenty-three riders failed to complete the course.

The following year she took her place once again amid a field exclusively male competitors. This time she finished second to last, a mere twenty-three minutes behind the winner and only a fraction behind the five riders ahead of her. Fourteen riders failed to finish. This was to be her final Lombardia—the organizers now had their big-name riders back from the war and no longer needed the extra publicity that came with pitting a woman against the men. Armando, like those managers and race organizers before him who had enthusiastically promoted women's racing in the 1890s, had lost interest as soon as the financial motivation ceased to be so compelling. I don't doubt he thought Alfonsina was a formidable and impressive rider, but he had no real interest in changing the status quo and opening cycling up to women. In fact, the race rules were tightened up, and women were no longer permitted to enter. To this day, Il Lombardia, as it's now known, is open only to men. There is no women's version. Alfonsina remains the only female entrant of this classic one-day race.

I imagine she was somewhat surprised when six years later Armando came cap in hand to ask the thirty-three-year-old to compete in another of his men-only races, this time what was and still is one of the most famous and demanding races of all, the multistage Giro d'Italia, also known as the Corsa Rosa on account of the pink jersey worn by stage winners. Again, they needed her surprise appearance to help create some media buzz since a handful of the usual star riders weren't taking part—they had demanded fees to show up and since the organizers refused to give in and the riders were holding firm, the two sides had reached an impasse. To maintain the public's interest, Armando needed the greatest Italian woman cyclist of the day to provide drama and excitement. Alfonsina couldn't pass up this opportunity to show the world what she—and by extension, her gender— was capable of in her country's legendary "Grand Départ," an iconic race on a level with the Tour de France.

In 1924, the route was a punishing 2,245 miles long, with stages ranging from 155 to 260 miles, many of which involved some long mountain climbs. By comparison, the 2019 edition was marginally shorter but with no stage longer than 144 miles. And there is a huge disparity in the quality of road surfaces now compared to then, as well as the weight of bikes. Alfonsina and her contemporaries rode steel machines that had no gearing and which weighed close to twice as much as the carbon frames of today's bicycle.

Armando entered his secret publicity weapon under the name Alfonsin Strada, though it's unlikely he was fooling anybody, since she was a household name. When the riders crossed the start line in Milan on May 10, headed nearly two hundred miles away to Genoa, anyone who still might have doubted that Alfonsin was Alfonsina now had incontrovertible evidence that *he* was indeed *she* in her signature black shorts and sweater emblazoned with her name.

On most of the early stages she finished between forty-five minutes and a few hours behind the lead rider, but she wasn't always last over the line, and hung on in there in the face of much adversity while two-thirds of her competitors dropped out. The ecstatic crowds who lined the streets to watch her pass, showering her with flowers and gifts, lifting her from her bicycle to hold her aloft when she'd completed another stage, must have helped keep her going. A crash in terrible weather during the seventh stage on unpaved and icy mountain roads in the south left her with a painfully damaged knee, but she pushed on to finish that day's 189-mile route.

The following day Alfonsina came close to abandoning the race: she was still in pain and afflicted with multiple tire punctures when her handlebars gave way and she resorted to fixing them with a broomstick to get her to that day's finish line. The accident resulted in her official expulsion from the race since she had arrived at the day's end point in Perugia long past the cutoff.

However, with her participation the talk of Italy and beyond, she was too valuable an asset for Armando to let it end there. Although she wouldn't be officially recorded as having finished the race, he paid her to complete the remaining stages regardless. It wasn't her last crash, but her grit and determination saw her through to the very end. On the final day, she rode back into Milan thirty-three hours behind the winner, Giuseppe Enrici, but a hero to the people waiting to see her finish. Even the king of Italy sent his congratulations to the Queen of the Cranks.

When it came to registering her place for the 1925 Giro, she was surprised—and doubtless angered—to find her application was blocked by the very people who had called on her the previous year to help drive precious column inches. Alfonsina had served her purpose, and now that they had all the star male riders they needed to ensure the public stayed interested, she was surplus to requirements. They never had any plans to change the rules and let women compete long term, or to launch a women's version (that wouldn't happen until 1988, too late for Alfonsina). It was, and would remain, a men-only competition with no further exceptions.

It wasn't the end for Alfonsina. She continued to compete for more than a decade in races where she was welcome. In 1938, she broke another women's hour record with 20.24 miles, which would hold for seventeen years. Eventually she retired to run a bike shop in Milan with her second husband, another former racing cyclist, and with the passing years her achievements began to fall into obscurity, like those of Tillie, Louise and countless other female racing cyclists before her. Her new husband had hoped to write a book about her incredible career, but died before he could get a publisher interested.

Alfonsina died of a heart attack in 1959, and the remarkable story of the only woman to have ever competed in her country's world-famous Giro was all but forgotten. That is, until the first decade of the following century when she finally got the biography, and consequently acclaim and acknowledgment, she had more than earned. Were she alive today, she would be pleased, I'm sure, that women can finally race the Giro, albeit in a women-only version, but she might wonder why the women aren't racing as far or receiving anywhere near the amount of money or media coverage as the men.

CHAPTER ELEVEN

CYCLING LIKE A GIRL

"In the Rosslyn they were all lesbians..."

In 2005, the art critic and cyclist Tim Hilton received a letter in which the correspondent told him she'd like to "gouge his eyes out." He had just published a well-reviewed book about cycling, *One More Kilometre and We're in the Showers*, and possibly hadn't expected to provoke this violent reaction. The would-be eye gouger was—perhaps even more surprisingly—a woman in her nineties. She had taken offense at comments he'd included about the cycling club she'd belonged to for decades, the Rosslyn Ladies Cycling Club. It wasn't the only critical letter he received from disgruntled members, but it was the only one threatening physical violence. His reference to the club is brief, little more than a page, but what his critics were vehemently objecting to was the inclusion of the following unverified hearsay:

> *In the Rosslyn they were all lesbians, it was said. Or they were all so voracious that no man was safe in their company.*

*Warn your son against them. None of them was married.
Or, said another story, they kept their club membership
secret from their husbands. They kept a list of hated male
riders. When someone was on that list the Rosslyn Ladies
would gather on a hill to jeer and taunt him. They did a lot
of knitting.*

These were remarks Tim had heard over the years, from
sources who were unlikely to have met any Rosslyn members. To
them the club was a mythical group on whom to project various
contradictory prejudices about women who cycle competitively.
Apart from the unfounded gossip, Tim hadn't managed to un-
cover anything much that was based on fact—undoubtedly another point of contention for the women.

The Rosslyn Ladies' achievements weren't the stuff of myth—
they were legendary. Most of the members are now in their sev-
enties, eighties and nineties and they no longer race. But in their
heyday, they were a formidable force on the road and track,
women who rode steel and were as strong as steel. Founded in
1922, it was the longest-running women's cycling club in the U.K.

Pat Seeger first joined the Rosslyn in 1946, at the age of
twenty. Now ninety-two, she was one of the club's most successful road racers. When I visited her at her home in rural Essex, we
talked in her sitting room surrounded by her many medals and
trophies. She grew up in the borough of Haringey in North
London—only a few streets away from where I live now—and
was taught by a boyfriend to ride a bike when she was fifteen. He
persuaded her to join his mixed club, which then had only a
handful of women members.

After she married (to another cycling boyfriend), she decided
to join the all-women Rosslyn, which still had some of its founders as active members. One was Nellie, who told Pat that in the

early years they often had stones thrown at them, as well as insults like "fast hussies," when they rode out together from Hackney. It's possible that Tim Hilton's incensed poison-pen letter
writer had been on those rides with Nellie and had endured
such abuse.

Pat tells me that she joined the Rosslyn because the club was always in the cycling press on account of winning (as well as organizing) so many races. That their results were recorded at all was
thanks to Evelyn Parkes, who had founded the U.K.'s Women's
Road Record Association in 1934. Decades of women's cycling and
not being given recognition made her realize that if women's records were ever going to be formalized, she'd have to do it herself,
even if the official cycling organizations wouldn't accept them.

For despite the achievements of Tillie, Lisette and other stars
who came before, the suitability of women racing was still being
hotly debated well into the twentieth century. In 1937, British
cyclist Albert Lusty declared that women racing was not just
"injurious to the game itself," but also to "the interests of the
nation." In the decades before the second wave of feminism of
the 1960s, despite women having joined the workforce en masse
during two world wars, it was still widely accepted that women's
place was in the home, that they should leave the sweaty stuff to
the men and stick to the housework and childrearing, tasks Albert saw as in "national interests."

Albert would have been happier in the Netherlands, where
women's racing was banned in the 1930s and '40s, and anyone
wanting to compete had to do so outside the country. After
moving to Belgium, Dutch cyclist Mien van Bree, won many big
races, only for newspapers in her country to declare that she
should have "stayed home, in her kitchen." Times have indeed
changed; the Netherlands has more than embraced women's
competitive cycling, with the likes of Marianne Vos, Annemiek

van Vleuten and Anna van der Breggen dominating the sport internationally in road, track, Cyclo-cross and mountain bike. It's a shame the turnaround came too late for Mien.

The mother of American cyclist Nancy Neiman Baranet, the four-time U.S. national champion who in 1956 competed in a short-lived precursor to the women's Tour de France, subscribed to the view that a woman's place was in the home and refused to watch her daughter compete. When Nancy joined a cycle club in Detroit, her mother was appalled, protesting, "What will the neighbors think?" Nancy's father had only agreed to her riding a bike in the first place because he was more opposed to the idea of women driving cars.

Cycling wasn't alone in this; sportswomen across the board were meeting resistance if they wanted to participate in longer or harder events. In running, they could take part in the Olympics (unlike women's cycling prior to 1984), but the longest race before 1960 was just 200 meters. There had been an 800-meter event in the 1928 Games, but it was dropped after it was inaccurately reported that those who finished collapsed or fainted after crossing the line. Women were not allowed to enter marathons until 1972, though a number had attempted to unofficially run in them. In soccer, the women's game had thrived in the U.K. during World War I and after, but in 1921, the U.K.'s Football Association banned them from playing at their club grounds after they declared it an unsuitable sport for women, a ruling that wasn't lifted until 1971.

The Blonde Bombshell and the Mighty Atom

Coventry-born Eileen Sheridan, now in her nineties, often raced against Pat and other Rosslyn ladies in the 1940s and became one of the greatest competitive cyclists of the twentieth century, earning her the nickname "the Mighty Atom" because of her immense power, speed and diminutive stature of just under five feet. In her memoir she describes how when she started getting into competitions, she wasn't exactly welcomed with open arms. At her first audax, a long-distance ride of 140 miles to be completed in twelve hours, she was the only female entrant. The organizers, believing that a woman would hold everyone else back, tried to persuade her husband to take her home before it started. Eileen refused to drop out. Fifty miles into the ride, they stopped asking if she was surviving, and after a hundred miles, having proved she could more than keep up, she says she was finally accepted as "one of the gang, initiated and admitted to the inner circle."

When she joined her mixed local club, the Coventry CC, she says she was again made to feel that she and her bike had "strayed into a world where they were sadly out of place." On her first ride, the leaders kept upping the pace to try to drop Eileen, who they assumed wouldn't be able to keep up. She more than held her own. She was often the only woman out on rides with the club, so she was the one required to pour the tea when they stopped for a break, but she could easily outpace most of her fellow members. In the words of one magazine at the time, she "rocked the racing world, setting up completely new standards for women's records," some of which would remain unbeaten for decades.

Marguerite Wilson, the U.K.'s first professional female cyclist, dubbed "the Blonde Bombshell" and whose records Eileen would go on to beat, had met similar resistance and skepticism in the 1930s. Before cycling, she had tried athletics, attempting to set up a women's club in her hometown of Bournemouth. She gave up and switched to cycling after it became clear that men at other athletics clubs "resented the intrusion of women into their pastime." She didn't think her parents would approve of her decision, so she would creep out of the house with her homemade racing outfit hidden in her bag.

She was soon winning races and looking for greater challenges. In 1937, she entered her first twelve-hour race—organized by the Rosslyn—in which competitors endeavor to cover as much distance as possible in that time. Her male peers told her that it takes "a man to ride a twelve," but the eighteen-year-old knew she could prove them wrong. She traveled to the race after finishing work on a Saturday afternoon, snatching a few hours' sleep in the car. The youngest entrant, she nevertheless finished with 209.25 miles. The next female rider was seven miles behind.

When Eileen entered her first twelve-hour in 1949, people again underestimated her. On the day, she completed the 223-mile women's course with forty minutes left on the clock, leaving the race organizers no choice but to direct her onto the men's course so she could continue until the time was up. She finished with 237.628 miles, beating the existing women's national record by seventeen miles. Taken alongside the men's results, her distance placed her fifth overall. For this and other results that year, she was awarded women's British Best All-Rounder at a glitzy ceremony in London.

Remarkably, there were "not a few" who refused to believe her results, with some accusing Eileen of cutting a section of the course or suggesting there had been an error adding up her distance. She told herself she would beat, or at least equal, her record the following year to prove the doubters wrong.

Once again, she ran out of course and had to go onto the men's. Extremely challenging weather meant she finished a mile short of her previous record, but fifteen miles ahead of the next woman. In the men's race, half the field dropped out because they couldn't handle the conditions. That year she won the Best All-Rounder again, as well as the prestigious Bidlake Memorial Prize, an award given to a British cyclist for their contribution to the sport. It had only been open to women since 1939, when it was won by Marguerite, Eileen's record-breaking predecessor.

End-to-End

This should have been the proof needed to shut the doubters down; it was certainly enough to convince the Hercules Cycle company to sign up Eileen as a professional cyclist in 1951. They wanted her to break the twenty-one long-distance place-to-place records—such as Land's End to London, Liverpool to Edinburgh and London to York—that had been set by Marguerite in the late 1930s and early '40s, again for Hercules. These events had just one rider, and they started as early as two a.m. to avoid traffic, the country roads lit by the cyclist's front light and the headlights of the Hercules team car following the regulation one hundred meters behind. Eileen set about bettering each of Marguerite's already extraordinary records. The most daunting of these was the End-to-End—872 miles from Land's End, the most southerly point in Cornwall, to John o'Groats, in the far north of Scotland.

Marguerite's End-to-End had taken place in August 1939, as the country was on the brink of war with Germany. Only one woman, Lilian Dredge, had taken on the challenge before. Thirty-two-year-old Lilian had completed the arduous ride in 1938 with a time of 3 days, 20 hours and 54 minutes, but not without battling much prejudice from within the cycling world about her ability to manage such a feat of endurance. Apparently, as a result of the scrutiny she was under, Lilian opted to get some sleep each night to avoid looking too exhausted. The effortlessly glamorous Marguerite, on the other hand, decided she could better Lilian's time by seventeen hours if she only slept when absolutely necessary. She reached the hotel in John o'Groats more than twenty hours faster, in 2 days, 22 hours and 52 minutes, with only three hours of those sleeping. Afterward, she said that it wasn't the lack of sleep that was the problem, it was the loneliness, since she was someone who loved to talk. Nevertheless, after a warm bath, followed by a large breakfast, she jumped back into the saddle. She wanted to try for the 1,000-mile record by pedaling 130 additional miles, as Lilian had done before her.

When she finally unmounted in Wick at the end of the ride, she had made an incredible record of a thousand miles—with 36,000 feet of climbing—in 3 days, 11 hours and 44 minutes (compared to Lilian's 4 days, 19 hours and 14 minutes), a time only two men had previously bettered. She later said she'd felt that she had the energy to do another thousand. If she hadn't already done more than enough to disprove the theory that "it takes a man to do a twelve" wrong, then she certainly had now. However, all around her the town was in total darkness; unbeknownst to Marguerite and her team, war had officially been declared during the record attempt, and the country was now under enforced blackout every evening. She had achieved something remarkable, but understandably her celebrations were marred by the terrible news. She arrived back in London to the sound of the first air-raid sirens.

Marguerite continued to set records during the first few years of war, but her attempts were thwarted by wartime measures— the removal of road signs, sudden roadblocks and the cessation of weather forecasts, which were crucial to planning long rides that require advantageous conditions. In 1941, she had to put cycling aside completely to join the war effort, volunteering as an ambulance driver in Southampton. She told a fellow cyclist that she would "never be able to forgive Hitler" for putting an end to her career.

She got back into the sport when she relocated to Canada in 1948 with her husband, Ronnie, but when she joined a Canadian cycling club, she was required to prove herself once again. On her first rides the men did their utmost to try to drop her as quickly as they could, much as Eileen had experienced in her early days. The Canadians were "astonished" that instead of being left in their dust, Marguerite could more than keep up. She started competing in amateur races and the men became less hostile toward the speedy Brit. When she eventually returned home, the U.K.'s National Cyclists' Union refused to grant her an amateur racing license because she had previously raced as a professional. This, combined with a back injury, signaled the end of her days as a competitive cyclist.

Marguerite would have seen her records tumble as Eileen set to work on bettering each and every one. On June 9, 1954, the Mighty Atom set off to take on the jewel in Marguerite's crown, her End-to-End and one thousand miles, the latter having remained unbeaten for fifteen years. Eileen had been in Cornwall for weeks, carefully preparing for this mammoth ride, but as she set off from Land's End on her steel bicycle with three gears (like Marguerite before her), it turned out to be far from the clement summer weather the team had expected. It wasn't long before Eileen was doing battle with strong crosswinds and unseasonably cold rain.

By the time she reached Exeter, 120 miles away, she was already thirty minutes down on the schedule she needed to keep to in order to improve on Marguerite's record. Nevertheless, she rode for twelve hours straight without taking her feet from the pedals, refueling with food stored in a canister on her handle-bars. Her first break off the bike was momentary, just long enough to put on warmer clothing and some bike lights for the moonless and rainy night of riding ahead of her.

After twenty-four hours and over 450 miles, including some tough climbs in the Lake District, she came across a group of expectant journalists who hoped by this point she would stop for her first proper break and update them on her progress. She just pedaled on past. At the 470-mile mark, the cold finally got to her, so she stopped to warm up in the caravan being towed behind her, changing her wet clothes and filling up on hot soup by the gas fire. She allowed herself a fifteen-minute nap which—unbelievably—she says left her feeling "wonderfully fresh" and ready to tackle the next eight hundred miles. Even so, her manager insisted on carrying her onto her bicycle to preserve her energy.

On the road again, she battled strong headwinds and torrential rain while struggling up the big hills over the Scottish border—it a low point point of the ride and Eileen suffered. Yet she wasn't about to give in and eventually the rain eased off. After Perth, she was cycling into her second night, through the Grampian Mountains, which loomed eerily out of the darkness, snowdrifts visible in their crevasses, the temperature plummeting. After 673 miles, frozen feet and blistered hands forced another brief stop to thaw out in the caravan. Her manager wrapped more tape round the handlebars to save her injured hands as Eileen put on a second pair of gloves before heading into the darkness.

It wasn't until she'd completed seven hundred miles and was suffering badly from the cold that she relented and took a nap—for thirty minutes. As dawn broke on the third morning, blue skies and sunshine helped lift her spirits during a slog over more

Scottish mountains. But the break in the weather didn't last; as the day wore on she was again up against the wind once more, enduring cold and intense tiredness. She persevered and finally reached her destination of the John o'Groats Hotel that evening, in a total of just 2 days, 11 hours and 7 minutes. She had beaten Marguerite's record by 11 hours and 45 minutes.

After a bath and snooze of just under two hours in total, she was back in the saddle for another 130 miles in the hope of adding the thousand-mile record to her wins. This last push was grueling, with prolonged lack of sleep and physical exhaustion so acute that she began to hallucinate. First, she started seeing people who were directing her the wrong way, then in the hedges in the darkness on either side of her, large and brightly colored animals, including polar bears, appeared. Before long she was dodging imaginary obstacles on the road ahead. After sixty miles, it was too dangerous to continue so she slept for an hour, but of course it wasn't anywhere near enough, and when she set off again, she was falling asleep while turning the pedals. After another thirty miles, she had to stop and sleep for an hour to minimize the very real possibility of a crash. Her manager forked food into her mouth because her hands were too sore to hold the cutlery.

Once on the road again, she was buoyed by the reemergence of the sun and the appearance of Lilian Dredge, that first female 1,000-mile record holder, cheering her on as she approached the last twenty miles. It put a spring in her pedal stroke, and by the time Eileen neared the John o'Groats Hotel for the second time, her pace had quickened to an average of eighteen to twenty miles an hour. She arrived back at the hotel's front door with 3 days and 1 hour on the clock, a mammoth 10 hours, 44 minutes ahead of Marguerite's own thousand. Only one man at that point had recorded a faster time, and it was forty-eight years before

Eileen's record was broken, when Lynne Biddulph did the same route in 2 days, 16 hours and 38 minutes.

Housewives and Hardmen

Cycling culture celebrates those who suffer. This is why the big multistage races like the Giro d'Italia and Tour de France are so long and, to mere mortals, seem impossibly challenging.

The sport's icons are given the godlike status of "hardmen" on account of the epic amounts of pain they overcome to win. Men like Andy Hampsten and Bernard Hinault have gone down in history for races in which they have persevered and triumphed through dangerous amounts of snow, ice and sub-zero temperatures, conditions which forced many others to abandon the race; riders like Fausto Coppi, who was compared by some to the crucified Christ when he was close to complete physical and mental breakdown during the 1951 Tour de France; or Louison Bobet, winner of the Tour for three consecutive years in the early 1950s, but at the expense of saddle sores that resulted in such serious tissue damage that large amounts of his flesh had to be surgically removed.

By contrast, Eileen was described by one writer as a "dainty lady." And in a 1956 British Pathé short film where she is shown feeding her baby daughter and putting her to bed before starting her training, cycling on rollers and lifting weights in the garage, the commentator lists her incredible records, then ends by saying "No wonder she wins races, she has to in order to get back to catch up with the housework." It's hard to imagine them saying the same about Louison Bobet, who won the Tour de France less than two months after Eileen was on the road to John o'Groats and who held himself in such high regard that he often referred to himself in the third person—although I doubt he did that much vacuuming when he was off the bike.

Eileen wouldn't have been offended by the film; she was as proud of being a wife and mother as she was of her achievements on the bike. But throughout her career she continually came up against the idea that women should leave the cycling, and all the pain, suffering and glory that comes with it, to the men. One audience member at an event in 1953 told her it was "wrong" for women to compete in sports and that she should stay in the kitchen. Yet what she, Marguerite and Lilian before her went through during their record attempts involved an epic amount of endurance and suffering—although thankfully no surgery. They could more than handle the pain; like the bikes they rode, they were made of steel. They were unbeatable, and having to fit their training and racing around a packed schedule of work, childrearing and housework wasn't about to stop them riding to victory.

Before Eileen turned professional and could give up her job to focus on her training, she would carefully manage her schedule to make sure she always had time to train. This would involve rising early to get her household chores done, sometimes even baking a cake, leaving just enough time to cycle to the office, pedaling at breakneck speed through the streets, straight through the car showroom where she worked, and dismounting at her desk. She had the evenings free to cover as many miles as she could. While doing chores like the washing up, she would be working on the strategy for her next race.

When Eileen was pregnant with her first child, Clive, in 1946, she did feel a slight sense of trepidation, writing in her memoir that she was worried that the "happy and longed-for event" might "put an end to my racing career." After the birth, a friend asked Eileen if she had put racing behind her for good. Six months later the friend had her answer when Eileen was back on her bike and winning races, showing that motherhood was no barrier. Her doctor had told her to refrain from cycling for a year after giving birth, but within seven weeks she was back in the saddle again.

As her later remarkable records show, her greatest achievements were still ahead of her. It wasn't long before baby Clive was joining Eileen on her training rides, where he would sleep in a little trailer attached to her husband's bike. When Clive was bigger, she placed him in a seat on the back of her bicycle, his weight providing an extra training challenge, particularly when going uphill.

Pat Seeger of the Rosslyn Ladies was another mother who didn't see why the birth of her son, Tony, meant the end of her racing days. She tells me that during her pregnancy she continued going out on her bike until she could no longer fit comfortably behind the handlebars. After Tony was born, she too put him in a sidecar trailer so she could join the others on the weekend club runs. In those days there was less traffic on the road, so many members with small children did the same.

The Yorkshire Housewife

By the time Eileen took the decision to retire—after breaking and still holding all twenty-one existing records held by the Women's Road Record Association by 1955—another British cyclist who would come to be considered one of the greatest athletes of all time and who embodied the "hardman" ideal was also putting in the miles with her baby in a sidecar.

Beryl Burton was nineteen when she gave birth to Denise in 1956, and her astonishing decades-long international career was very much ahead of her. Denise accompanied Beryl to all her races from when she was a tiny baby, along with her dad, Charlie. Before Beryl met Charlie, she had barely been on a bike. They had met at the clothing factory in Leeds where they both worked, and soon started dating, with Charlie, a keen cyclist and amateur racer, lending Beryl a bike so they could ride together.

There was little to indicate then that Beryl would go on to have the stellar career on the bike that she eventually did. As a child she had been struck with rheumatoid fever shortly after unexpectedly breaking down in the middle of her 11-plus school exam, and so failing. The illness left her temporarily paralyzed and with limited speech, keeping her in the hospital for nine months, then off school recovering for over a year, resulting in her leaving school at fifteen. She was warned by her doctor to avoid strenuous exercise as they believed the illness had weakened her heart. But when she fell in love with cycling, she didn't give it a second thought. She had found something she enjoyed and through sheer determination—an attribute that was at the core of all she achieved—could succeed in. And so she began powering past the competition. She later described her astonishing career as "retribution" for having endured such trauma.

In 1957, the year after Denise was born, Beryl won three national titles. Two years later, she raced on the track in Liège in Belgium and won her first world title. Her career is so lengthy and outstanding that it's impossible to describe in its entirety here—we don't even have an accurate record of how many races she won as they are so numerous, possibly close to a thousand according to some sources. What we do know is she achieved seven gold world titles across track and road, plus dozens of national championships, and she held the U.K. Road Time Trials Council's women's Best All-Rounder title (the same award Eileen won twice) for twenty-five consecutive years. She was the first woman to go under an hour for twenty-five miles, two hours for fifty miles, and under four hours for a hundred. Some of her record times remain unbeaten to this day. Yet she never turned professional. She worked out her own training programs and her career was entirely self-funded.

Beryl was such a dominant force in the sport that for decades few could beat her, much like the Belgian Eddy Merckx, who became an unstoppable force in European cycling at that time. While the press dubbed Eddy "the cannibal" for his determination, it's telling that Beryl was most frequently referred to as the "Yorkshire housewife." She did at least benefit from women's world records finally being officially recognized, unlike her predecessors. In 1955, the Union Cycliste Internationale (UCI) had finally relented and announced it would recognize women's world cycling records. That year Daisy Franks recorded the first ever "official" women's hour record at the Herne Hill Velodrome. This volte-face was largely thanks to Eileen Gray, a British former track cyclist whose own frustration about the lack of medals or titles for women competitors, and limited opportunities to race, led her to set up the Women's Cycle Racing Association and campaign for the women's side of the sport to be recognized internationally. She met a lot of opposition, particularly from the Netherlands, a country which even in the 1950s didn't think women should race.

Eileen eventually made many of her adversaries see sense, and in 1958, the UCI held the inaugural women's Road World Championship race in France—sixty-five years after the first men's one—which was won by Elsy Jacobs from Luxembourg. The Luxembourgers, however, had yet to come onboard with women's racing: Elsy may have been crowned world champion, as well as holding a new hour record that was unbroken for fourteen years, but she couldn't compete to be a national champion in her own country because women were not eligible at that time. Luxembourg belatedly woke up the following year, doubtless after recognizing they had some serious homegrown talent, and Elsy was finally able to add national champion to her growing list of palmarès in 1959.

One of the British women that Eileen Gray chose to represent Britain at that first Road World Championships was Eileen Cropper. Decades later she told a journalist about the huge gulf between the way the women's and men's teams were treated at the event, with a limited budget requiring the women's team to pay for most of their equipment themselves. At eighty-four, she was still outraged by the inequality, describing their accommodation as a "doss-house," three to a room. She recalled how race adjudicators employed guesswork to decide what order the riders came over the line after the winner. There was quite a difference too in the press coverage of the men's and women's races: "If the men did anything it was all over the papers" while "the women were ignored."

The resistance to female interlopers in a man's world continued, and Eileen Gray witnessed it repeatedly in her role of assisting women's teams competing at home and abroad. Once, while accompanying a team of British women to a competition in Leipzig, a member of the men's team sneaked off with all their spare inner tubes and tires (equipment they'd had to pay for themselves), in an attempt to scupper their chances. It didn't work and the team triumphed, coming home with gold, silver and bronze medals. Another time, the celebrated British cyclist Reg Harris had women banned from one track. This understandably enraged Eileen, who said later "it would have been nice to have had even a little of the amount of help that he's had. But we were never going to get it."

Discrimination only succeeded in making Eileen and her

team "more determined to succeed." She continued to push for equal opportunities in her later role as president of the British Cycling Federation, where her tireless campaigning to get women's cycling into the Olympic Games finally bore fruit in 1984.

According to Denise Burton, Beryl's daughter, her mother too refused to let anything stand in the way of her success, and many now consider her one of the greatest cyclists of all time. Like Eileen Sheridan, Beryl fitted her cycling around work and family life, doing more and more miles each evening after her already strenuous day job on a Yorkshire rhubarb farm. This work involved "carrying, lifting, bending, digging, all day long in all weathers" and left her body aching. After downing tools on the farm each evening, she would get on the bike, pedaling up to five hundred miles a week, often under the supervision of her boss, Norman "Nim" Carline, who was a formidable time-trialist.

Although her husband was a passionate cyclist, Beryl wasn't expected to stay home with the washing up so he could race— though she certainly managed to squeeze in her share of the housework when she wasn't training or heaving rhubarb. As Beryl began to win nearly every competition she entered, Charlie left his own racing days behind so he could support her fully. He was the reason she had taken up the sport, but he recognized she had the potential to become a true legend. Her daughter has since said that Beryl couldn't have achieved the victories she did without Charlie's support. He was her mechanic and driver (when they could afford a car and no longer had to cycle hundreds of miles to get to a race), he looked after Denise during her long hours of training and was her rock through good and bad during four decades of competing. Eileen Sheridan's husband, Ken, was similarly supportive, getting her bike ready when she put Clive to bed so she could get out to do some miles, encouraging her back on the bike after the birth of both her children, and helping her work out a training regime.

When their wives progressed from winning women's races to overtaking the men, there were more than a few feathers ruffled elsewhere. The "housewives" hadn't just entered this man's world; they were threatening to beat them at their own game. Eileen Sheridan sensed how it would go down when, in a 50-mile time trial in 1945, she passed all the other women competitors who had set off before her and started catching up with the men's field whose last rider had started off ten minutes before the women. No one had expected the women to catch up, but Eileen was so strong that she easily made up the time. As she drew up alongside the first man, she knew his pride would take a knock and said to him sympathetically, "Golly, isn't this tough," as she sped ahead. Eileen Cropper was less sympathetic when a male competitor in a time trial begged her not to pass him, responding, "Sod off, I'm passing you."

Beryl was such an outstanding cyclist that she became accustomed to frequently bettering men's times and distances. In 1967, Beryl entered a twelve-hour time trial in Yorkshire. As with Eileen Sheridan's 50-mile race, the women rode the same course as the men but were staggered some distance behind them. Beryl had soon passed all the other women in the field, and started catching and passing the men. At this point there was a twenty-one-mile gap between the men's and women's twelve-hour records; although many had anticipated that Beryl would rack up the most miles of all the women entered, no one expected that the "Yorkshire Housewife" was capable of bridging that gap to trouble the men's record.

After a hundred miles, she was only two and a half minutes down on the men's favorite, Mike McNamara. Another hundred miles and she had gained a couple of seconds on him. After 250 miles, with over eleven hours in the saddle and the sun starting to set, she had passed all ninety-eight other male cyclists in the event and could see Mike ahead of her. She had—extraordinarily—closed the gap between the men's and women's records and was about to pass him. At that moment even Beryl, who was more than used to overtaking men, was overcome by the immensity of the moment, writing in her autobiography: "I froze, the urge in my legs to go faster and faster vanished as though with the click of a switch. Goose pimples broke out all over me, and for some seconds I just stared at his heaving shoulders, the sweat-stained jersey. I could hardly accept after all those hours and miles I had finally caught up with one of the country's great riders."

She quickly recovered and was soon overtaking him in what has gone down as one of the most legendary moments in cycling history: as she pulled up alongside Mike—a man on course to make a new men's record, but who had no idea he was about to be overtaken by Beryl—she offered him a Liquorice Allsort. He took it, thanking her as she pulled ahead and continued on her record-breaking ride.

Even then, she felt conflicted: "There I was, first on the road, ninety-nine men behind me, not knowing whether to feel elated or sorrowful. Mac was doing a sensational ride but his glory, richly deserved, was going to be overshadowed by a woman." This was unusual for Beryl; in other races when she passed the men, she quite rightly had no qualms. One of her competitors recalled her shouting out, "Eh, lad, you're not trying" as she flew past. Mike's dented ego aside, she had much to celebrate. She had cycled 277.5 miles in twelve hours, beating the existing women's record by nearly forty miles. It was five miles more than the previous men's twelve-hour record. Mike had made a new record too, with 276.52 miles, but he hadn't managed to surpass Beryl. It was on account of this that she was awarded her third Bidlake Memorial Prize, the only time in the history of the prize it's been given to the same cyclist more than twice. It took two years for another man to beat her distance. It was fifty years before another woman improved on it—despite the technical developments in the interim—when, in 2017, Alice Lethbridge achieved 285.65 miles.

It seems that Mike never quite recovered from the shock of his defeat by a woman, since he refused to talk about that day. Beryl, on the other hand, was granted the opportunity to take part in the Grand Prix des Nations in Cannes the following year, the first and only time a woman was allowed in this prestigious time trial in its seventy-two-year history. She had to ride before the men, and her time was unofficial, but she finished so far ahead of expectations that the last few laps, which took place in the velodrome, occurred while another race was still taking place—no one had expected her to arrive back so soon. The Grand Prix was won by "the Phoenix," Felice Gimondi, but Beryl was only twelve minutes slower and just one minute behind the last man, all of whom were highly decorated, full-time professional cyclists.

She continued setting records into the early 1980s and was awarded her twenty-fifth and final consecutive Best All-Rounder in 1983. She never stopped cycling. Fittingly, but tragically, she died on her bike when out delivering invites to her fifty-ninth birthday in 1996. She had been scheduled to take part in a 10-mile national time trial the following weekend. Many believe her heart gave out from being pushed so hard for decades. Her lengthy list of achievements is unique and phenomenal in the cycling world, one in the eye for anyone who thinks women aren't up to it, though sadly we will never know what she might have achieved had women been allowed to compete in the Olympics. If she'd had the benefit of later technological advances in bikes and training, I can only guess her records would be even more astounding and unbeatable.

Now that more women have the opportunity to partake in tougher sporting events, we are seeing evidence that, in the world of ultra-endurance events, which would include something as arduous as Beryl's twelve-hour or Eileen and Marguerite's End-to-Ends, the gap between the sexes starts to level out, with women regularly beating the men, much as Beryl showed all those decades ago. In 2016, Alaskan Lael Wilcox was the first to finish the 4,200-mile Trans Am Bike Race, which crosses the United States from the Pacific to Atlantic coasts. The previous year she had set a new women's record on the Tour Divide, a 2,745-mile mountain-bike route the length of the Rockies, from Canada to the Mexican border.

Then, in 2019, Germany's Fiona Kolbinger made history as the first woman to win the punishing Transcontinental Race outright, cycling 2,485 miles from Bulgaria to France in 10 days, 2 hours and 48 minutes. She crossed the finish line over six hours ahead of the next person. In the world of ultra-endurance running that same year, the U.K.'s Jasmin Paris won the tough 268-mile Montane Spine Race. She broke the existing record by twelve hours, sleeping for just seven hours out of over eighty-three hours on the trail. On top of this, she also managed to find time to express milk for her baby.*

---

* Remarkably, women's capabilities in sports are still doubted by some, and in a revealing 2019 YouGov poll, one in eight men said they thought they would be able to score a point off Serena Williams, possibly the greatest tennis player in the world right now.

Dirt Grrrls

Beryl had broken new ground for women cyclists, and by the time she retired from international contests in the mid-1980s, women's cycling was entering a new era which, although still a long way from being equal to the men's, was finally presenting women with long-overdue opportunities to prove what they were capable of. And the more they proved they could hold their own in competition, the harder it became for critics to say they would be better off sticking to the washing up. Any doubters who still required further proof need only look at a scene emerging on the West Coast of America in the 1970s and early '80s, where a group of women cyclists were riding hard and fast over the concept of the "dainty lady."

The origins of mountain biking (MTB) are contested ground, but it's generally accepted that a group of cycle-mad hippies living in Marin County in the late 1960s and '70s played a major part in inventing what was then a new type of bike and riding style. Many were competitive road cyclists who found the scene conformist and rule-obsessed. After all, this was just over the bridge from San Francisco's Haight-Ashbury district, the epicenter of the counterculture movement, psychedelia and the summer of love.

To let off steam, the group took to riding around the dirt tracks of Mount Tamalpais on old balloon-tire cruisers from the 1930s and '40s that they had scavenged from junkyards—the type of heavy (44-pound plus) bikes that the likes of Joan Crawford had once promoted, and now, due to their weighty construction, proved a more robust option for off-road biking. These adapted bikes became known as "clunkers." Enthusiasts began to create their own bikes that were more suited for their style of fast downhill riding over rough ground.

It started out as a collaborative and anticonsumerist scene, with bikes made from salvaged parts, a pure DIY ethos, but would end up making a huge amount of money for some of the early founders when the scene exploded into the mainstream in the mid-1980s. The development of the mountain bike was a revolution in cycling and is now such a significant part of the industry that it's hard to imagine there was a time when people just didn't think of venturing off tarmac. Those who did feel the urge, found there were no bikes designed to handle the terrain. It was a new frontier, one that was adrenaline fueled, exhilarating, brought you closer to nature, away from cars and urban areas, but could also result in some seriously nasty, even fatal, spills.

Downhill MTB riders descend at high speeds down steep and technical courses, often off-season ski slopes, covered in rocks, ruts, tree roots and other obstacles. It's fast and furious and all over in around five minutes. The first ever downhill event, which became known as the Repack race and ran sporadically from 1976 to 1984, took place on a steep two-mile stretch of near-vertical fire road on Tamalpais. If you look at photographs of these early races, it's a challenge to spot a woman among the lineup of men tearing down the trail in jeans and work boots. Some of those men became famous, like Gary Fisher, whose name is synonymous the world over with mountain bikes. It remains an uncompromisingly dangerous sport, especially back then when the bikes were still a long way from having evolved into the kind of machines you can buy today, which are lighter in weight with added advantages like suspension and disc brakes.

What isn't obvious from those early photos is that many of them were taken by a woman. And when she wasn't behind the camera, Wende Cragg would join the men on the Tamalpais trails and down the Repack course.

From its origins, MTB has tended to have a reputation for being a tough and stereotypically "masculine" sport. It is aggressive, dirty and sometimes dangerous—all the things women have traditionally been encouraged to stay away from. It's true that there are many more men taking part, even today, than women. There have, however, always been women who have helped shape, define and progress the sport over the decades, women who have helped recast to "ride like a girl" as something fast, fearless and unapologetically dirty.

In the mid-1970s, when Wende first started fat-tire biking, she was for some time the only woman among her group of pioneering enthusiasts out on the trails. She still lives in Fairfax, the town nestled at the foot of that mountain, and I talked to her via e-mail about what it was like to be part of this new movement in cycling. She describes the small group she cycled with, which included her now ex-husband Larry and a few local male friends and neighbors, as something more akin to a "tribe" who felt themselves to be "the lone explorers of a new world that had just opened up to us." She liked the fact they were "under the radar" and just doing their own thing.

However, she admits she nearly didn't fall for mountain biking at all. Her first ever foray on a 55-pound "behemoth" up the peak in August 1975 left her swearing she would never get back on again. It was hot and dusty, there was a lot of pushing the weighty machine on the uphill, and she found the narrow paths down the mountain, or single track, quite terrifying. Unlike the others she rode with, she was at more of a disadvantage as she hadn't been a cyclist at all up until that point. What got her back on the bike was the extent to which the experience made her feel so connected to the stunning scenery on her doorstep. As she got more adept at handling the challenging terrain, as well as her cumbersome bike, she grew progressively more adventurous, enjoying the "thrill of discovery" of both self and surroundings. It became something she just had to do: "the perfect fit for my innate desire for fun and adventure. The sense of freedom and jubilation was intoxicating and addicting, and before long, it became apparent I needed my daily 'fix.'"

The races began as a "lark," but went on to become highly competitive—participants were always relieved when they reached the finish line alive. For the first eighteen months, she was the only woman riding and racing on Mount Tam. Far from putting her off, she says that it never really occurred to her that she was the "lone ranger" as the only woman. As a child she had always been more drawn to the games played by her brothers than her sisters and was used to being the token "tomboy." This may explain why she didn't find the situation that daunting or unusual, allowing herself to be too much "in the moment" to give it a second thought. It seemed to her that the bike was an "equalizer," with the power to "transform gender and cultural restrictions."

Wende says it wasn't always about racing downhill as fast as possible. Some days the group would just relax and enjoy the scenery, picnicking by the river with their dogs, berry and mushroom picking along the way. Not that she shied away from the racing side—she still holds the fastest woman's Repack race time down that two-mile "sinuous and ruthless" 1,300-foot descent, complete with cavernous ruts and holes, giant rocks, hairpin turns and endless obstacles that caused countless falls, some more serious than others.

Wende also ventured farther afield with her bike, and in 1978, traveled to Colorado with five other members of the Mount Tam group, where she became the first woman to take part in the now legendary Pearl Pass Tour. The event still takes place today and is an infamously punishing thirty-eight-mile, then two-day, route from Crested Butte to Aspen via the 12,700-foot Pearl Pass along an old mule path once used to bring ore down from the mines. The Colorado group that had created the tour two years previously had been on the verge of pulling out and leaving it to the Californians and their superior bikes, but when they realized Wende would be doing it too, their machismo stopped them giving in.

Wende describes the ascent up to the pass as more about "tenacity and endurance" than speed, with many sections involving carrying or pushing the bikes, passing over multiple icy streams. The rocky and narrow descent into Aspen the following day was a "brutal shakeup" and nothing short of "a true test of fortitude." This edition of the event has since gone down in legend as one of the pivotal moments in the birth of the sport. The Pearl Pass Tour remains a serious undertaking, not for the fainthearted; one can only imagine the fortitude it required in 1978 when everything was a lot more rudimentary, to say the least.

When MTB exploded in the mid-1980s and the races became increasingly serious and regulated, with corporations coming in to sponsor riders, Wende admits it wasn't really something she wanted to play a part in. She feels incredibly proud of having been a pioneer in the sport, "especially as a female on the forefront of a boom that eventually went worldwide and changed the face of the cycling industry forever." Her photo archive, now stored at the Marin Museum of Bicycling, is an important record of the birth of the sport and her unique position within it. She tells me she feels a huge sense of joy whenever she sees a girl "straddling a fat-tire bike." The sport has changed in so many ways, not least the bikes and the many types of MTB, which includes cross-country, enduro, freeride and others—and there are more women hitting the dirt and single track than ever before.

Many of today's female competitors would have been inspired by the incredible women competing in races as it became professionalized in the 1980s and '90s, some who rode with Wende in the early days and others who came after, leaving an indelible mark in what was still an overwhelmingly male-dominated sport.

There were riders like Denise Caramagno, one of the few women who crossed over with Wende at those early races and is responsible for coming up with the now ubiquitous phrase "fat-tire," which she used to name the magazine she cowrote, *Fat-Tire Flyer*, the first devoted to the sport. Or Jacquie Phelan, who stood out on the start line of races for her unorthodox outfits which included polka-dot tights and a helmet with a rubber duck glued on top. She switched from road racing to MTB in the early 1980s, winning the first race she entered. Jacquie was a national champion for three years in a row from 1983, back when there were no separate men's and women's races because there were still so few female competitors. Another was Juli Furtado, whose brief but stellar career (sadly cut short by a diagnosis of lupus) started with the first UCI MTB world championships in 1990, where she won in the cross-country (XC) race, and ended with her representing the United States at the Olympics in 1996. At the point of her retirement, she held a Guinness World Record for holding the most first-place finishes in MTB (male or female), which at that time exceeded the combined total wins of the most successful man and next most successful woman.

The Missile

One downhill competitor from the 1990s particularly stood out, not only for her formidable skill and domination of the competition, but for her audacious bad-ass attitude, which saw her catapulted to something close to rock star status. Missy Giove was definitely no "dainty lady," she was "the Missile," a punk-rock icon who embodied the phrase "go big or go home." Among numerous other major wins, she bagged eleven World Cup medals in downhill, putting her body through all kind of punishment in the process. She was a highly skilled rider, but hurtling down the toughest and most technical downhill courses in the world at close to 60 mph is guaranteed to result in some spills.

A journalist once described her race style as "like a nuclear bomb exploded here, here, and here, all the way down the course." Which may in part explain why her tally of broken bones was so high, an estimated thirty-eight, including both kneecaps and heels, ribs, collarbone and pelvis. She endured multiple concussions, and in one particularly terrible accident at the 2001 World Championships, she suffered a brain hemorrhage. It's a sobering medical record, and certainly nothing to celebrate, particularly since the effects of the hemorrhage were a big part of her decision to retire in 2003, but it does convey the fearlessness and commitment that so defined her.

"I'm not afraid of death, I wouldn't be who I am if I was," Missy once told an interviewer. "I love that experience of flying. It's a very liberating feeling to not be worried about anything but that one moment." Her philosophy was about seizing the day: "You're only here once and that's it. You better live it up." For over a decade there was almost nothing that would stop her getting back on her bike, sometimes straight after a new break. She was unmissable at the start line, with hair that ranged from dreadlocks to short bleached-blond crop or dyed two-tone to match her bike, multiple piercings and tattoos, and with unusual lucky charms that made headlines, including the desiccated body of her pet piranha, Gonzo, that hung from a necklace, and the ashes of her beloved dog Ruffian, which she sprinkled in her bra before each race. A huge personality and an outstanding athlete, she was invited on television talk shows with the likes of Jon Stewart and Conan O'Brien, as well as guest-hosting on MTV— programs that wouldn't normally take the time to talk to stars of niche sports. At races, legions of teenage boys lined up for her autograph.*

Missy grew up in New York and first got paid to ride a bike delivering Chinese food as a teen in the city. She always found the city suffocating and longed for the mountains, eventually jumping on her bike to relocate to Vermont, where her grandparents lived. It was there she got into downhill skiing, winning the junior national championships in 1990, and earning herself a college scholarship in the process. It says a lot about her level of grit that when she was starting out and couldn't afford a lift pass, she would just hike up to the top of the slopes to ski down.

As part of her off-season training, she discovered mountain biking and immediately fell in love. That same year, she packed her tent and hitchhiked from Vermont to Colorado for the first ever UCI World MTB Championships, the same event where Juli

---

* If you type "Missy Giove" into an Internet search engine today, the first thing that will come up is her arrest for smuggling a large quantity of marijuana across states in 2009. It would be odd not to mention it, as it was a story that shocked many in the sports world. I'm not going to go into the rights and wrongs of what she did, instead focusing specifically on Missy's significant contribution to women's mountain biking, which I don't believe is negated by what came later.

Furtado won the women's XC. She acquired a race license and rode in her first downhill competition, where she was spotted by John Parker, manager of Yeti, Juli's team, who immediately handed her a team jersey after recognizing that the gutsy and maverick rider would be a winning addition.

Her career went from strength to strength, with spectators always guaranteed an electrifying and exhilarating performance as Missy shredded the trails at full throttle. A commentator at the 1999 MTB World Cup in Les Gets, France, summed up Missy and her career: "She's a wild rider, probably one of the wildest in the women's field today. But despite that wildness she's so consistent, usually in the top three."

Within a few years of joining Yeti, she was winning world championships and World Cup medals consistently until 2001. During that time, she moved on to elite team Volvo-Cannondale, which was throwing a lot of money into the sport and their riders at that time. Missy starred in ads for Reebok, was photographed by Annie Leibovitz and even featured in a computer game. The cycling press couldn't get enough of her, filling column inches on her supposed bitter rivalry with dominant French MTB and BMX racer Anne-Caroline Chausson.

Even with men's racing dominating the media spotlight so much, Missy succeeded in getting them to pay attention. And she didn't have to compromise to do so. She once told a journalist that she thought it was a "cool thing" she could be a role model while not having to look like Barbie. Moreover, she has never shied away from being open about her sexuality.

Sport has a problematic history with homosexuality, something it still struggles with. Many athletes in the public eye have felt unwilling to reveal their sexuality for fear it will lose them lucrative sponsorship deals or they will suffer homophobic attacks. None more so than in the hypermasculine world of male

soccer, where according to some reports the problem of homophobia is getting worse, not better, with homophobic chants
often still heard at matches. When the U.K.'s Justin Fashanu
came out in 1990, he suffered such abuse that it's widely believed
it was a significant factor in his suicide eight years later. Since
then no other professional soccer player in the U.K.'s Premier
League has come out. It's a very different picture in women's
soccer today, with Megan Rapinoe, along with around forty
other players and coaches in the 2019 Women's World Cup, openly
gay or bisexual. It's taken a while to get to that point, though.

This is an incredibly nuanced issue that needs a whole book to
explore, but it's true to say that sports have been so deeply associated with stereotypes of red-blooded, heterosexual masculinity—
those hardmen—that it has struggled to accept anyone seen as
deviating from "the norm." Athletic women, on the other hand,
have long been typecast as gay because they deviate from what
constitutes acceptable femininity, much like when the teen pro-
tagonist in the 2018 film *The Miseducation of Cameron Post* is
sent to a Christian conversion camp to "cure" her of being gay:
the adults in charge conclude that her attraction to girls was triggered by her love of running.

The conflation of women's sports and homosexuality led to
the Rosslyn ladies and others being labeled lesbians, even when
it was untrue. For sportswomen who were in fact gay, to come
out risked confirming deep-seated and erroneous prejudices and,
more crucially, being treated with hostility. They were also
likely to earn less: tennis star Martina Navratilova estimated she
lost $10 million in endorsement deals when she came out in the
1980s. She was one of the first sports superstars to be openly gay
and met a fair amount of animosity for it. By contrast, a 2019
photo of Swedish soccer player Magdalena Eriksson celebrating
her team's entry into the quarterfinals of the World Cup by kiss-

ing her girlfriend, Danish player Pernille Harder, was seen
around the world and widely celebrated. Not that the problem
has gone away entirely, but it shows we are now at a point when
prejudices around female sexuality and sports might finally be
eroding.

Cycling, like many sports, remains in thrall to an outdated
hypermasculine and heterosexual ideal of hardmen, a culture
that Philippa York, a former professional cyclist who transi-
tioned from male to female after having competed at the highest
level of the sport, has said means that "anyone thought to be
different has been singled out for ridicule or presented as some
kind of danger." She has been open about her own transition in
the hope that the sport will become more progressive, breaking
down barriers around gender and sexuality.

Back in the 1990s, homophobia was rampant across many aspects of society, so it's understandable few people in sports, unlike Martina and Missy, were willing to be openly out. Missy
also once said she thought being openly gay meant she made less
money, but she had no regrets: "it's important to represent who
you are because it gives other people strength." She was out and
proud, talking about her girlfriends and being photographed for
gay magazines, showing there was nothing shameful about being
a gay woman doing sports or anything else she chooses. Many
have felt MTB, as a newer discipline, has always been more open
and progressive, which may explain why her sexuality wasn't the
issue it might have been had she been in a more traditional sport.

Missy thrived in the fast, dangerous and exhilarating environment, never doubting she could ride as hard as those in the
men's field. It became part of her DNA, and in 2015, aged forty-
three, twelve years after her retirement, she made an appearance
on the course at the UCI World Cup at Windham. Her wife, who
had been diagnosed with cancer, had wanted to see her race at a

world championship, and so Missy got back on the bike. Though she had barely ridden in the last ten years, she finished sixteenth on the day. She hadn't expected to win but told reporters she hoped to be an inspiration to others. It's good advice from a woman who had never allowed anything to hold her back and who wasn't about to let age get the better of her.

U.S. ultra-endurance athlete Rebecca Rusch, who didn't even start competing in MTB until she was thirty-eight, would agree with Missy. She has since gone on to win national and world championships in XC and twenty-four-hour MTB races, earning her the title "Queen of Pain" and a career that is one of the most inspirational in any sport. Meanwhile, Missy's former nemesis, Anne-Caroline Chausson, also now in her forties, has survived ovarian cancer and is back on her bike.

Depth of Field

Many in MTB feel that their sport is inclusive and welcoming, less snobbish and rule-obsessed than older disciplines like road cycling, but it's impossible to get away from the fact that it too has far fewer women taking part than men, and even fewer from diverse ethnic backgrounds. It's difficult to obtain figures on the gender split, but in 2016, one U.S. MTB magazine estimated that its readership was around 15 percent female, which led them to calculate as few as two in ten people out on the trails are women, whereas in a sport like running it's equal—in 2015, 57 percent of all finishers in running races were female.

Sabra Davison, a former professional mountain biker, and her sister, Lea (an Olympic-level competitor), were often the only women on their team when they started out in the early 2000s. There were also noticeably far fewer women on the start line at races. When I spoke to her on the phone from her home in Vermont, she told me that they both felt incredibly encouraged and supported by the male riders around them. She admits that her experience wouldn't be for everyone: "When you are truly just an individual standing on your own. a lot of people find that a hard space to be in."

As a result, she and Lea created Little Bellas, a nonprofit MTB mentoring program for girls aged seven to sixteen to learn and ride together, to foster a sense of "community and camaraderie" which they hope will encourage more girls into the sport. Their cofounder, Angela Irvine, only learned to mountain bike at forty by trying to keep up with her male friends along the trails, so she knew all too well how having a more female-friendly space could encourage greater diversity. Sabra tells me the goal was to make the sport more "approachable" by creating a space where girls "feel safe and invited" since "it's potentially not a sport that naturally lends itself to that."

Their organization has chapters across the country and is so successful they have waiting lists of up to four years in some areas. They offer scholarships to ensure everyone has a chance to join, regardless of family income, as well as sponsors who subsidize the entry fee for each girl to keep costs at a minimum. This is just one of many groups across the United States and Europe now helping the sport become more diverse and open by providing supportive spaces for women, people of color and LGBTQ cyclists. This is an idea that goes back as far as the 1980s, when Jacquie Phelan founded her legendary WOMBATS, the Women's Mountain Bike & Tea Society, a series of camps to encourage women into a sport that was then even more white and male-dominated than it is today.

That sense of being outnumbered in the sport is something Anissa Lamare knows intimately. Twenty-three-year-old Anissa, or Suri to her friends, comes from the northeastern Indian city of Shillong, part of the mountainous region of Meghalaya, which translates as "the abode of the clouds." Nestled between Bangladesh and Bhutan, with peaks that reach nearly 6,600 feet, as well as high-mountain and lush tropical lowland forests, Meghalaya is ideal territory for off-road biking.

The tribes of the province have traditionally operated a matrilineal system, with inheritance passed down to the youngest daughter, a rarity today in India and elsewhere. Yet despite the region's female-centric stance, in its MTB competitions there is no category for women. The same is true in races in other regions in the country. Which means that Anissa, who first took up downhill MTB when she was seventeen, has been forced to enter in the men's category, first in the junior men's races and now the elite men's. The same was true for Wende forty years ago, as the only woman taking on the Repack race on Mount Tam against a field of men.

Like California back then, the sport in India today is very much at a nascent stage, with infrastructure and participation a long way behind Europe and the United States. The cost of a bike alone is enough to put it out of reach of many. Anissa believes she is probably the only woman taking part in downhill races in the country, because she has yet to come across any other female competitors at the events she has attended to date. There is no Indian equivalent of Little Bellas to get more girls and women to the start line, so Anissa stands out as a pioneer, making tracks that hopefully others will one day follow. She tells me over e-mail that when she signed up to her first competition— riding a BMX bike, as that was all she had—she knew almost nothing about the sport. She didn't even own a helmet. But once she'd experienced the overwhelming exhilaration of racing down the mountain, she was hooked. And she managed to get placed in the top ten.

Anissa immediately started saving up to buy a proper mountain bike. The nearest shop was three hours away; since she didn't want to return without a bike, she ended up coming home with one that was far too big. At under five feet, and in a country where there is almost no market for women's MTB, finding one that fit was always going to be a challenge. The frame was so outsized that in competitions she would resort to borrowing a friend's bike to get down the course, before once again saving for a (secondhand) bike designed for someone her height. She lovingly named her new mount Muse.

Rather than feeling put off by being the only girl out riding and competing, she initially liked being unique. But it wasn't long before the novelty wore off and she started longing to bike with and compete against her own gender. A lack that made her feel, because she couldn't legitimately compete as a woman, that ultimately there was no future for her in the sport. When she moved to Bangalore, over 1,800 miles south, to complete a master's degree in political science, she was forced to put a hold on competing entirely since the nearest MTB trails are over thirty miles away. The decision, she says, "hit me hard"; without biking as a release, she feels "life is just going to be filled with emptiness." She briefly considered dropping out of her course, but she knew that ultimately she couldn't because of the responsibility she has to support her family financially in the future.

She has stuck with it and will graduate in summer 2020. However, she has told her family that she intends to take time out after graduating to focus on competing in MTB again. Her desire to be on the bike, training for competitions, is, she tells me, "the part of me that will never die." Anissa hopes that she will make it to Europe, to finally test her skills against other women. Perhaps by that point, she won't be the only woman in India shredding the downhill trails. Just as Wende was once in the vanguard of MTB in the United States, it surely follows that Anissa will not be the lone pioneer for much longer. Perhaps one day she, or those that follow in her tire-tread marks, will also start their own Indian version of Little Bellas for a new generation of girls who will never know what it's like to not have a category of their own.

CHAPTER TWELVE

CAN YOU SEE US NOW?

For Want of a Yellow Jersey

In a turnout on a stretch of road heading south toward the Pyrenees out of the town of Limoux in Aude, southwest France, a group of women are pulling bikes out of vans. It's 7:30 a.m. on July 20, 2019, and after several weeks of scorching temperatures, it's currently drizzling with a slight chill in the air. Tomorrow, this road will be lined with spectators who will watch the participants of the 2019 Tour de France start out on stage fifteen, which this year is a challenging 115 miles—with over 14,000 feet of total climbing—ending on the summit of the Prat d'Albis.

The women getting onto their bikes today are going to be cycling that same route. They have also completed all fourteen prior stages, each one the day before the men take their turn, and will continue to do so right up to the final miles on the Champs-Elysées in Paris. There is no publicity caravan traveling ahead of them to hype up the crowds, no advance motorcade clearing the streets and filming them from every angle, and no press conference at the finish. This isn't the women's Tour de France, because there isn't one. These women are taking on the full 2,162 miles and 170,600 feet of climbing (the most mountainous in the Tour's history), as a protest against the failure of one of the world's most popular sporting events to allow women to compete.

Among the group are a team of thirteen French cyclists called the Donnons des Elles au Vélo J-1 (which roughly translates as "give her the bike") who have been riding every stage of the Tour for the last five years. This year they are joined by ten international riders named the InternationElles. Members of the general public are also encouraged to join them on each stage, but today it's just me hanging on to their back wheels as we head toward the mountains.

The first section moves along a fast road following the Aude River before we head gently uphill, passing forests and the ancient Château de Puivert. As we progress, other riders join the back of the group and villagers cheer us on, having heard about these women who are taking on the Tour. I hang at the back with the international team, none of whom has taken part in such an intensive and unrelenting event before, though more than a few are serious athletes with a history of competing in tough challenges such as Ironman triathlons. The Tour, however, is on another level. It's generally considered to be one of the most challenging endurance events of all, and though the women aren't racing each other, it is still an outstandingly demanding test. Many have had to take sabbaticals from their jobs, and a number have small children back at home, including Pippa, who gave birth to her son eleven months ago and only stopped breastfeeding him three times a day a few weeks before she flew out to Europe from her home in Australia.

Yesterday was another grueling mountain stage, 69 miles that ended with the 6,939-foot Col du Tourmalet, an iconic and punishing Tour de France climb. They then had to travel to the start line for the next stage, as well as get their bikes and kit ready for another long day. At most the group managed five hours' sleep. Yesterday's clothes are now hanging in the back of the InternationElles' support van to dry. It's true to say that no rider in the peloton of the official Tour will have to spend their time out of the saddle worrying about having a functioning bike or a clean pair of cycling shorts—they have teams of support staff, as well as luxurious buses kitted out with multiple washing machines and comfy beds. They also have nutritionists and chefs, and onboard masseurs to ease their overworked muscles. Apart from a skeleton support crew of four, these women have few such luxuries. And with no prize money to be won, they are funding the ride themselves.

When we start the climb up Montségur, the first mountain of the day, I find it hard to believe that the group is now on their fifteenth day as I watch most of them power up toward the Cathar castle on its peak. I'm left pedaling behind with a few others who are either feeling a little less fresh after so many mountainous miles or reserving their energy for the rest of the long day ahead. As we make our way up the more than nine miles of grinding ascent, people who've pitched their camper vans and tents at the side of the road, keen to make sure they have a good spot on the iconic mountain to watch the official race tomorrow, shout encouragement. It helps me push onward, as well as gives me just a tiny taste of the Tour de France experience from the other side.

The parents of Carmen, one of the InternationElles, have come down from the Netherlands to support her and appear near the top to rally her on. At the summit we regroup, refueling on bananas and energy bars under what are now clear blue skies, before the exhilarating and well-earned descent down the other side. It's at this point I leave the group to head back in the direction of the start, slightly relieved I won't have to tackle the three brutal remaining climbs, one of which is known as "the Wall."

The InternationElles handled it just fine and over the remaining six days, the two groups take on everything the Tour route planners were inflicting on the men the following day. What they perhaps hadn't bargained for was that temperatures in Nimes would soar to a hellish 118 degrees Fahrenheit, forcing them to resort to cooling off in a car wash. Or that they would ultimately end up riding a longer total distance than the men when an extreme hailstorm in the Alps, the day after the heat wave, caused icy conditions and then a mudslide on stage nineteen, resulting in the men's race being canceled midway.

As they pedaled up that iconic Parisian street toward the finish line, what they had more than proved was that if a group of amateur riders were able to handle it, then there is no question the pro women are more than capable.

They aren't the first to protest women's exclusion from this race. It's rumored that in 1908, a Frenchwoman named Marie Marvingt tried to enter, but after being refused, rode the entire course before the official race started. There doesn't seem to be any conclusive evidence to back this up, but I don't doubt Marie was more than able to do it. I can't go into all her incredible sporting and other achievements here, which range from swimming the length of the Seine to winning medals at the Winter Olympics, setting women's aviation records, disguising herself as a man to pilot bombing missions in World War I and working as a resistance fighter in World War II, but in short she is one of the most decorated French women in history and has the biography to match. Marie cycled two hundred miles from

Nancy to Paris when she was eighty-eight which, along with everything else, does suggest she would have been more than up to the challenge in 1908.

Fact or fiction, it highlights the extent to which women have been calling out the unfairness of this exclusion for almost as long as the race has existed, but it's far from the only inequality to have persisted in women's cycling. In fact, there's quite a list, including a hefty gender pay gap, fewer racing opportunities and less sponsorship, little or no media coverage, and a lack of diversity in general. Women's professional cycling is now finally changing for the better, though, thanks in part to a long line of inspirational activists—many professional cyclists themselves—who are calling on the sport to do better. They are disrupting what racer Nicole Cooke called the "sport run by men, for men" and pushing for change.

"Cycling Is Much Too Difficult for a Woman"

The absence of women from cycling's biggest and most watched event, the Tour de France, has had a complicated history. In 1984, the Amaury Sport Organization (ASO), the organizers of the Tour, launched the Tour de France Féminine. This eighteen-stage race offered something as close to the men's race as there had ever been, even if the UCI, the sport's governing body, would only allow a total maximum distance of no more than 620 miles compared to the men's 2,500 miles. The women raced before the men, finishing around two hours ahead each day, in front of the same crowds who were waiting to watch the men go past. This was the same year women's cycling finally entered the Olympics, and although it was just one event, it felt like a significant turning point. U.S. cyclist Connie Carpenter-Phinney (then just Carpenter), who won gold at that first women's Olympic road race, said she felt that "we were really going somewhere." Then the initial optimism around the women's Tour began to fizzle out because the press were so focused on the men's race. Many remained unconvinced women should be doing such a thing, not least former Tour de France winner Jacques Anquetil, who wrote in one paper that although he had "absolutely nothing against women's sports," he felt that "cycling is much too difficult for a woman. They are not made for the sport. I prefer to see a woman in a short white skirt, not racing shorts." Laurent Fignon, the winner of the 1983 Tour, was similarly unimpressed by women racing: "I like women, but I prefer to see them doing something else."

Two years later the women's event was down to just two weeks; and after another three years, the ASO had pulled out. The women's stage race limped on until 2009, going through a name change to Grande Boucle Féminine Internationale because the ASO saw any use of the word "Tour" as an infringement of their trademark. It suffered other problems too: chronic lack of sponsorship, riders not getting paid and the organizers going into serious debt. By 2009, its final outing, it was down to four stages.

The Grande Boucle Féminine was dead, but out of the cold ashes La Course emerged in 2014, a new women's race once again organized by the ASO. This long-overdue rethink was all down to campaigning by pro cyclists Marianne Vos, Emma Pooley, Kathryn Bertine and triathlete Chrissie Wellington. Its fifth edition took place the day before I joined the InternationElles on their stage fifteen and was won by Marianne.

So if the women have a race, why are these twenty-three women still protesting? Because while the men get twenty-one days of racing and the chance to compete for $2.6 million, the women get only one day with a total prize pot of just $25,000. As a result, it gets nowhere near the coverage of the men's mammoth contest. When Marianne went to the press conference after an exhilarating victory, she arrived to a room full of empty chairs and a handful journalists, one of whom tweeted "Embarrassing that one of the sport's greatest ever riders gets ignored like this." Mark Cavendish, one of the top men's pro cyclists and someone who has been vocal about the lack of equality in the sport, also tweeted "this genuinely makes me sad & embarrassed about where my sport is at."

It can sometimes feel like the Tour's infamous podium girls, the women who hand bouquets to the stage winners as they plant a kiss on their cheek, are more visible than the women of La Course. In 2013, pro cyclist Peter Sagan was seen on live television groping podium girl Maja Leye after he came second at the Tour of Flanders, which says a lot about how these women are viewed. This anachronistic tradition has long been called out for its inherent sexism, and in 2018, in the face of vocal opposition and petitions, the Tour organizers suggested they would finally end it. This was at the same time that the World Darts Championship and Formula One auto racing dropped their controversial "walk-on" and "grid" girls. The ASO decided not to follow through; instead it doubled down, announcing it would continue after all.

The Tour isn't the only race that matters, and there are other opportunities for women to take part in multiday road races that are more equivalent to the men's. Alfonsina Strada would, I'm sure, be pleased to know that sixty-four years after she made her grand Tour debut, the Giro finally launched a women's version, initially known as the Giro Donne and today it is known as the Giro d'Italia Internazionale Femminile, or Giro Rosa. At ten stages, it is currently the longest women's road race (though at one point it was sixteen), and for a few years it was the only multistage women's race, or Grand Départ. However, Alfonsina may wonder why its participants can only hope to win a fraction of what the men do: in 2018, overall winner Annemiek van Vleuten was awarded $1,250, which she then had to share with her teammates, while the winner of the men's race scooped $128,217. That same year, Chris Froome was paid $1.5 million just to take part.

Hard as it is to believe, it's a lot better than it was: in 2014, Marianne Vos received just $593 for making overall winner, compared to Nairo Quintana's $220,000. Women's cycling falls substantially short in prize money compared to many sports. Female tennis players at the world Grand Slams receive equal money to the men—thanks to the campaign work of former pro and activist Billie Jean King. In marathon running, track and field, and swimming, male and female finishers almost always receive the same. In soccer, the most popular sport, there is a huge gender pay gap, with players from the FA Women's Super League in 2019 being paid on average 2 percent of the earnings men command in the Premier League. This led to the U.S. women's team suing for equal pay after winning their second FIFA World Cup in a row. The U.S. men's soccer team has never made it to the semifinals, but had they got to just that stage, they would have been paid substantially more, around $550,000 each compared to the women's $90,000. While grossly unfair, it's much more than anyone competing in the Giro Rosa can hope to earn.

In many other races, it's a similar story. In the 2019 Tour of Flanders, the winner of the men's race received $22,000. The first woman over the line, Marta Bastianelli, got $1,400. The women's race was just under seventy miles shorter, but it's hard to agree it should be worth more than twenty thousand dollars less. It seems there hasn't been much progression since 1984, when Marianne Martin from the United States won the first ever women's Tour de France and received just over $1,000 compared to the men's winner, Laurent Fignon, who took home over $104,000. Marianne later said that taking part had left her out of pocket, though she never regretted it.

In women's professional cycling, lack of prize money and modest—or even no—salaries means many work other jobs on top of their racing and training to survive financially. It's telling that Olympic medal–winning cyclist Emma Pooley, who came second overall in the Giro Rosa in 2011 and 2012, told a journalist that she earned more money coming third in a triathlon in the Philippines than she has ever done cycling. Before her retirement, American Mara Abbott had won the Giro Rosa race twice, as many times as Vincenzo Nibali has won the men's event, but while he has earned millions, Mara says she lived a fraction above the poverty line. She is also an Olympian, but had to earn money outside of cycling to support herself during her racing career. Nicole Cooke, a Giro winner and Olympic gold medalist, alleged she wasn't even paid her team salary for three months in the run-up to the 2012 Olympics.

If Women Compete in a Cycle Race and No One Watches, Should They Get Paid?

Iris Slappendel, a retired competitive cyclist from the Netherlands, knows the problems faced by women in professional cycling intimately—she didn't get paid for six years of her career. In 2017, she decided to investigate just how endemic the gender pay gap is and surveyed around two hundred female road cyclists on their pay and work conditions. What she found was that a third of respondents made less than $6,500 a year, and the majority had to work a second job to survive. Over half of those who did receive a salary had to give some of it back to their team to pay for essential expenses.

Like Eileen Gray and other activists before her, Iris realized no one was going to fight to make changes for women's cycling on their behalf. Far from being sympathetic to the cause, one representative of the men's cycling union asked her, "Do you really think women are professional cyclists?" So Iris decided she would have to do it herself. Out of this came The Cyclists' Alliance, a union fighting for equality across all aspects of professional women's cycling, along the lines of the Women's Tennis Association set up by Billie Jean King in 1973 to push for the rights of women players.

Iris says that in her experience "women's cycling still feels like the last topic on the agenda of many stakeholders." It speaks volumes that in 2019 the sport's governing body, the UCI, has only two women on its eighteen-member management committee. Emma Pooley, who has been vocal about inequality on the women's side of the sport, once said that she thinks she is viewed by the industry as "some kind of weirdo, radical feminist" and "quite unpopular in some parts" as a result.

Iris has pushed hard for her members' rights. So far she has secured an agreement that by 2020, teams who take part in the elite series of women's road races known as the Women's WorldTour will have to pay their riders a minimum salary of $17,500, which will then rise to match men's Continental Teams salaries of $34,400 by 2023, as well as offering other essential benefits like pensions.

It's definitely a start, but she feels frustrated that she and others are required "to be activists just to be treated equally" and that for too long they were expected to "settle for less and not complain, simply because we are women." She thinks that one of the biggest problems blocking equality in road cycling is that there is so much money tied up in the big men's races. You only have to look at the hefty prize pots of the big races and the fact that the average UCI Men's WorldTour team has a budget of over $19 million, compared to an average women's team budget of around $195,000, to see that's evident. She thinks that this is due to the extensive media exposure of the men's races, with so many televised globally, bringing the sponsors and money flowing in.

Visibility is something that still holds women's racing back, with few events televised. The Giro Rosa, currently the longest women's race, has been notoriously hard to watch outside of Italy, though in 2019, highlights were streamed online after the race. It doesn't help that the race runs at the same time as the Tour de France, meaning that the world's media and cycling fans are almost exclusively focused on that race, which is broadcast live around the world. In an interview with the *Guardian* in 2016, Mara Abbott said that "it gets depressing" when "nobody knows what you're doing and you go off to races in the middle of nowhere and nobody's there." This led her to the conclusion that "so often money represents significance." It's a vicious circle, since the lack of coverage also means that sponsors are less willing to get onboard and so there is less money to go around to make a race people want to watch. Road racing also differs from stadium sports like soccer, in that it can't sell pricey tickets to fans, which makes it entirely reliant on sponsorship and selling media licenses.

The Tour de France has the most exposure of any race in the world, and as a result it's the richest. It's also a race which exposes the huge gulf in resources, money and attention between the men's and women's side of the sport at its most extreme level, inequalities that Emma Pooley has described, understandably, as making them look and feel like they are "second best." Connie Carpenter-Phinney feels now that in many ways women's racing has "flipped backward" since the 1980s and that "women cyclists struggle so much today to be seen."

Iris believes the audience is there, but they just aren't being given the opportunity to view the races. This is backed up by the 2016 Rio Olympics, where the women's road race was the fifth most watched event in France. And look at the incredible audience figures for the 2019 FIFA Women's World Cup, watched by over a billion viewers worldwide, with more media rights licenses granted to broadcasters than ever before. There are few people—not least one of the world's leading flag-bearers for misogyny, President Donald Trump—who don't know who Megan Rapinoe is. This watershed moment led to FIFA committing to expand the tournament from twenty-four to thirty-two teams in 2023.

Beyond the Road

It's not all glaring inequality in the world of women's cycling. In some disciplines things are much better, even if the gender pay gap hasn't quite closed. In mountain biking, women now get the chance to race in many elite competitions on the same course, for the same amount of time, and for the same prize money as men. The women's events are equally popular too: in 2018, the viewership on Red Bull TV for the women's World Championship event jumped from 99,000 the previous year to 233,000, putting it on a par with the men's event. Sabra Davison, who runs Little Bellas, the U.S.-wide organization encouraging more girls into the sport, tells me that women's MTB cross-country races now often attract more viewers than the men's. She thinks this is partly a result of the women's races often being more entertaining and unpredictable since there isn't one woman dominating every competition.

The sport has come a long way since 1990, when Jacquie Phelan was mistakenly handed the sixth-place prize envelope for the men's competition. It contained a check for $500. The one meant for her was just $45. In 2013, when Sabra got involved with the USA's Pro Mountain Bike Cross Country Tour, which was being held in her home state of Vermont, she was shocked to discover that women would only receive 65 percent of what the men did. She and her sister Lea approached the sponsor, who responded by increasing their contribution to the extent that the women came away with more money than the men. They all felt this would make a strong statement about the inequality at that time. Sabra tells me that when there is more money at stake, it is harder to make it equal. Men's elite road racing is a prime example, with top cyclists like Chris Froome earning as much as $3.9 million a year. She believes that where there are such big figures in contention, it makes for "a more electrified and politicized environment" and one that's harder to change.

Muddy and Equal

Cyclo-cross, which emerged in France and Belgium in the early 1900s, is another area where the women's side has now equalized in almost every way with the men. Races are fast and muddy laps for up to an hour over a short course (1.5 to 2 miles) which includes a variety of terrain—pavement, wooded trails, grass, steep hills, as well as obstacles over which the riders have to carry their bicycle. The woman responsible for pushing for positive change is Helen Wyman, British national champion from 2006 to 2015 and trailblazer for women's cycling.

I met Helen, along with her dog Alonso and two young female cross riders she is training, in a beautiful village in the Languedoc, southwest France, where she lives and trains. It was a sweltering June day and I had cycled twenty-five miles over some big hills from the village where I was living. I guessed she wouldn't bat an eyelid about me turning up sweaty and in cycling clothes to interview her. I was right.

In 2012, Helen was invited to join the UCI's Cyclo-cross Committee and took that as her opportunity to completely transform the way women were viewed and treated in the sport. The process was "brutally hard" and she had to fight for the changes she made. The first significant change she achieved was getting the women's UCI races moved from a morning slot, when few showed up to watch, to just before the men's race. It cost nothing, so it was difficult to refuse. This meant that journalists who previously hadn't shown up at the women's races were now there at the finish line and giving them media coverage.

The organizers of the prestigious DVV Cyclocross Series in Belgium, in an effort to show they lead the way, then committed to put all their women's races on live TV. They were an instant success; audiences have grown rapidly and they now have 93 percent of the men's viewing figures. Helen tells me that after her races were televised, she would be recognized in Belgian supermarkets, which shows just how far the sport has come from those days when the women's races, in their graveyard slot, were almost invisible. She believes that audiences "don't care what gender they are watching, they just want a good battle" and that "arguably 90 percent of the races this year have been more interesting for the women than the men."

Another significant change Helen got the UCI to commit to was to guarantee that by 2021, women's races would be fifty minutes long and every single race would have equal prize money. With men only riding ten minutes more than the women, it's very hard to make the case they deserve five times as much cash. Helen feels that women in competitive cycling have too often been "expected to do it more for love" than financial reward. While she says it's vital that you love it, "you also need to live," for as she says, "it doesn't cost more to have a penis." Now one World Cup cross race will be worth six times what the winner of the Giro Rosa currently has to share with her team. She hopes that women in the sport are on their way to achieving financial parity with their male counterparts.

Like Sabra, Helen believes that change is all down to economics: "As soon as you show that the women's sport holds a value, that they can get a piece of that pie, then suddenly they are interested." The DVV now has a sponsor who has come in specifically for the women's race and puts in more money than it costs to run it. She believes this is the clincher for supporting women in the sport: "When you see that you can't think any differently, they want us because it gets them more."

After Helen's stint on the commission, women's Cyclo-cross is in a strong position and there are now more women taking to the start line at races. She is aware, though, that young women between sixteen and twenty-three are more likely to leave sports than any other group, so before she left the commission, she had the UCI commit to including a junior women's category (for fourteen- to sixteen-year-olds) at all national and international championships, as there has been for men for decades.

Despite announcing her retirement in 2018, Helen remains committed to supporting up-and-coming women riders and recently crowdfunded to pay the fees for a hundred women under the age of twenty-three to enter the U.K. national cross championships. She also organized the first junior women's race in 2018, the Helen100 Trophy, with a prize fund equal to that of the junior boys.

Helen has also raced in many women's road races but feels less optimistic about the pace of change there. She sees it as very much "an old boys club," and with the huge amounts of money pouring into men's road racing, she thinks it's almost impossible to change the minds of an organization like ASO, which runs the Tour. Helen has ridden La Course and felt that it was "basically a little sideshow." Lizzie Deignan, a pro cyclist who has taken part in the event several times, feels similarly and told me that "we are there as a token gesture. It's more insulting than complimentary."

Instead of trying to force the ASO to do the "morally right thing," Helen thinks that it makes more sense to focus on working with organizers who are already invested in making the sport equal. She raced in the U.K.'s first Ovo Energy Women's Tour in 2014, which now runs over six days and is one of the most prestigious women's road stage races in the world. Since 2018, they have awarded the same prize money as they do for their men's race, the Tour of Britain. She felt the difference between this and La Course was stark, which she puts down to how the organizers "set off in the beginning to make it a successful event." The Women's Tour works closely with local schools, showing them that it's normal for women to be racing on bikes by incorporating the women's teams into lessons, from math to art. This is in sharp contrast to when the InternationElles stopped at a school en route through France and the children showed them their Tour de France artwork, which of course featured only male riders.

There are other races that stand out for equalizing prize money and demonstrating that they are invested in women in the sport. The Colorado Classic dropped their men's race altogether in 2019 and more than doubled the prize money for their women's four-stage race ($30,000 to $75,000—$5,000 more than the men received). They also organized free live TV streaming coverage with female commentators. The same year it was announced there would be a new women's race to rival the Giro Rosa, the Battle of North. This ten-stage race will launch in August 2021 and riders will race across Denmark, Sweden and Norway, presumably for significantly more money than its Italian competitor offers. The organizers have already said they are sure of attracting millions of TV viewers and thousands of spectators along the course. Unlike the Giro Rosa, they won't have to compete for media coverage with the Tour de France.

With other races stepping up to offer women riders better opportunities, why does it matter that the Tour de France currently only runs a one-day women's race? Not least when many female pro riders don't want a road race as long and hard as the French Grand Départ. Activists like the InternationElles aren't asking for a carbon copy of a race that is arguably too long; they want to be offered something that bridges the gulf between the men's and women's experience. The Tour de France is one of the most watched sporting events in the world. It is certainly the most popular cycling event and the only race most of its audience will watch each year. It's possible that the impression they come away with is that women aren't up to it. There is more than enough evidence to prove that's false, but if you're a young girl watching the race on TV, how are you going to know that?

The day I rode stage fifteen, it was announced that the UCI

had held talks with the Tour organizers about committing to a women's stage race. An ASO spokesperson later said, as if they had only just worked this out despite the years of campaigning, "women cyclists need a race which is to them what the Tour de France is to the men and we need to find a solution for that."

The phenomenal success of the FIFA Women's World Cup in its home country may have helped convince them that there was money in women's sports, but I like to think that years of pressure from those who have been calling them out on their lack of interest in the women's side of the sport has helped with that shift. There was justifiable outrage when just a few months later, the Tour organizers announced the route of the 2020 race, with La Course still a one-day event, this time on a flat 90 kilometers of laps around the Champs-Elysées in Paris. The 2019 Road Race World Champion, Annemiek van Vleuten, responded by describing it as a "step back."

Bike Baby Gone

Lizzie Deignan (née Armitstead) was a schoolgirl in Yorkshire when it first occurred to her that a career in cycling might be possible. It was 2004 and British Cycling's Olympic Talent Team had come to try out pupils and identified Lizzie as having a natural talent. Lizzie proved them right, winning silver in the 2012 Olympic road race and being crowned World Race Champion in 2015 and British National Road Race Champion four times. She has a long list of other palmarès to her name in track and road.

I spoke to Lizzie on the phone on a break from her training for the 2019 UCI Road World Championships, which would take place on home soil and pass through her hometown of Otley. The run-up to this race, compared to when she won in 2015, has been radically different. Almost exactly a year ago, she gave birth to her first baby, Orla. Lizzie and Italian Marta Bastianelli were likely to be the only mothers taking part in the event, though many riders in the men's race have children. In women's cycling there are only a handful of pro riders who have children and are still racing.

Iris Slappendel of the Cyclists' Alliance thinks the reason for this is largely financial. As well as successfully pushing for higher wages for riders on the top teams, she secured eight months' paid maternity leave clauses for riders competing in WorldTour teams, a benefit that is standard in many job contracts in Europe but was absent in women's cycling. There's no doubt that it's a challenge to race and raise children. Iris recalls being away 180 days of the year; had she had children, that would have been impossible unless there was someone taking on the childcare. What definitely doesn't help is not having a job which offers you any sort of financial buffer during pregnancy and looking after a small baby, when you are unable to train and race. Iris also thinks that cycling is still quite traditional, and that women have generally felt they had to choose between their career and children. With the new maternity clause in place, she hopes women will no longer be in a position where they have to choose between career and children.

Lizzie tells me that when she was growing up, she assumed that having children would mark the end of her career. With so few women with children in the professional peloton, it's easy to assume that's just how it is. However, seven months after having Orla, she took part in the Amstel Gold Race. Two months after that, she was overall winner of the Ovo Energy Women's Tour.

She hopes that other riders, seeing her return to racing, will no longer "correlate being pregnant with the end of their career." Lizzie may have felt similarly inspired by Kristin Armstrong, who two years after giving birth won a gold medal in the individual time trial at the 2012 Olympics. At thirty-nine, Kristin was then the oldest rider to have won the event. When she did it again at Rio in 2016, she made history as the oldest female cyclist to win an Olympic medal and the first rider to win three gold medals in the same discipline.

With new research showing that pregnancy pushes the body closest to the maximum limit for human endurance, it makes sense that women can return even stronger. When Lizzie won the 2019 Ovo Energy Women's Tour, she was incredibly emotional, describing how the result felt like a "massive validation" after all the doubts she'd had over whether her return was the right decision. In the months post-birth, when she was juggling a tiny baby, sleep deprivation and getting back on the bike to train, an experience she has described as "overwhelming" and "difficult"—she looked to fellow cyclists like Laura Kenny and Sarah Storey, who had successfully resumed their cycling careers after having children. If they could do it, then it wasn't as impossible as it might have felt at four a.m. while feeding Orla and knowing she would have to be on the bike a few hours later.

They helped by giving advice about how to manage her pregnancy as an elite athlete, since she found there was little information out there to help her navigate this unknown territory. She admits it's "not for every woman," but she believes there needs to be a "re-education for everybody," so they're aware it's possible to exercise more during pregnancy than women are led to believe.

She tells me that she is luckier than many of her peers in that she was able to take time off. It came as a surprise when the new women's team Trek-Segafredo signed her up while she was six months pregnant—a decision all the more remarkable in the cycling world, where it's all about being at the peak of physical performance. Lack of financial support for athletes during pregnancy and maternity is widespread throughout the sports world. Not least with Nike, a company that has released ads proclaiming their investment in gender equality, but in 2019 was called out for hypocrisy by some of the female athletes they sponsored. These women revealed that the company suspended their pay when they became pregnant.

When Olympian Alysia Montaño, one of the top three runners in the world, became pregnant, she was informed by Nike that they would pause her contract and stop paying her until she returned to running races. She broke with Nike and later released a video which turned their famous slogan "Dream Crazy"—used in an ad where viewers are told to "believe in something, even if it means sacrificing everything"—against them: "If we want to be an athlete and a mother, that's just crazy . . . Believe in something, even if it means sacrificing everything, like maybe your contract, your pay." She exposed their positive messaging around women in sports as hollow, just about selling sneakers rather than actual investment in equality.

Sports companies often put confidentiality clauses into their contracts to stop athletes from disclosing details, but when Alysia left Nike she was able to reveal that the company has the right to reduce an athlete's pay "for any reason" if a specific performance target isn't met. They make no exception for childbirth, pregnancy or maternity. When she was eight months pregnant with her first child, she ran a major 800-meter race and came seventh. Six and ten months after her daughter's birth, still breastfeeding, she won national championships. She had to use tape to hold her torn abdominals together. Alysia did this partly to prove it's possible to be a mother and still have a successful sports career, but also because her new sponsor, Asics, had threatened to stop paying her after expressing doubts she would be ready to come back within the time frame they had set.

Another Nike-sponsored athlete, Kara Goucher, revealed that she signed up to a half marathon scheduled three months after the birth of her son because Nike had suspended her pay until she started racing again. When her son got dangerously ill and was hospitalized, she had to keep training instead of being with him twenty-four hours a day as she would have wanted, something she says she will never be able to forgive herself for, though she felt she had little choice. The company had requested she keep her pregnancy secret for four months so they could announce it in a newspaper on Mother's Day as part of their brand promotion around equality.

It's telling that in 2019 all the executives negotiating contracts at Nike are men.

Lizzie's new team took a different approach, perhaps because it has two women directors. They are committed to giving "exactly the same opportunities to women, always considering they are women, so pregnancy could be part of their life." Lizzie strongly believes that improving rights for mothers in sports is "all part of the fight for equality" and Trek has been vocal about helping improve parity between men and women, not least hiring women's cycling activist Kathryn Bertine as an ambassador for equality. Lizzie tells me she felt trusted by the Trek team to do what was right for her, such as missing training camps because she was breastfeeding and choosing when it was right for her to return to racing—something she felt was "a completely open-minded and new approach."

Lizzie is aware that every pregnancy and baby is different, and she was lucky that she was able to keep cycling—though not hard—until three days before giving birth. She then took six weeks off before getting back on the bike. She knows that in such a competitive environment many women don't feel able to risk taking time out to have a baby, knowing that childbirth could result not just in the loss of their contract, but also their peak fitness. But at least the new maternity clause for top-level riders will give them more financial security.

Lizzie is in the fortunate position of being supported by her husband, Philip, who retired early from his own professional road racing career to become a full-time dad. Though she felt she'd been "thrown in at the deep end" initially, she says that like any mother returning to work, "you just manage, you just do it." She regained her fitness quicker than she expected, and even though her team put no pressure on her, she returned to competing nearly two months ahead of schedule. She says being a mother has rekindled her love of cycling, that before her pregnancy she was winning but not always enjoying it.

She feels her life is more balanced, that being a mother means cycling is now "just my job and I have to get it done," and as a consequence the wins are more rewarding. She also finds her training rides give her an important "mental break" from childcare and that she's lucky to have a job that, when she's not racing, only takes her away from Orla for four hours a day. She strongly believes that every woman has the right to choose when they want to have a baby and to be supported by their employer, even in the world of sports. She hopes that cycling teams will start including paternity rights so that male riders don't risk losing a contract if they too choose to take time out for the birth of their children.

Representation Matters

If you do manage to find women's cycle racing on TV, it's not obvious who might be a mother, but it is plain to see that it's a very white sport. So much so that when amateur black British track cyclist Yewande Adesida turns up at races, she is often the only black woman there.

I met twenty-six-year-old Yewande in London just before she headed to Newport for a race the following day. She tells me that before she got into cycling, she had been a competitive rower, but when she realized she wasn't going to excel as she'd hoped, she decided to look for another sport. She had previously been recommended to take up track and field, a sport with much more racial diversity. Instead, she decided to follow the advice of those who told her she would be a good fit for track cycling. She tells me that the lack of diversity in the cycling world wasn't that much of a surprise to her, since rowing is also overwhelmingly white and elitist. Even so, when she first got into track cycling, not seeing anyone else who looked like her at the start line made her wonder if "maybe I've picked another sport that I shouldn't really be doing because no one like me does it."

If she'd read about the experiences of Natnael Berhane, the only black African cyclist to take part in the 2019 Tour de France, then it's understandable she would have felt that way. In 2015, Natnael was racing for Team MTN-Qhubeka, the first African team to take part in the Tour de France. When he competed in the Tour of Austria that same year, he was racially abused by a cyclist from another team. If this wasn't bad enough, MTN-Qhubeka said this was far from an isolated incident for their black African team members.

Professional cycling has long struggled to be racially inclusive, as we saw in chapter 5 with the League of American Wheelmen introducing a ban on nonwhite cyclists. They made that decision at a time when African-American cyclist Major Taylor was leaving his opponents standing, winning national and international medals across the United States and Europe. As well as being barred from racetracks on account of the color of his skin, throughout his career he was subjected to vile verbal and physical abuse from fellow cyclists and fans. In one incident he was choked by a rival to the point of unconsciousness. One of the highest-earning athletes in the world in his heyday, he died destitute and forgotten.

As recently as the 1970s, the U.K.'s first black British cycling champion, Maurice Burton, relocated to Belgium because he could no longer endure the racial abuse directed toward him at races in his home country.

Yewande is quick to point out that she's never experienced any sort of racism on the track and that people have always been massively encouraging, but that hasn't stopped doubt creeping in from time to time. She worried more about making mistakes, because she felt she already stood out as more often than not the only black woman on the track: "I still had that thought in the back of my mind that maybe I should try something else that someone suggested, like track and field." Joining an all-women's cycling club, Velociposse, helped. They invited her to become a member after seeing her cycling at Lee Valley Velodrome. At that point, the idea of joining a cycling club was "really intimidating," but an all-women club felt like it would be a "safer environment." They were able to loan her a track bike, so she didn't have to commit to buying before she'd decided whether to stick with the sport.

Her time with Velociposse helped her grow confidence on the track, as well as her sense of belonging there, and affirmed that she had made the right choice. Two years on, she juggles a PhD in sports biomechanics with competing with mixed-team SES Racing, specializing in sprint events. These tactical races have two riders battling it out over distances from 250 to 1,000 meters. They start extremely slowly, with each rider watching the other's every move, before one initiates the high-speed sprint to the finish.

For someone who initially felt the track might not be a suitable choice because of the absence of other women who looked like her, Yewande is aware that her participation might make others think that they belong. Self-promotion doesn't come naturally, but she feels it's important to be visible and an active voice in the sport: "I know what a difference it can make being able to see someone that looks like you, and so for that reason I don't mind it."

Though there are times she would rather just get on and ride her bike, by doing interviews and using social media, she knows she is helping break down barriers about who the sport is for and encouraging more people into competitive cycling. Yewande believes that brands need to step up and show that cycling is much more diverse than the picture that comes from races like the Tour de France, where the peloton is overwhelmingly white and a large proportion of ads make use of that same demographic.

In 2019, Yewande was chosen by a well-known company that makes bicycle components, many of which end up on the bikes of pro riders from MTB to road, to front the campaign for their most important product launch in some years. In their images, she is seen flying along, crouched over the handlebars and owning the road, the landscape a blur behind her. After the ad went out, she received messages from people who told her it had inspired them to get on a bike. She thinks that other companies should be doing more to use similarly diverse images: "there are black cyclists out there, people need to open their eyes more and look a bit deeper."

When Yewande first got into track cycling and was struggling to find other black women in the sport, she was unaware that in the United States a cyclist had set out to become the first female African-American pro road cyclist. Ayesha McGowan took up cycling in her twenties so she could get to university faster. She instantly fell in love, finding it also helped her through a period of depression, and was soon dabbling in track racing before moving on to road, winning a state championship soon after. Like Yewande, she looked for a mentor from a similar background, but not finding one, she decided she would have to become that person for others like her.

Ayesha now competes in professional races and is sponsored by major international brands, but she's yet to achieve her ultimate goal of joining a professional racing team. She has said that "simply existing in this sport as a black woman is its own form of advocacy" but she goes much further than that and has become one of the most visible and proactive forces for change, pushing the industry to be more inclusive, particularly for women, women of color and people with disabilities.

Through her popular social media accounts, blog and podcast, as well as media interviews, Ayesha details her journey into competitive cycling, empowering others to do things they might once have thought impossible, as well as turning the spotlight on other women of color in the cycling world. This includes cyclists like thirteen-year-old Maize "aMAIZEn" Wimbush from

Maryland, who hopes to be the first African-American woman to compete in a cycling event at the Olympics. In a film Ayesha made with Nike, she says while it's obviously about winning, at the same time there's a wider goal of making the sport more diverse. "It's about showing up and claiming my space and knowing that I deserve to be there. If I don't show up to these pro races, then there are no other black women in them."

When I asked Iris Slappendel of the Cyclists' Alliance about the lack of diversity in cycling, she says the sporting world is "still very traditional" and that it "makes a big thing out of every thing or person that's not 'ordinary' or they're not familiar with." Justin Williams, an African-American from impoverished South L.A., experienced this when he entered the elite and rule-obsessed world of professional road cycling. He has described how the experience nearly broke him: "Being involved in a sport that is primarily white, it was hard not to be alone and it ultimately cracked me." He has now created his own team, Legion of Los Angeles, whose members don't conform to outdated stereotypes of how a racing cyclist ought to look or behave. A team who he hopes will inspire the next generation and break down barriers, with riders who "wear Jordans, listen to rap really loud at races" and who are also "going to be a part of the conversation."

In Rwanda, a country with no history of women's bike racing, the Africa Rising Cycling Center aims to get black women from across the continent into the sport. This nonprofit organization, which has successfully gotten many black African cyclists into the international men's professional peloton, is helping do the same with their black African female riders. One of their most successful female cyclists is Jeanne d'Arc Girubuntu. In 2009, Jeanne had watched cyclists compete in the Tour du

Rwanda and immediately thought that was something she wanted to do. That race is men only, but it didn't put her off. Six years later she had made it onto her country's national cycling team, the lone female member, traveling to the United States for the UCI World Road Championships, making history as the first black woman from Africa to compete at the event. Jeanne hopes that by becoming a visible force in cycling in the country, and internationally, she will help make cycling more acceptable for women in Rwanda, where gender norms are still quite traditional.

With black African cyclists like Natnael Berhane and Tsgabu Grmay now a core part of the peloton in the big European road races like the Giro d'Italia and Tour de France, black women from Africa are finally making their mark in elite international races. Eyeru Tesfoam Gebru from Ethiopia made cycling history when, in 2018 at the Tour Cycliste Féminin International de l'Ardèche, she was awarded the title of Most Combative. She is the first black African woman to hold a jersey in a professional race. Like Jeanne, she benefited from training at the center in Rwanda and has gone on to become part of the new UCI women's team, WCC, which was formed in 2019 with nine riders from around the world. Eyeru now takes part in elite international road races alongside fellow African Desiet Kidane Tekeste.

Africa Rising hopes that with more support of women's cycling in the continent, which is chronically underfunded, they can continue to expose the incredible talent of African women who would previously have struggled through lack of access to training and opportunities to get anywhere near the international elite women's races. In so doing, they hope to change the landscape of the women's international cycling scene forever.

Where Now?

Lizzie Deignan has said that women's professional cycling is "at a point now where we cannot go back." With activists and advocates for the sport like Helen, Iris, Ayesha, Sabra, Yewande and so many others pushing successfully for change, I think she's right. It's been a long time coming and there is still a good distance to go in making the sport as equal, diverse and inclusive as it should be.

Look at the details of the women's road race that was planned (then postponed) for the 2020 Tokyo Olympics and you will see we aren't there yet. A maximum of 67 women were scheduled to compete over the 137-kilometer course, whereas there were 130 places in the men's 243-kilometer race. And this was supposed to be the most gender-equal Games yet, with 49 percent of participants women.

For progress to continue in the right direction with the next generation, there needs to be much more exposure, because if no one can see it, then how will they know what's possible?

If a true women's Tour de France ever does become a reality, the impact would undoubtedly raise the profile of women across every aspect of the sport. French children will be drawing pictures of the likes of Annemiek van Vleuten, Marianne Vos, Lizzie Deignan and Eyeru Tesfoam Gebru. And girls around the world will know that riding a bike, even racing on a bike, is something they can do too.

The narrative of women being the sideshow to the men's main event needs to end and the spotlight needs to shine bright on the strong, diverse and talented women who are taking to the start line across the sport. Girls around the world need to see women they can identify with and think they can do that too. Women also need to be treated like professionals with pay, prizes and races that aren't insulting, as well as working conditions that treat them like human beings. They should be able to participate in a sport where they are as visible and respected—and by turns celebrated—as their male counterparts: Cycling Queens.

KEEP ON PEDALING

We opened in Cambridge, 1897, with a female effigy on a bicycle being used as a warning to those "New Women" studying at Girton College to keep out of territories claimed by the male students as their own, particularly higher education and cycling. We end in the same city, but in 2020, where it's abundantly clear the protest ultimately failed. Cambridge is now teeming with women students, like every university in the U.K., but what's more unusual is that the proportion of women on bikes is greater than anywhere else in Britain.

Cambridge, with the highest number of bike commuters in the U.K., is now dubbed the capital of cycling. If you visit the city, the whir of wheels and ding of bicycle bells might make you think you're in the Netherlands. On the Hills Road alone, a busy artery connecting the train station to the center, at least five thousand cyclists pedal the busy stretch each day. And it doesn't take in-depth research to see why cycling might be so popular with residents and visitors alike: the city is crisscrossed with an extensive network of safe and protected bike lanes, as well as multiple bridges dedicated to cyclists and pedestrians that cross the River Cam. The city has invested in its active travel infrastructure, prioritizing bikes and walking over cars so you don't need to do battle on the roads each day just to get to work or the shops. Superstar classicist Mary Beard has cited her bicycle commute to the university, which includes a scenic path along the river, as guaranteed to improve her mood. She will not be alone: the physical and mental health benefits of cycling have been proven beyond doubt.

And like major Dutch cities, half of those on two wheels in Cambridge are women, which is in stark contrast to the rest of the country, where it's on average 27 percent, or often far less, with similar or worse figures in the United States, Australia and Canada. But wherever you have a good network of bike lanes, you get a more even gender split, which is the case in Germany, Denmark and the Netherlands. In 2011, a street in New York City with no bike lane was shown to have only around 15 percent of users who were women compared to 32 percent using the dedicated lane on a street nearby. In Philadelphia, women on bikes went up by 276 percent where cycling infrastructure was installed.

Women tend to be more risk-averse than men, for myriad social and cultural reasons, which explains why better cycling infrastructure can shift the gender balance significantly. While in most countries, women aren't being told they shouldn't bike—unlike their Victorian sisters—a lack of safety on the roads disproportionately impacts their willingness to participate, holding them back. To emulate the Netherlands, Denmark, Cambridge and elsewhere—from children going to school to those still pedaling long past retirement, with an equal gender split—it's obvious more needs to be done to keep everyone safe from cars and trucks.

Despite its great age, I believe the bicycle's role in the future can be just as important as in the past—if not more so. Not many people in Cambridge would think that their city would be improved by more fossil fuel–reliant vehicles and fewer bicycles. We are at a critical point for our health and that of the planet: 2019 was one of the hottest years ever, with record-breaking temperatures across the globe, culminating in deadly fires decimating large swaths of Australia, destroying fragile ecosystems. It is clear that we need to drastically cut our carbon emissions, and make it more attractive for people to journey by bike—or on foot—instead of by car, which could have a significant impact. In the U.K., transport is the largest source of greenhouse gas emissions, and air pollution causes forty thousand premature deaths a year. At present, 60 percent of journeys between one and two miles in the U.K. are done by car. Convert these trips to bike or foot and it would have a hugely positive impact on people's health and the environment. Electric bikes could also play a significant role in this shift, attracting those who might not see themselves as fit enough for regular biking. The huge increase in cyclists recorded on new protected bike lanes in cities like London and elsewhere proves that if the infrastructure is built, then we will come and use it, gladly, and women most of all.

But if all this makes it sound rather worthy, let's not forget that cycling is also immensely pleasurable. It would be a shame for only a minority to experience all that it has to offer. And with more people cycling, the more our governments will, hopefully, be compelled to provide better infrastructures to meet their needs.

· · ·

I could easily not have gotten hooked on cycling. At school I loved exploring the woodlands and open spaces of Bristol by bike with friends. We were often in trouble for roaming farther than allowed. But as I progressed through my teenage years I got into punk rock and joined a band, and my bike mostly gathered dust in the shed. I had never identified as sporty and I remember one school sports report where the teacher wrote, "I'd like to comment on Hannah's progress this term, but I've not seen her." Many other women cyclists tell me they too hadn't enjoyed gym classes at school, but rediscovering bikes in their twenties changed their perception of themselves. In fact, there are some pro women riders who started late, like Ireland's Orla Walsh who took up cycling in 2015 to get to college cheaply and quickly. A dedicated party animal until that point, with no prior interest in sports, by 2017 at age twenty-eight, she was on the national cycling team.

I may not be racing, but cycling plays a significant role in my life. It didn't start with commuting (that came after) but a need to escape. Rides have since become longer, faster and an increasingly important part of my life. Now most of my holidays, both in the U.K. and abroad, revolve around the bike.

That isn't to say my relationship with cycling isn't uncomplicated. I live with a potentially fatal heart condition, which can be brought on by strenuous exercise. I feel fit and able and my ultrasound heart scans have all been normal—and possibly always will be—but people with my rare condition, Marfan syndrome, are at 250 times greater risk of aortic dissection (a tear or rupture between layers of the aortic wall) than the general population. And it is very often fatal. One cardiologist suggested I just cycle on the flat, but my current doctor is more relaxed and thinks I can judge what might be pushing it. There is no exact measure and there are no guarantees, but I wear a heart rate monitor and make sure I am never straining or too out of breath.

I need to navigate my way around doing what I love so that it doesn't kill me. I can't ignore my condition, but I can keep pedaling even if I know I won't be challenging anyone to a race up Mont Ventoux. Instead I will be taking it slowly and steadily, which allows me more time to take in the scenery. I also know that I could always opt for an e-bike to give me a little boost for the tough stuff. Many others with varying physical barriers, whether it's age or disability, continue to cycle with the use of adapted or e-assisted bicycles and tricycles. In fact, a bicycle can be a mobility aid for those who find it less painful than walking, and even a correction to balance issues. A tandem can mean a nonsighted person can get in the saddle too.

I don't have to stop cycling and I hope you don't either. And if you don't cycle already, I hope the stories here might inspire you to start.

Getting on your bike is only the beginning of many new stories and adventures.

ACKNOWLEDGMENTS

I am immensely grateful to everyone who agreed to be interviewed for this book: Fatimah Al-Bloushi, Yewande Adesida, Wende Cragg, Sabra Davison, Lizzie Deignan, Shannon Galpin, Jenny Graham, Jenni Gwiazdowski, Anissa Lamare, Dervla Murphy, Zahra Naarin, Iris Slappendel, and Helen Wyman. Without your generosity this idea would have gone nowhere; you are the beating heart of women's cycling today. I hope I've done justice to both the stories you've told me and your passion. I would also like to mention the Bike Project, which is doing incredible work and has let me play the most miniscule part in that. Keep doing what you are doing.

Thanks too to my brilliant and peerless agent, Patrick Walsh, who saw something in my scrappy initial ideas and committed to helping develop it into something much more resembling a solid and persuasive outline for a book. John Ash, also at PEW, played a significant role in this too.

Here I must also give credit to Andrew Franklin, friend, colleague, committed cyclist and experienced publisher, who was the person who gave me the belief that I might be capable of writing a book and the motivation to organize my thoughts and take the terrifying step of getting some words down. I do not think there would be a book at all if he hadn't been so insistent I could do it. I'd also like to mention Hannah Westland, who gave much encouragement from the start, and Diana Broccardo, who has been unfailing in her support, not the least agreeing to my writing sabbatical. Valentina Zanca, Drew Jerrison and Anna-Marie Fitzgerald deserve special mention too for being excellent people to work with.

I am hugely appreciative of all those involved at every stage of making this into a proper book; their efforts are immense. My editor Jenny Lord, whose judicious editing and wise guidance, not to mention endless enthusiasm—as well as patience with my inability to anticipate how long it might take to write a book—have been invaluable. Thanks to the rest of the team at W&N who have worked hard to make sure the book happened, including Rosie Pearce, Kate Moreton, Virginia Woolstencroft, Brittany Sankey, Anne O'Brien and everyone else involved in getting the book into the world. Otto Von Beach, the illustrator of the UK edition, deserves special mention here too.

Marya Pasciuto has indefatigably and astutely guided the process on the other side of the pond at Penguin Random House US. I'm grateful to the efforts of everyone involved there including Becky Odell, Caroline Payne, Susan Schwartz, Alice Dalrymple and Jill Schwartzman. I am truly indebted to Katie Zaborsky, who enthusiastically commissioned the book there before she moved on.

To the friends who read early drafts or even just put up with me endlessly talking about women and cycling, you are all great. As well as everyone who made suggestions, introduced me to people I should talk to, and gave me new ideas. You are too numerous to mention by name, but thank you.

My parents, John and Sylvia; and siblings, Jon, Nick and Emma; have played a major role in this book coming into being by nurturing in me a love of cycling and the outdoors. You are the reason I can cycle at all, and the bike rides I've been on with you are now part of my DNA. I also don't think any present will top that Christmas when "Father Christmas" left a note by my bed attached to a piece of string which led all the way downstairs to a new bicycle.

The biggest thanks of all goes to Mike, without whose support and encouragement this book wouldn't have seen the light of day. Your readings of the very rough, early drafts and multiple reworkings were always the most thoughtful and incisive. You also kept me fed and the fires burning—literally, when that was our only form of heating in Villelongue—when I was glued to the laptop too long. You always find the best bike routes and are my favorite cycling, and everything else, partner.

NOTES

CHAPTER 2

24 "rabid disease commonly known as cyclomania": *Cycling*, 1895. Consulted at the British Library, London.

24 "look sweet on the seat of": Harry Dacre, "Daisy Bell (Bicycle Built for Two)," 1892.

26 "the intricate figures performed by the cyclists": *Munsey's Magazine*, 1896. Consulted at the British Library, London.

27 "a bird, sailing over flower-covered prairies": Helen Follett, "Honeymoon on Two Wheels," *Outing* 29 (1896–97).

27 "at the cost of some thousands of pedal strokes": Eve Curie, *Madame Curie: A Biography*, trans. Vincent Sheean (Garden City, NY: Doubleday, Doran & Co, 1937).

28 "Bus drivers were not above": Helena Maria Swanwick, *I Have Been Young* (London: Victor Gollancz, 1935).

29 regularly called her a "hussy": Evelyn Everett Green, *Cycling for Ladies* (1896). Consulted at the British Library, London.

31 "wild women of the usual unprepossessing": Ethel Smyth, *The Memoirs of Ethel Smyth* (London: Viking, 1987).

32 "Now and again a complaint arises": Marguerite Merington, "Woman and the Bicycle," *Scribner's Magazine* 17 (June 1895).

33 "has done more to emancipate women": Nellie Bly, "Champion of Her Sex: Miss Susan B. Anthony," *The World*, February 2, 1896.

34 **"the devil's advance agent"**: Charlotte Smith, as quoted in Sue Macy, *Wheels of Change: How Women Rode the Bicycle to Freedom* (Washington, DC: National Geographic, 2011).

35 **"bring about constant friction"**: R. L. Dickinson, as quoted in Patricia Vertinsky, *Eternally Wounded Women: Women, Doctors and Exercise in the Late Nineteenth Century* (Manchester, UK: Manchester University Press, 1990).

37 **"the haze, the elusiveness, the subtle suggestion"**: Arabella Kenealy, as quoted in Kathleen McCrone, *Sport and the Physical Emancipation of English Women: 1870–1914* (London: Routledge, Taylor & Francis Group, 2014).

37 **"I have seen them rapidly decline"**: James Beresford Ryley, *The Dangers of Cycling for Women and Children* (London: H. Renshaw, 1899).

38 **"hardly lets me stir without special"**: Charlotte Perkins Gilman, *Herland and The Yellow Wallpaper* (London: Vintage, 2015).

39 **"The woman's desire to be on a level"**: Silas Weir Mitchell, *Doctor and Patient* (New York: The Classics of Medicine Library, 1994).

40 **"When women began to understand the needs"**: "A Lady Doctor's Views on Cycling," *The Hub*, September 1897.

40 **"there is nothing in the anatomy"**: W. H. Fenton, "A Medical View of Cycling for Ladies," *The Nineteenth Century* 39 (May 23, 1896).

CHAPTER 3

44 **"not in that dress"**: "Lady Haberton and the Hotel Keeper," *Pall Mall Gazette*, April 5, 1899.

45 **"abominable. It smelled of spirits"**: "Bloomers Condemned," *Dunstan Times*, June 2, 1899.

46 **"use boyish gestures and talk"**: *The Lady Cyclist*, March 1896. Consulted at the University of Warwick Library online, www.warwick.ac.uk/services/library.

46 **beleaguered "great war"**: Elizabeth Sanderson Haldane, *From One Century to Another: The Reminiscences of E. S. Haldane, 1862–1937* (London: MacLehose & Co., 1937).

48 **"By force of habit"**: Florence Pomeroy, *Reasons for Reform in Dress* (London: Hutchings & Crowsley, 1884).

48 **"the pressure on the large vessels"**: Victor Neesen, *Dr. Neesen's Book on Wheeling: Hints and Advice to Men and Women from the Physician's Standpoint* (London: Forgotten Books, 2018).

50 **"I can do the work for 16 cows"**: Diana Crane, *Fashion and Its Social Agendas: Class, Gender, and Identity in Clothing* (Chicago: University of Chicago Press, 2000).

51 **"a costume that caused hundreds"**: "She Wore Trousers," *National Police Gazette*, October 28, 1893.

52 **"a lamentable incident"**: *Cycling*, September 1893. Consulted at the British Library, London.

52 **"a caricature of the sweetest"**: *Yorkshire Evening Post*, as quoted in "Womanly Cycling—Part Two," *The Victorian Cyclist*, February 15, 2015, https://thevictoriancyclist.wordpress.com/2015/02/15/womanly-cycling-part-two/.

52 **"congratulate Miss Reynolds"**: *Bicycling News*, as quoted in Sheila Hanlon, "Tessie Reynolds: The Stormy Petrel in the Struggle for Women's Equality in Cycle Racing and Dress," May 12, 2015, http://www.sheilahanlon.com/?p=1830.

53 **"I protest, in the name"**: *The Daily Telegraph*, 1893.

54 **"Parisian women are riding"**: *Cycling*, June 1894. Consulted at the British Library, London.

57 **"Let it visibly announce"**: Oscar Wilde, "The Philosophy of Dress," *New-York Tribune*, April 19, 1885.

CHAPTER 4

66 **"my beautiful picture gallery"**: Frances Willard, *Writing Out My Heart: Selections from the Journal of Frances E. Willard, 1855–96*, ed. Carolyn Gifford (Urbana, IL: University of Illinois Press, 1995).

66 **"the earthly anchor"**: Kathleen Fitzpatrick, *Lady Henry Somerset* (London: Jonathan Cape, 1923).

67 **"born with an inveterate"**: Willard, *Writing Out My Heart*.

73 **"peculiarities of figure"**: *The Lady Cyclist,* March 1896. Consulted at the University of Warwick Library online, www.warwick.ac.uk/services/library.

79 **"weary and worn out"**: *The Lady Cyclist*, September 1896. Consulted at the University of Warwick Library online, www.warwick.ac.uk/services/library.

80 **"trying to find"**: "Celebrating International Nurses Day," Access Sport, April 17, 2017, https://www.accesssport.org.uk/News/celebrating-international-nurses-day.

CHAPTER 5

88 **"cease to be such"**: And all other quotes relating to Kittie Knox quoted in Lorenz J. Finison, *Boston's Cycling Craze, 1880–1900: A Story of Race, Sport, and Society* (Amherst, MA: University of Massachusetts Press, 2014).

91 **"women like me"**: "Women and Biking: A Case Study on the Use of San Francisco Bike Lanes," Women 4 Climate, accessed March 2019, https://w4c.org/case-study/women-and-biking-case-study-use-san-francisco-bike-lanes.

92 **"I have to admit that"**: Elly Blue, "An Interview with Monica Garrison of Black Girls Do Bike," *Bicycling*, March 4, 2016, https://www.bicycling.com/news/a20015703/an-interview-with-monica-garrison-of-black-girls-do-bike/.

93 **"this is what freedom"**: *Ovarian Psycos*, directed by Joanna Sokolowski and Kate Trumbull-LaValle (Los Angeles: Sylvia Frances Films, 2016), documentary, 72 min.

96 **"We're not about who can ride"**: Denise Florez, "Latina Bicyclists Answer Macho Bike Culture with Their Own Chain Gang," *Los Angeles Times*, September 22, 2013, https://www.latimes.com/local/la-xpm-2013-sep-22-la-me-psyco-riders-20130923-story.html.

99 **"Riding a bicycle often attracts"**: Tom Coghlan, "Women Defy Fatwa on Riding Bicycles," *The Times*, September 22, 2016.

101 **"girls deserve to have"**: Zahra, as quoted in Shannon Galpin, "Revolutions," *Sidetracked*, accessed April 2019, https://www.sidetracked.com/cycling-in-afghanistan/.

109 **"encouraged women to exercise"**: Alicia Buller, "Princess Reema: It's Time to Focus on Saudi Women's Capabilities, Not Their Clothes," *Arab News*, March 10, 2018, https://www.arabnews.com/node/1262466/saudi-arabia.

112 **"fills my heart with joy"**: Sadeeya A. Nadim, "Saudi Women Conquer Jeddah Streets on Bicycle," *Gulf News*, February 3, 2019, https://gulfnews.com/world/gulf/saudi/saudi-women-conquer-jeddah-streets-on-bicycle-1.61705902#.

CHAPTER 6

114 **akin to a "football scrummage"**: Mike Hill, "Day a Preston Heroine Was Arrested," *Lancashire Post*, February 17, 2017.

117 "a considerable handicap": Sylvia E. Pankhurst, *The Suffragette Movement: An Intimate Account of Persons and Ideals* (London: Longmans, Green & Co, 1931).

117 "She would disappear from me": Ibid.

117 "There were usually some slow": Ibid.

119 "the common tragedy": Ibid.

125 "stand up for the oppressed": Eveline Buchheim and Ralf Futselaar, eds., *Under Fire: Women and World War II* (Amsterdam: Verloren Publishers, 2014).

130 "Once I ran into a dog": Simone de Beauvoir, *Letters to Sartre*, trans. and ed. Quintin Hoare (London: Vintage Classics, 1993).

130 "I pedaled on": Simone de Beauvoir, *The Prime of Life*, trans. Peter Green (London: Deutsch, Weidenfeld and Nicolson, 1963).

130 "I only wanted to eat up the kilometers": Beauvoir, *Letters to Sartre*.

132 "the moment my legs begin": Henry David Thoreau, "Walking," in *The Writings of Henry David Thoreau* (Boston: Houghton Mifflin, 1894).

133 "I like to have space to spread": Virginia Woolf, *The Diary of Virginia Woolf*, vol. 5, ed. Anne Olivier (London: Hogarth Press, 1980).

133 "scarcely make head": Beauvoir, *Letters to Sartre*.

134 "pedaling so indolently": Beauvoir, *The Prime of Life*.

135 "intoxicated by the swift": Ibid.

135 "leave espionage to those": Ibid.

136 "I had lost a tooth": Ibid.

136 "a childish sense": Ibid.

137 "reduced to a condition": Ibid.

138 "saved us from literally starving": Ibid.

139 "back on the road in front": Ibid.

140 "pedaled across the railway": Ibid.

140 "on a little journey all alone": Ibid.

CHAPTER 7

145 "What would become of us": Henry David Thoreau, "Walking."

146 "thirst for longer flights": Lillias Campbell Davidson, *Handbook for Lady Cyclists* (London: Hay, Nisbet & Co, 1896).

147 "*inside* the movie": Juliana Buhring, *This Road I Ride: My Incredible Journey from Novice to Fastest Woman to Cycle the Globe* (London: Piatkus, 2016).

148 "some considerable peril": A. C. Pemberton, Harcourt Williamson, C. P. Sisley, and Gilbert Floyd, *The Complete Cyclist* (London: A. D. Innes & Co., 1897).

149 "the observed of all observers": Martha, "We Girls Awheel through Germany," *Outing* (April–September 1892).

150 "prophecies of broken limbs": Margaret Valentine Le Long, "From Chicago to San Francisco Awheel," *Outing* (October 1897–March 1898).

151 "She has two spare": Davidson, *Handbook for Lady Cyclists.*

152 "being stared at as": Elizabeth Robins Pennell, "Cycling," in *Ladies in the Field: Sketches of Sport*, ed. Beatrice Violet Greville (London: Ward & Downey, 1894).

152 "Hers is all the joy": Ibid.

153 "The world is our great book": Ibid.

157 "I am told I made a record": Elizabeth and Joseph Pennell, *Over the Alps on a Bicycle* (London: T. F. Unwin, 1898).

157 "a big German frau": Ibid.

158 "People may object that I rode": Ibid.

158 "immortalize the name and": Ibid.

159 "I was doing this thing": Ibid.

160 "dine with the fifty": Ibid.

160 "wept over the sublimities": Ibid.

162 "courage, endurance and enthusiasm": Fanny Bullock Workman and William Hunter Workman, *Sketches Awheel in Fin de Siècle Iberia* (London: T. F. Unwin, 1897).

163 "Don Quixotian days": Ibid.

163 "enabling us an entire": Fanny Bullock Workman and William Hunter Workman, *Algerian Memories: A Bicycle Tour over the Atlas to the Sahara* (London: T. Fisher Unwin, 1895).

164 "not so far advanced": Workman, *Sketches Awheel in Fin de Siècle Iberia.*

164 "with much the same awe-inspired": Ibid.

165 "there seemed to be no chance": Ibid.

165 "the women stared": Ibid.

166 "not a pleasant place": Ibid.

166 "gaunt, wolfish-looking": Workman, *Algerian Memories.*

166 "one must look deeper:" Ibid.

167 "light may fall upon": Fanny Bullock Workman and William Hunter Workman, *Through Town and Jungle: Fourteen Thousand Miles-a-Wheel among the Temples and People of the Indian Plain* (London: T. Fisher Unwin, 1904).

CHAPTER 8

171 **"love of the great-out-of-doors"**: Marya McQuirter, "Women's (Bike) History: 3 Days, 5 Women, 250 Miles," The League of American Bicyclists, March 20, 2013, https://www.bikeleague.org/content/womens -bike-history-3-days-5-women-250-miles.

173 **"I had never known holidays"**: Mrs. Cattaneo, as quoted in James McGurn, *On Your Bicycle: An Illustrated History of Cycling* (London: John Murray, 1987), 146.

177 **"young and fit and ready"**: "Billie Fleming: Happy 100th Birthday," *Cycling Weekly*, May 6, 2014, https://www.cyclingweekly.com/news/ latest-news/billie-fleming-happy-100th-birthday-121964.

180 **"If I went on doing this"**: Dervla Murphy, *Wheels Within Wheels* (London: Eland Books, 2010).

181 **"completely trapped and miserable"**: Ibid.

183 **"exalted by the realization"**: Ibid.

186 **"a hideous bit of business"**: Davidson, *Handbook for Lady Cyclists*.

187 **"series of interiors"**: Rebecca Solnit, *Wanderlust: A History of Walking* (London: Verso Books, 2001).

188 **"seized with sudden envy"**: Anne Mustoe, *A Bike Ride: 12,000 Miles around the World* (London: Virgin Books, 1991).

191 **"the more that doubt"**: Jenny Tough, "El Miedo (The Fear)," YouTube video, January 17, 2019, https://www.youtube.com/watch?v=Y4f4UTm Kc1U&feature=emb_logo.

CHAPTER 9

200 **"audacious and unprecedented"**: Peter Zheutlin, *Around the World on Two Wheels: Annie Londonderry's Extraordinary Ride* (New York: Citadel Press, 2008).

204 **"drains your morale"**: Buhring, *This Road I Ride*.

209 **"was nothing to qualify me"**: Ibid.

210 **"another being, I just lose all sense"**: Ibid.

213 **"a kind of meditation"**: Ibid.

215 **"circus freak show"**: Ibid.

216 **"people want to think income"**: Belinda Goldsmith and Meka Beresford, "India Most Dangerous Country for Women with Sexual Violence Rife," Thomson Reuters Foundation, June 27, 2018, https:// poll2018.trust.org/stories/item/?id=e52a1260-260c-47e0-94fc-a636b19 56da7.

CHAPTER 10

225 **"a sport run by men, for men":** Michelle Arthurs-Brennan, "Nicole Cooke: 'Cycling is a Sport Run by Men, for Men,'" Total Women's Cycling, January 24, 2017, https://totalwomenscycling.com/news/ nicole-cooke-evidence-british-cycling.

228 **"no one can have any idea how":** Louise Armaindo, as quoted in M. Ann Hall, *Muscle on Wheels: Louise Armaindo and the High-Wheel Racers of Nineteenth-Century America* (Montreal, Quebec: McGill-Queen's University Press, 2018), location 1,221 in Kindle eBook.

231 **"is not, nor can it ever be, a fit thing":** *Cycling*, August 1894. Consulted at the British Library, London.

231 **"if carried to excess":** Pennell, "Cycling."

233 **"instead of a demonstration of limbs":** "The Cyclists at the Drill Hall," *Sheffield & Rotherham Independent*, December 31, 1889, on Six Day Cycle Race, "1889—Sheffield," http://www.sixday.org.uk/html/1889_ sheffield.html.

238 **"speediest of all cyclists":** "Lisette to Ride in Chicago," *The Inter Ocean* (November 20, 1898): 32. Archived newspaper accessed at https://www .newspapers.com/clip/19907033/amelie_le_gall_1898/.

240 **"disgraceful exhibition":** Margaret Gast website, last updated May 1, 2012, http://nagengast.org/nagengast/Gast/index.html.

CHAPTER 11

247 **"gouge his eyes out":** Nicholas Pyke, "We're Not Deviants Say the Cycling Ladies," *The Independent*, August 28, 2005.

247 ***"In the Rosslyn they were all":*** Tim Hilton, *One More Kilometer and We're in the Showers* (London: Harper Perennial, 2004).

249 **"injurious to the game itself":** Albert Lusty letter in *Cycling*, August 1937.

249 **"stayed home, in her kitchen":** Mariska Tjoelker, "Mien Van Bree," in *Ride the Revolution: The Inside Stories from Women in Cycling*, ed. Suze Clemitson (London: Bloomsbury Sport, 2015).

250 **"What will the neighbors think?":** Nancy Neiman Baranet, *The Turned Down Bar* (Philadelphia: Dorrance & Company, 1964).

251 **"one of the gang":** Eileen Sheridan, *Wonder Wheels* (London: Nicholas Kaye, 1956).

251 **"rocked the racing world":** *The Bicycle*, February 27, 1946. Consulted at the British Library, London.

252 **"resented the intrusion"**: William Wilson, *Marguerite Wilson: The First Star of Women's Cycling* (Poole, UK: CMP, 2016).

252 **"a man to ride a twelve"**: Ibid.

256 **feeling "wonderfully fresh"**: Sheridan, *Wonder Wheels.*

263 **"If the men did anything"**: Jeremy Wilson, "'Sod Off, I'm Passing You': Pioneering Cyclist Eileen Cropper's Amusing Take on Beating the Men and Fending Off Their Advances," *The Daily Telegraph*, September 19, 2019.

263 **"It would have been nice"**: Belinda Sinclair, "Interview: Eileen Gray," British Cycling, June 2, 2010, https://www.britishcycling.org.uk/article/spor20100602-Interview—Eileen-Gray-CBE-0.

264 **"more determined to succeed"**: Ibid.

264 **"carrying, lifting, bending"**: Beryl Burton, *Personal Best: The Autobiography of Beryl Burton* (Huddersfield, UK: Springfield Books, 1986).

265 **"Golly, isn't this tough"**: Sheridan, *Wonder Wheels.*

265 **"Sod off, I'm passing you"**: Wilson, "'Sod Off, I'm Passing You.'"

275 **"like a nuclear bomb exploded"**: "The Champion Mountain Biker Turned Drug Smuggler," VICE, November 20, 2018, https://www.vice.com/en_us/article/wj3nvb/the-champion-mountain-biker-turned-drug-smuggler-missy-giove.

275 **"I love that experience of flying"**: Ibid.

275 **"You're only here once"**: Jason Sumner, "MTB News and Notes: Missy on Being Missy," *VeloNews*, April 23, 2004, https://www.velonews.com/2004/04/mountain/mtb-news-and-notes-missy-on-being-missy_5945.

279 **"anyone thought to be different"**: William Fotheringham, "Philippa York: 'I've Known I Was Different Since I Was a Five-Year-Old,'" *The Guardian*, July 6, 2017.

279 **"it's important to represent"**: Sumner, "Missy on Being Missy."

CHAPTER 12

290 **"we were really going somewhere"**: Aliya Traficante, "What I Have Learned: Connie Carpenter, Women's Cycling's First Olympic Gold Medalist," Ella Cycling Tips, December 8, 2017, https://cyclingtips.com/2017/12/learned-connie-carpenter-womens-cyclings-first-olympic-gold-medalist/.

290 **"cycling is much too difficult"**: Isabel Best, "Remembering the Golden Era of the Women's Tour de France," *The Daily Telegraph,* July 5, 2019.

294 **"Do you really think women are":** Rachel Sturtz, "Meet the Billie Jean King of Cycling," *Outside*, July 24, 2019.

296 **has "flipped backward":** Traficante, "What I Have Learned."

312 **"Being involved in a sport that":** Johnny Long, "US Road Champion Justin Williams," *Cycling Weekly*, June 3, 2019.

BIBLIOGRAPHY

BOOKS

Atkinson, Diane. *Rise Up, Women!: The Remarkable Lives of the Suffragettes.* London: Bloomsbury Publishing, 2019.

Atkinson, Diane. *Suffragettes in the Purple White & Green.* London: Museum of London, 1992.

Atwood, Kathryn J. *Women Heroes of World War II: The Pacific Theater; 15 Stories of Resistance, Rescue, Sabotage, and Survival.* Chicago: Chicago Review Press, 2017.

Bailey, Rosemary. *Love and War in the Pyrenees: A Story of Courage, Fear and Hope, 1939–1944.* London: Weidenfeld & Nicolson, 2008.

Bair, Deirdre. *Simone de Beauvoir: A Biography.* London: Vintage, 1991.

Baranet, Nancy Neiman. *The Turned Down Bar.* Philadelphia: Dorrance Publishing, 1964.

Beauvoir, Simone de. *Letters to Sartre.* Translated by Quintin Hoare. London: Vintage Classics, 1993.

———. *The Prime of Life.* Translated by Peter Green. London: Deutsch, Weidenfeld and Nicolson, 1963.

———. *The Second Sex.* Translated by H. M. Parshley. London: Vintage, 1997.

Buchheim, Eveline, and Ralf Futselaar, eds. *Under Fire: Women and World War II.* Amsterdam: Verloren Publishers, 2014.

Buhring, Juliana. *This Road I Ride: My Incredible Journey from Novice to Fastest Woman to Cycle the Globe*. London: Piatkus, 2016.

Burton, Beryl. *Personal Best: The Autobiography of Beryl Burton*. Huddersfield, UK: Springfield Books, 1986.

Clemitson, Suze, ed. *Ride the Revolution: The Inside Stories from Women in Cycling*. London: Bloomsbury Sport, 2015.

Crane, Diana. *Fashion and Its Social Agendas: Class, Gender, and Identity in Clothing*. Chicago: University of Chicago Press, 2000.

Crawford, Elizabeth. *The Women's Suffrage Movement: A Reference Guide 1866–1928*. London: UCL Press, 1999.

Cunningham, Patricia, and Susan Voso Lab, eds. *Dress and Popular Culture*. Bowling Green, OH: Bowling Green State University Popular Press, 1991.

Curie, Eve. *Madame Curie: A Biography*. Translated by Vincent Sheean. Garden City, NY: Doubleday, Doran & Co, 1937.

Davidson, Lillias Campbell. *Handbook for Lady Cyclists*. London: Hay, Nisbet & Co, 1896.

——. *Hints to Lady Travelers at Home and Abroad*. London: Iliffe & Son, 1889.

Dodge, Pryor. *The Bicycle*. Paris: Flammarion, 1996.

Erskine, F. J. *Lady Cycling: What to Wear & How to Ride*. London: British Library, 2014.

Everett-Green, Evelyn. *Cycling for Ladies*. 1896.

Finison, Lorenz J. *Boston's Cycling Craze, 1880–1900: A Story of Race, Sport, and Society*. Amherst, MA: University of Massachusetts Press, 2014.

Fischer, Gayle V. *Pantaloons and Power: Nineteenth-Century Dress Reform in the United States*. Kent, OH: Kent State University Press, 2001.

Fitzpatrick, Kathleen. *Lady Henry Somerset*. London: Jonathan Cape, 1923.

Galpin, Shannon. *Mountain to Mountain: A Journey of Adventure and Activism for the Women of Afghanistan*. New York: Saint Martin's Press, 2014.

Gilles, Roger. *Women on the Move: The Forgotten Era of Women's Bicycle Racing*. Lincoln, NE: University of Nebraska Press, 2018.

Gilman, Charlotte Perkins. *Herland and The Yellow Wallpaper*. London: Vintage, 2015.

Greville, Beatrice Violet, ed. *Ladies in the Field: Sketches of Sport*. London: Ward & Downey, 1894.

Guroff, Margaret. *The Mechanical Horse: How the Bicycle Reshaped American Life*. Austin, TX: University of Texas Press, 2016.

Haldane, Elizabeth Sanderson. *From One Century to Another: The Reminiscences of E. S. Haldane, 1862–1937.* London: MacLehose & Co, 1937.

Hall, M. Ann. *Muscle on Wheels: Louise Armaindo and the High-Wheel Racers of Nineteenth-Century America.* Montreal, Quebec: McGill-Queen's University Press, 2018.

Hallenbeck, Sarah. *Claiming the Bicycle: Women, Rhetoric, and Technology in Nineteenth-Century America.* Carbondale, IL: Southern Illinois University Press, 2016.

Hargreaves, Jennifer. *Sporting Females: Critical Issues in the History and Sociology of Women's Sports.* London: Routledge, 1993.

Harris, Kate. *Lands of Lost Borders: A Journey on the Silk Road.* New York: Dey Street Books, 2018.

Herlihy, David V. *Bicycle: The History.* New Haven, CT: Yale University Press, 2004.

Hilton, Tim. *One More Kilometer and We're in the Showers.* London: Harper Perennial, 2004.

Jennings, Oscar. *Cycling and Health.* London: Iliffe & Son, 1893.

Jordan, Pete. *In the City of Bikes: The Story of the Amsterdam Cyclist.* New York: Harper Perennial, 2013.

Jungnickel, Kat. *Bikes and Bloomers: Victorian Women Inventors and Their Extraordinary Cycle Wear.* London: Goldsmiths Press, 2018.

Lightwood, James T. *Cyclists' Touring Club: Being the Romance of Fifty Years' Cycling.* London: Cyclists' Touring Club, 1928.

Macy, Sue. *Wheels of Change: How Women Rode the Bicycle to Freedom.* Washington, DC: National Geographic, 2011.

Marks, Patricia. *Bicycles, Bangs, and Bloomers: The New Woman in the Popular Press.* Lexington, KY: University Press of Kentucky, 1990.

McCrone, Kathleen. *Sport and the Physical Emancipation of English Women: 1870–1914.* London: Routledge, 2014.

McGurn, James. *On Your Bicycle: An Illustrated History of Cycling.* London: John Murray, 1987.

Mitchell, Silas Weir. *Doctor and Patient.* New York: The Classics of Medicine Library, 1994.

Murphy, Dervla. *Full Tilt: Ireland to India with a Bicycle.* London: Pan, 1967.

———. *Wheels Within Wheels.* London: Eland Books, 2010.

Mustoe, Anne. *A Bike Ride: 12,000 Miles around the World.* London: Virgin Books, 1991.

Neesen, Victor. *Dr. Neesen's Book on Wheeling: Hints and Advice to Men and Women from the Physician's Standpoint.* London: Forgotten Books, 2018.

Pankhurst, Sylvia E. *The Suffragette Movement: An Intimate Account of Persons and Ideals.* London: Longmans, Green & Co., 1931.

Pemberton, A. C., Williamson Harcourt, C. P. Sisley, and G. Floyd. *The Complete Cyclist.* London: A. C. Innes & Co., 1897.

Pennell, Elizabeth and Joseph. *A Canterbury Pilgrimage.* London: Seeley and Co, 1885.

——. *Our Sentimental Journey through France and Italy.* London: Longmans & Co., 1888.

——. *Over the Alps on a Bicycle.* London: T. F. Unwin, 1898.

——. *To Gipsyland.* London: T. F. Unwin, 1893.

Pomeroy, Florence. *Reasons for Reform in Dress.* London: Hutchings & Crowsley, 1884.

Purvis, June, and Sandra Stanley Holton. *Votes for Women.* London: Routledge, 2000.

Pye, Denis. *Fellowship Is Life: The National Clarion Cycling Club, 1895–1995.* Bolton, UK: Clarion Books, 1995.

Ritchie, Andrew. *King of the Road: An Illustrated History of Cycling.* London: Wildwood House, 1975.

Ryley, James Beresford. *The Dangers of Cycling for Women and Children.* London: H. Renshaw, 1899.

Sheridan, Eileen. *Wonder Wheels.* London: Nicholas Kaye, 1956.

Smith, Robert A. *A Social History of the Bicycle: Its Early Life and Times in America.* New York: American Heritage Press, 1972.

Smyth, Ethel. *The Memoirs of Ethel Smyth.* London: Viking, 1987.

Solnit, Rebecca. *Wanderlust: A History of Walking.* London: Verso Books, 2001.

Swanwick, Helena Maria. *I Have Been Young.* London: Victor Gollancz, 1935.

Sykes, Herbie. *Maglia Rosa: Triumph and Tragedy at the Giro d'Italia.* London: Bloomsbury, 2013.

Thoreau, Henry David. *The Writings of Henry David Thoreau.* Boston: Houghton Mifflin, 1894.

Vertinsky, Patricia. *Eternally Wounded Women: Women, Doctors and Exercise in the Late Nineteenth Century.* Manchester, UK: Manchester University Press, 1990.

Ward, Maria E. *Bicycling for Ladies.* New York: Brentano's, 1896.

Wellings, Mark. *Ride! Ride! Ride!: Herne Hill Velodrome and the Story of British Track Cycling.* London: Icon Books, 2016.

Whitmore, Richard. *Alice Hawkins and the Suffragette Movement in Edwardian Leicester*. Derby, UK: Breedon Books, 2007.

Willard, Frances E. *A Wheel within a Wheel*. New York: Fleming H. Revell, 1895.

———. *Writing Out My Heart: Selections from the Journal of Frances E. Willard, 1855–96*. Edited by Carolyn Gifford. Urbana, IL: University of Illinois Press, 1995.

Wilson, William. *Marguerite Wilson: The First Star of Women's Cycling*. Poole, UK: CMP, 2016.

Woolf, Virginia. *The Diary of Virginia Woolf*. Edited by Anne Olivier, vol. 5. London: Hogarth Press, 1980.

Workman, Fanny Bullock, and William Hunter Workman. *Algerian Memories: A Bicycle Tour over the Atlas to the Sahara*. London: T. Fisher Unwin, 1895.

———. *Sketches Awheel in Fin de Siècle Iberia*. London: T. F. Unwin, 1897.

———. *Through Town and Jungle: Fourteen Thousand Miles-a-Wheel among the Temples and People of the Indian Plain*. London: T. Fisher Unwin, 1904.

Zheutlin, Peter. *Around the World on Two Wheels: Annie Londonderry's Extraordinary Ride*. New York: Citadel Press, 2008.

MAGAZINES

Bicycle—Active January 4, 1876–June 25, 1895, published in London; archived issues accessed at the British Library, London.

Bicycling News—Victorian publication, active 1936–1955, published in London; archived issues accessed at the British Library, London.

Casquette

Cycling—Active June 6, 1957–April 25, 1964, published in London; archived issues accessed at the British Library, London.

Cycling Weekly

Cycling World Illustrated—Victorian publication, active November 25, 1896–August 4, 1897, published in London; archived issues accessed at the University of Warwick Library online, https://warwick.ac.uk/services/library/.

Cyclist

The Cyclists' Touring Club Gazette—Active 1899–1923, published in London; archived issues accessed at the British Library, London.

The Hub—An illustrated journal for wheelmen and -women. Victorian publication, active 1886–1898, published in London; archived issues accessed at the British Library, London.

The Lady Cyclist—Victorian publication, active 1895–1897, published in London; archived issues accessed at the University of Warwick Library online, https://warwick.ac.uk/services/library/.

The Outing Magazine—Victorian publication, active 1886–1905, published in New York; archived issues accessed at Hathi Trust Digital Library, www.hathitrust.org/.

Rouleur

The Wheelwoman—Victorian publication, active 1886–1899, published in London; archived issues accessed at the British Library, London.

JOURNAL ARTICLES

Fenton, W. H. "A Medical View of Cycling for Ladies." *The Nineteenth Century* 39 (May 23, 1896).

Grand, Sarah. "The New Aspect of the Woman Question." *North American Review* 158 (1894): 270–76.

Hanlon, Sheila. "At the Sign of the Butterfly: The Mowbray House Cycling Association." *Cycle History* 18 (Spring 2008).

Merington, Marguerite. "Woman and the Bicycle." *Scribner's Magazine* 17 (June 1895).

WEBSITES

Throughout my research, I consulted a number of online publications for information and to verify facts. Below is a list of the ones I used most extensively.

www.bicycling.com
www.bikemag.com
www.cyclingtips.com
www.dirtmountainbike.com
www.dirtragmag.com
https://mmbhof.org
www.pinkbike.com
www.playingpasts.co.uk
www.podiumcafe.com
www.sheilahanlon.com
www.sidetracked.com
www.singletrackworld.com

www.sixday.org.uk
www.sustrans.org.uk
www.totalwomenscycling.com
www.velonews.com

FILMS

Al-Mansour, Haifaa. *Wadjda*. Berlin, Germany: Razor Film Produktion, 2013. 98 min, https://www.amazon.co.uk/Wadjda-Waad-Mohammed /dp/B00J5SD2IU/ref=sr_1_2?keywords=wadjda+film&qid=1580246077 &s=digital-text&sr=1-2-catcorr.

Borden, Lizzie. *Born in Flames*. St. Paul, MN: The Jerome Foundation, 1983. 79 min, https://vimeo.com/ondemand/borninflames.

"Housewife Cyclist." Isleworth, UK: British Pathé, 1956. 1:19. https://www .britishpathe.com/video/housewife-cyclist.

"Hyde Park Bicycling Scene." London: BFI, 1896. https://www.dailymotion .com/video/x6ti1zp.

Menzies, Sarah. *Afghan Cycles*. Seattle, WA: Let Media, 2018. Documentary, 90 min. https://www.afghancycles.com.

Moore, Sarah. "Missy Giove—The Champion Mountain Biker Turned Drug Smuggler." VICE Sports. November 20, 2018. 13:32. https://www.vice .com/en_us/article/wj3nvb/the-champion-mountain-biker-turned -drug-smuggler-missy-giove.

Racing Is Life: The Beryl Burton Story. Narrated by Phil Liggett. London: Bromley Video, 2012. DVD, 130 min.

Sokolowski, Joanna, and Kate Trumbull-LaValle. *Ovarian Psycos*. Los Angeles: Sylvia Frances Films, 2016. Documentary, 72 min. http://www .ovarianpsycosdocumentary.com.

INDEX

ABOUT THE AUTHOR

Hannah Ross grew up in Bristol and Bath and now works for an independent publisher in London. When she isn't working on other people's books or writing her own, she is usually on a bike. She belongs to a local cycling club and volunteers for a charity helping refugee women learn to ride bikes. Whenever she can, she packs up her saddlebags and heads for the open road, and now she doesn't feel she's really traveled anywhere unless it's on two wheels. Given the choice, Hannah would always rather be (slowly) pedaling up mountains than almost anywhere else. She also spends too long thinking about the next bicycle she really "needs" to own.